S0-ADI-462

INNER LIVES OF DEAF CHILDREN

INNER LIVES OF DEAF CHILDREN

Interviews and Analysis

MARTHA SHERIDAN

Foreword by Patricia Elizabeth Spencer
and I. King Jordan

Gallaudet University Press   *Washington, D.C.*

Gallaudet University Press
Washington, DC 20002

© 2001 by Gallaudet University.
All rights reserved. Published 2001
Printed in the United States of America

Library of Congress Cataloging-in-Publication Data

Sheridan, Martha.
  Inner lives of deaf children : interviews and analysis / Martha Sheridan ; foreword by
  Patricia Elizabeth Spencer and I. King Jordan.
      p. cm.
  Includes bibliographical references and index.
  ISBN 1-56368-102-1 (alk. paper)
      1. Deaf children—Case studies. 2. Deaf children—Interviews. 3. Deafness—
  Psychological aspects—Case studies. 4. Deafness in children—Case studies. I. Title.

  HV2391. S58 2001
  362.4'2'083—dc21
                                                                    2001023027

∞ The paper used in this publication meets the minimum
requirements of American National Standard for Information
Sciences—Permanence of Paper for Printed Library Materials,
ANSI Z39.48-1984.

To my loving husband, Michael,
My beautiful son, Christopher,
Joseph and Marilyn Sheridan,
And all deaf and hard of hearing children everywhere.

CONTENTS

FOREWORD

IN THIS book, we meet deaf children—in their own worlds, in their own words, in a way that emphasizes their unique personalities and experiences while demonstrating the experiences and ideas they share. In taking this very personal and humanized approach to exploring the lives and attitudes of deaf children, Martha Sheridan's work reflects and extends emerging trends in research in the social sciences and, specifically, research about deaf people.

Research techniques evolve as we learn from our past experiences and find ways to better capture the essence of the phenomena we want to study. Readers whose image of research consists of dry statements filled with numbers and strange Greek symbols will be especially pleased with the approach to research taken by the author of this book. The writing here reflects current trends toward qualitative instead of quantitative data analysis. Qualitative research has many variations but all include an in-depth and naturalistic look at the topic to be studied. The qualitative researcher looks for patterns—patterns showing similarities across the participants as well as patterns of individual variation. Instead of using numbers to summarize and provide an "average" group description, qualitative researchers focus intensively on relatively few informants or participants toward the goal of understanding the subtleties of the topic being studied. In this approach, the research participants do not lose their individuality in "averages."

Note that we use the words *informants* and *participants* to describe the people on whom qualitative research focuses. The term *subject* has been intentionally discarded by those who conduct qualitative research. This distinction in terms is made to remind the researcher, the reader of the research, as well as the participants themselves that it is the participants, not the researchers, who are the experts on the topic. For example, in the context of the study reported in this book, who knows more about the reality of being a deaf child than a deaf child him- or herself? With this acknowledgment, the researcher's role is clarified. The researcher is a seeker of the knowledge already attained by the participants, not an expert from outside who looks dispassionately into the world of the participants or who "studies" them as though they were in a laboratory.

However, the researcher is not a mere recorder of the words or actions of the participants. In fact, the researcher's cognitive and analytical skills are key to the quality of a qualitative research study. Unable to rely on statistics or other formulaic approaches for analysis, qualitative researchers are, in fact, themselves the analytic instruments. They work best when they start with a theoretical approach and apply that approach consistently (in this case, a phenomenological approach is taken to the study), looking for patterns, commonalities, and explanations in real-life words for the phenomena they study. Martha Sheridan wanted to define the worldview of deaf children to find out how they see themselves, what their joys are, and what challenges they face. She also sought to ascertain what roles communication skills and modalities, their own and others', play in their lives. In short, she set out to discover how deafness and the communicative challenges it provides are reflected in the personal lives of individual deaf children.

Another important research trend represented in this book is that of communities being studied by persons who themselves are members and who can relate to and communicate fluently with the informants. This trend is especially welcome in the deaf community, which has often suffered from the misinterpretations of "outsider" researchers who either failed to communicate fluently with those whom they studied or who inadvertently imposed their own hearing cultural values on the interpretation of their data. In this case, the researcher has actually been a deaf child. Now, as an adult deaf professional who is fluent in communicating with the informants, she can reflect upon the information they give by referencing (perhaps even contrasting) her own experiences. She can conduct her analysis in the context of what it means to be deaf in America. With the increased awareness, both within and beyond the deaf community, of the abilities of deaf people, research is increasingly being conducted by people who are deaf. It may be that people who are themselves deaf are most sensitive to differences within and among deaf individuals. Thus, Martha Sheridan brings her own awareness to the topics she is studying and becomes a sensitive interpreter of the thoughts and feelings of the individual children whom she interviews.

Inner Lives of Deaf Children is an outgrowth of a dissertation written to fulfill requirements for the Ph.D. in social work. As such, it represents another growing trend—the increased frequency and technical sophistication of research conducted in the social work field toward the goal of adding to the knowledge base supporting social work practice.* As a faculty member in the Department of Social Work at Gallaudet University, Martha Sheridan trains students who will become social workers and provide services to deaf and hard of hearing children and adults. Her research about the understandings and experiences of deaf children has been directly useful in the programming she provides for social work students. This book gives access to that information to students in social science programs beyond those at Gallaudet. It represents an important contribution to the rapidly growing research base in the field of social work, one that ensures that the voices of deaf children form part of that generally available research base.

In reflecting emerging trends, this book is a groundbreaking work, incorporating a theory-based qualitative approach to social work related issues and providing information specifically about deaf children by having the children tell their own stories to someone to whom they can relate. We hope that its publication will encourage additional research of this nature with portions of the community of deaf and hard of hearing people, adults as well as children. It is important that members of the deaf and hard of hearing communities set the topics for such research so that they are relevant to the needs of the communities, so that the views of the participants themselves are respected, and so that people, rather than mere numbers or scores, become the focus of the analysis.

---

* See Council on Social Work Education. (1992). *Curriculum policy statement for baccalaureate and master's degree programs in social work education.* Alexandria, VA: Council on Social Work Education.

Despite the fact that this publication summarizes a complex and sophisticated research study, readers will find it fascinating, thought-provoking, and even fun to read. It is now time to sit back and let the children tell their stories.

PATRICIA ELIZABETH SPENCER
I. KING JORDAN

PREFACE

WHAT DOES it mean to be a child who is deaf or hard of hearing? What perceptions and experiences do deaf and hard of hearing children have? What do they have to say about themselves, their identities, their relationships, their futures, and their perceptions of their fit with their environments? If we truly want to know the answers to these questions, we need to allow these children to tell us their stories, perceptions, feelings, and thoughts in their own words, without the impositions of others. This book is a medium for the children's voices as they tell us about their lifeworlds—their images of themselves and others in their lives.

After reading the children's stories, which are excerpts from actual interviews, readers may wonder about deeper psychological meanings than those I address in this book. My intent is not to analyze the children and their lifeworlds from a psychological or psychoanalytic perspective, or to diagnose or to label them. The spirit of this book lies in the children's voices, their similarities and differences, and I believe it is important for readers to see what these children have to say. Furthermore, I believe it is important for readers to see the strengths these children possess.

My approach to the children's chapters, for the most part, bypasses attempts to match the children, their stories, and situations to existing literature and published research. I take this approach to allow for an appreciation of the realities that the children present, and to respect the autonomous voice of the child. Another goal of this book is to illustrate how deaf and hard of hearing children from diverse backgrounds approach and define their lifeworlds and themselves. Their voices have been absent from the traditional texts, which reflect how hearing adults perceive deaf children. The seven children in this study represent a cross-section of educational programs, communication methods, and ethnic and cultural backgrounds. They vary in gender as well as their hearing status and that of their parents and family members. The names of all of the characters, places, and some circumstances in the children's stories have been changed to protect their anonymity. Transcripts and video-tapes from interviews with the children and observations recorded in the form of field notes were used to identify themes and theories that arose in the research process.

This book describes the images that the children in this study have of themselves (both now and their projections into the future), of their relationships with others, and the communication they experience with family, teachers, and friends. The book also explores the mechanisms (called pathways) that the children and their families use to foster comfortable relationships, positive experiences, and growth. I hope that the images and pathways revealed in the following pages will be enlightening for deaf and hearing parents, family members, and friends of deaf and hard of hearing children, as well as for educators, professionals, researchers, and students in a variety of fields such as anthropology, education, sociology, social work, psychology, counseling, and human development.

Acknowledgments

Many people have contributed in one way or another to the completion of this book. First and foremost, I am grateful to the children who so unselfishly shared their lives and their views. Their contributions will allow many to understand the multiple meanings of being deaf. I would also like to thank the parents of these children for allowing them to participate in such a worthy project. Thank you also to the staff at the schools these children attended for their cooperation.

I owe a very special thank you to Dr. Patricia Spencer for approaching me with the idea of publishing my dissertation and for her confidence in my work and her ongoing support and encouragement. I thank my colleagues on the faculty in the Department of Social Work at Gallaudet University for their patience and encouragement while I focused on this book. Funding from the Gallaudet Research Institute and Gallaudet University Press and the advice and support of Dr. John Van Cleve, Ivey Pittle Wallace, and Dr. Thomas Allen is gratefully acknowledged.

I extend my appreciation to the colleagues who reviewed and commented on drafts of this book during its development: Dr. Patricia Spencer, Dr. Janet Pray, Dr. Carol Cohen, and Dr. Reginald Redding, of Gallaudet University; Dr. Joseph Walsh of Virginia Commonwealth University; Dr. Robert Pollard of the University of Rochester; and Patrick Vincent. I am especially grateful for the influential support of my anonymous reviewers.

I am grateful for the guidance of Dr. Keith Kilty, Dr. Virginia Richardson, Dr. Amy Reimenschneider, and Dr. Peter Paul throughout the research process and to my peers, Dr. Lee Shillito, Dr. Patricia Lemley, Dr. Annette Jefferson, Leigh Kirkpatrick, and Jean Parmir for their advice. Gratitude is expressed for the generous support of the Gallaudet University Graduate Fellowship Fund, Netcare Foundation, Pilot International, Quota International, and Delta Epsilon.

Finally, and very importantly, I owe a tremendous and very special personal thank you to my husband, Michael, and our son, Christopher, for their love, support, and endurance throughout this project.

INNER LIVES OF DEAF CHILDREN

1

Beginnings

"How do I start for the Emerald City?"

"It's best to start at the beginning. All you do is follow the yellow brick road."

"But what happens if I . . ."

"Just follow the yellow brick road."

—*The Wizard of Oz*, 1939

LIKE DOROTHY in the classic children's story *The Wizard of Oz*, our journey through life is full of surprises, and at each crossroad we are faced with experiences, mysteries, and challenges that help to determine what the future will hold. No crystal ball can foretell which critical events and experiences that occur in childhood will direct our later thinking and decisions. Becoming the person that we believe ourselves to be, the development of self-concept, is a lifelong process.

For all of us, certain events and personal characteristics stand out as we reflect back on our lives and what led to our self-perceptions and the decisions we made. For me, many of these reflections involve growing up as a deaf child in a hearing family, attending a hearing school, and not understanding at the time that I was deaf or what that meant. As an adult, I can now put those childhood experiences into perspective in the context of being deaf because now I understand its meaning.[1] But what being deaf means to me may be different from what it means to anyone else. No two deaf or hard of

---

1. The term *context* is used throughout the text to refer to singular or multiple circumstances that contribute to a person's situation, particularly in relation to the being or becoming of the person as deaf and the perspectives one holds on various aspects of his or her life.

hearing people are alike. Each of us carries a set of historical experiences, perceptions, relationships, and individual psychological and social realities that contribute to our unique perceptions of self and experience.

The symbolic interactive process of language and how we interpret communicative interactions informs our self-perceptions and our perceptions of others. The following story is just one example of how this process can play out in a deaf child's life. Trisha, a ten-year-old deaf girl, came to my office one day with tears streaming down her cheeks. "Can I talk to you?" she asked. Then she sat down in the seat next to my desk and with profound sadness she confided, "My mother doesn't love me anymore." She went on to tell me about a note her mother had written, which actually expressed the enormity of her love for Trisha. Trisha, however, had misinterpreted her mother's note. She explained that the note, which her mother had placed on her nightstand, read, "I couldn't love you more." This little girl's interpretation of her mother's words caused her much pain. Fortunately, I was able to help this little girl understand that the meaning of her mother's statement was different from the meaning she had perceived, and she left my office that morning recovering from her distress and carrying a renewed sense of herself, her mother, and their relationship.

Sociologists tell us that our self-perceptions and the meanings that we ascribe to situations are ever changing because our experiences and interactions—our biological, cognitive, and social realities—constantly change. Thus, the images that we have of ourselves as adults may grow out of or be different from those we had as children. Symbolic interaction is a sociological theory that explains how perceptions of self come from how we interpret our interactions with others (Mead, 1934; Berger, 1963). Cooley's (1970) *looking glass theory*, suggests that self-concept is a reflection of how we believe others see us, and these beliefs continue to develop in response to various interactions. We develop a sense of meaning in our lifeworlds from these social and environmental interactions (Walsh, 2000). Trisha's story is a small example of this theory at work. I mention symbolic interaction here because it sheds light on the value of the stories told by the children in this book, as well as the epistemology of the researcher.[2]

This book explores the perceptions of children who are deaf and hard of hearing and the meanings they give to their interactions with others. Every story told by a deaf child or adult about his or her experiences and lifeworlds will reflect the particular perceptions and interpretations of the storyteller.[3] My story is no different in that respect. I could share much with you about my own life experiences, but this book is not about me. However, it was my own life experience that led to my career as a social worker, a college professor, and a researcher in deafness. This book had its beginnings in my own childhood, and it is important for the reader, and for me as a researcher, to be aware of what part, if any, my own assumptions, experiences, interpretations, and perceptions play in the research process and the making of this book. Thus, symbolic interaction forms its backdrop.

MY STORY: ACKNOWLEDGING AND SITUATING THE SELF AS RESEARCHER

I struggle with how much to share about my childhood experiences, partly because I know that the story I tell is from my own perception of my childhood. If my parents were asked about my early years, their story would most likely be different. I struggle also because I grew up in a different era than the children in this book. Nonetheless, as a researcher, it is important for me to acknowledge my background and biases.

I was the second of four children in a Midwestern Irish Catholic family. My parents, older brother, Pat, and younger sister, Mary, are all hearing. My younger brother, Dan, and I are deaf. I became deaf at the age of three from measles and mumps, but it wasn't until

---

2. *Epistemology* refers to the *frame* through which one views the world, which influences our perceptions of situations, of others, and of interactions.

3. *Lifeworld* is a term I use loosely to refer to the general aspects of a person's life—one's self, perceptions, feelings, thoughts, events, experiences, relationships, and the systems with which people interact.

three years later, at the age of six, that a routine hearing screening offered to my first grade class confirmed this. Dan partially lost his hearing at fourteen months of age from encephalitis. He considered himself hard of hearing until he lost more hearing in adulthood and now identifies himself as deaf.

No support services were available to me while I was attending hearing schools between 1959 and 1973. As a result of late identification and a lack of appropriate educational support, my early educational and social experiences were difficult for me as well as for my parents. I have my memories from those years: memories of feeling different, of wanting to succeed and to find a place where I fit in. I understand now what I didn't understand during those years—I was deaf, not just experiencing a hearing loss. I wondered then why I wasn't getting the good grades I wanted. I recall sitting in a small summer school class of hearing students on the cool screened porch of a private school when I was seven years old. The grass was still wet from the early morning dew, and a misty ray of sunshine beamed in on us. Sitting at the top of the oblong table where we were grouped, I concentrated on the teacher. Unaware of the effect, she sat in the glare of the bright morning sun, which allowed me to see only her silhouette. With the side of her face to me, she faced the row of students in front of her; I was blinded by the sun and unable to see her face to speechread. I wondered what she was talking about and what the other children were doing.

Since my deafness was not identified until age six, I had lost valuable time and missed out on critical learning opportunities. Because of that and other factors—such as being placed in an unreasonably large first grade class of sixty students, having teachers who were not trained in deaf education, lacking awareness of opportunities for visual learning or communication, living during a time when modern technology was unavailable, and growing up in a family struggling for answers without proper guidance and no prior experience in deafness—I failed the first grade.

Before learning that I was deaf, my parents thought I was just not paying attention. I remember one evening while my mother was in the kitchen cooking dinner, my father sat down next to me on the sofa in the living room. Putting his arm around me, he gently asked if I knew what the word *concentrate* meant and proceeded to explain to me that paying attention in school would reap great rewards. During my first few years of school, my mother spent hours sitting with me at the dining room table, talking me through my homework. I imagine that she started out in loving and devoted commitment to my academic success and probably became increasingly concerned when she saw that her efforts to assist me were unsuccessful. Little did she know that I couldn't hear what she was saying, or speechread her, while my eyes followed her fingers as she pointed to the addition and subtraction problems on the paper in front of us.

When I was ten, I reached a turning point. My fifth grade teacher was astute enough to recognize that repeating a grade might help. Embarrassed and hurt that I wasn't going on to the sixth grade with the other students, I spent the summer preoccupied with not passing. It was a secret I shared only with my family and a couple of close friends. I wondered if it was all just a bad dream from which I might wake up.

My parents transferred me to a smaller school, where I repeated fifth grade. This gave my grades a huge boost and, with this new academic success, my self-esteem soared. Suddenly I liked school and I discovered learning. From then on, I spent hours at my school books and took pride in my work and grades. I felt a sense of mastery I had never felt before, and because I was a little older and taller than the other students, I excelled in athletics. I liked winning races, hitting home runs, staying in spelling bees until the end, being a cheerleader, and going to slumber parties, but there was still something missing. I knew I was different, but because I had no framework to describe that difference, no peers, no reference group, and no role models who were also deaf, I didn't understand what that difference was.

Upon transitioning to high school, friends dispersed into separate crowds. The new school was much bigger, with more teachers and a large student body. I found myself becoming increasingly isolated. One afternoon during my freshman year, I sat on the sofa in my family's sunlit living room having a mutually desired but laborious conversation with my mother. Mom would carefully enunciate her words, but she wasn't an easy person to speechread. I'd understand a word here and there and try to put them all together like the pieces of a puzzle. I asked her why I didn't have as many friends as the other kids appeared to have and why I didn't get invited to parties. She looked at me with a surprised expression on her face.

"You don't know why?" she asked.

"No."

"It's because you can't hear, and they don't understand that."

That was a revelation and a turning point in my life. Until that moment, I had only understood my deafness in a blur. I had never understood this difference between myself and others to be such a determining factor in my life. I had sensed a difference, and I knew that I couldn't hear, but never did it come together in such a revealing way. But still I did not realize all the implications regarding relationships, my future, language, and education. I did not know this wasn't just a *hearing problem*. The difficulties I faced were not because I had a hearing problem, but because the often-cruel world around me was full of barriers. That understanding was a long way off.

One cold and rainy weekend, I went shopping downtown with a friend. We went from store to store, riding escalators, trying on clothes we knew we could only dream of buying, and then stopping for a soda and fries before heading home. Waiting for the bus that day, I noticed a small group of deaf students wearing Ohio School for the Deaf varsity jackets. They seemed a little older than I was and they were signing. As I watched them, I felt a significant bond. I wanted to meet them; I wanted to learn to sign too. But where would I learn, who would I sign with? How could I talk to them if I didn't sign? I wanted to find out if we were alike. Was I deaf like them? The bond was there, and even though I didn't know them and they didn't know me, there was a link that somehow I wanted to explore. I felt a side of myself that I wanted to uncover. They saw me watching them and probably noticed my hearing aid. One of them smiled. I smiled back. They boarded their bus, and I boarded mine.

The first thing I did when I got home that afternoon was to look up the word "deaf" in the family's encyclopedia. I really didn't understand deafness and assumed that since I had some residual hearing that I was hard of hearing. I found only a paragraph or two along with a drawing of the manual alphabet. I sat with that book in my lap for an hour, reading the paragraphs over and over, and practicing fingerspelling. This was the beginning of exciting times to come.

Teenagers often spend a great deal of time mulling over their vocational options, and I was no different in that respect. As a junior in high school I had learned about Gallaudet University and while I was very interested in going there, I needed to weigh going away to school against attending a local university. I shared this dilemma with my mother.

"Do you want to know what I think you should do?" she asked.

"Yes."

Then she calmly but frankly said, "I'm not going to tell you what *I* think you should do. This has to be *your* decision."

With her statement came a new freedom, and a door opened for me to go in the direction that I desired. Yes, I was going to Gallaudet, and at long last, I was going to learn to sign! August 1973 is a month I will never forget. I didn't mind the heat and humidity because I was on the brink of a new and exciting journey in life. Exactly what that journey would entail was unforeseeable, but intuitively I knew that change was in the air and it just felt "right." I spent hours shopping, packing, and preparing for my trip to Washington, D.C., where I would become a college freshman at Gallaudet.

Gallaudet is a fully accredited university on a beautiful campus in northeast Washington, D.C. Like at any other university, students at Gallaudet hurry across campus to classes, sit on a grassy knoll to study or rest between classes, do research in the library, join sororities and fraternities, date, attend football games, play sports, practice cheerleading, and dance. The difference is that at Gallaudet, the students are deaf and everywhere you look people are signing. It is a visual learning environment where faculty, students, and staff share a common, yet diverse, cultural and language bond. Students come to Gallaudet from all over the world, from fifty states, and from various cultural, ethnic, racial, and religious backgrounds. But the diversity at Gallaudet stretches a bit further than it does at most universities. Chapter 2 and the chapters about the children in this book will help to explain what that diversity is.

Gallaudet was a major gateway for me. It was the pot of gold at the end of my search for self, and it represented the beginning of the rest of my life. It was at Gallaudet that I discovered what it means to be deaf. It was where I sealed that bond that I had only touched on that rainy afternoon waiting for the bus. At Gallaudet, at last, I was in an environment where I had access to everything and everyone around me. I embraced the friendships, the learning, the self-discovery, and the change that lay before me. Here, and with sign language, my love for learning blossomed. Learning became more than just a textbook experience; it became interactive, broad, experiential, accessible, and exciting. Learning was everywhere! There was a whole world out there waiting for me to explore and no barriers holding me back.

Why did Gallaudet and my immersion in the Deaf community mean so much to me? The answer to that question lies in my own story, the biopsychosocial and developmental experiences that I had, my own perceptions, and the meaning I ascribed to them. Many deaf adults have similar stories and share my love of Gallaudet and the Deaf community. But every deaf person is different. This diversity among people who are deaf and hard of hearing has presented a challenge to researchers who have traditionally not defined their population adequately.

My own history helped to shape my particular self-perceptions, values, my world views, and my place in life today. For all of us, the self is based on the context of contributing variables in our social, intellectual, biological, and emotional environments and how we shape these factors into a whole. My story is my perception. Had my parents told you their recollections, the story you just read may have been very different. Their perceptions would have been shaped within the context of living as hearing individuals. They had "a different center" (Padden and Humphries, 1988)[4] and viewed the world from a different "epistemology" (Harvey, 1989),[5] paradigm, or map. They were parents; I was a child. They grew up in a generation different from mine, in different schools, with parents of their own, and they "heard" what was happening around them. My

---

4. "A different center" is a phrase used by Padden and Humphries (1988) to describe the different assumptions that deaf and hearing people have about deafness and hearing.

5. Harvey (1989) describes an epistemology as the lens through which one views the world.

perceptions, on the other hand, were based on what I "saw." While parents, teachers, and other professionals in the lives of deaf children have their valid perspectives, the views of the children must also be heard. Only a deaf child—speaking from his center and his context—can truly say what it's like to be deaf.

Many years ago, while I was leaving the swimming pool one day, three little girls approached me. Curiously, they asked, "What's it like to be deaf?" Little did they know the complexity of their question. Realizing the impossibility of answering that on my way out the door and knowing they were referring to not hearing sounds, a variable quite separate from the cultural and social meanings of being deaf, I just laughed and said, "Nice and quiet." Hopefully the stories told by the children in this book will give those curious little girls who are, no doubt, all grown up by now, some answers to their question. It is my hope that the voices of the children in this book will be heard by those professionals working to develop programs for the deaf. Further, I hope that these chapters will also help the reader understand the importance of context in the children's unique developmental experiences and resulting perspectives—their lifeworlds.

INSPIRATION

In my doctoral program at Ohio State University, *The Spiritual Life of Children* by Robert Coles (1990) was required reading for a research class I took with Dr. James Lantz. In his book, Coles interviews young children from various cultural, religious, racial, and ethnic backgrounds about their perceptions of their spiritual lives. He takes the reader on a journey through the spiritual heritage and experiences of these children as they draw pictures and share their images of this intangible aspect of their lifeworlds. I was impressed by the vividness of the children's images and inspired by Coles's approach to uncovering the meanings that spirituality has in the lives of these children. I was moved by how cognitively and qualitatively different their perceptions were from what I imagined an adult's would be. Then it struck me: "Why hasn't anyone sought to understand the lifeworlds of deaf and hard of hearing children from the children's perspectives?" I wondered what the children would say.

What perceptions do they have of themselves and of others in their lives? What do they think about being deaf?

Most of the research on children who are deaf involves their educational and cognitive development, and much less has been done on their social development (Meadow-Orlans, 1990). Further, much of the literature and research in deafness describes the perceptions that others have of these children. I thought of how much we could learn from the children themselves by listening to their stories and images of their lifeworlds. What better way to learn than to ask them? Thus, I set out to explore in my dissertation how deaf and hard of hearing children experience and interpret their lifeworlds.

I wanted to learn from the child's perspective what it is like to be a deaf child in a hearing world that imposes communication, language, and cultural biases. What belief systems of belonging and culture exist? How do the children deal with issues of grief, which the literature reports their parents and significant others experience? What views do deaf and hard of hearing children have of themselves? What meaning do they attribute to their environmental experiences and their relationships? What do they report their experiences to be? What are their world views?

METHODOLOGY AND RATIONALE

The focus of the qualitative research described in this book is the exploration of the perceptions deaf and hard of hearing children between the ages of seven and ten have of the world they live in.[6] Particular attention is given to gaining information on how deaf and hard of hearing children view themselves and others in their lives in the context of the hearing world.

Seven children from a variety of backgrounds were selected through a process of purposive sampling for interviews.[7] One of the problems with existing research is that the variables and diversity

---

6. Qualitative research allows for the discovery of themes and theory through an inductive process of analysis. This method helps us to understand the meaning and world views that people bring to their interactions with their environments.

7. Purposive sampling is a nonrandom sampling technique used to identify participants in a research study. More specifically, *maximum variation* sampling, a purposive technique, was adopted in this study to allow the selection of participants from diverse back-

among people who are deaf are often not taken into consideration when research is designed (Lane, 1992; Lane, Hoffmeister, and Bahan, 1996; Moores, 1987; Schein and Delk, 1974). I wanted to use a methodology that would allow me to identify and describe the unique background and experiences of each child. That way, I could avoid lumping together descriptions of all deaf and hard of hearing children, yet look for common themes among the children in the study. It should be noted that this type of research avoids generalizing its findings to all deaf and hard of hearing children and instead gives information only about the children participating in the study.

I prepared a script of direct questioning to use with the children. My interview techniques involved asking the children to draw pictures for me about deaf children, their families, friends, and schools, and then asking them to tell me stories about their drawings. I also showed the children pictures cut out from magazines and asked them to tell me what was happening in those pictures. With both techniques, I asked the children specific questions, and then based on what evolved, I followed with additional questions until common themes began to emerge and I felt I had enough information to report. This method allowed me to identify similarities and differences among the children.

Additional problems noted in the literature on research methods and their applicability to children who are deaf and hard of hearing include the communication skills of the examiners (Lane, 1992; Lane et al., 1996; Levine, 1960), the ethics of establishing a knowledge base in deafness based on the perceptions of others, and a lack of consideration for context in the deaf person's life (e.g., Akamatsu, 1993/94; Foster, 1993/94; Pollard, 1993/94). These problems call for an examination of the appropriateness of research methods with this population.

The qualitative research methods that were used allowed for the identification of emergent themes of the boys and girls in the study. With all of the diversity that exists among deaf and hard of hearing people, these methods allowed me to take issues of communication, etiology, the presence of disability, definitions of deafness used for

---

grounds. This diversity was beneficial in portraying and preserving the uniqueness of each child while allowing for the identification of common themes across cases.

sampling, identity, appropriate research instruments, ethnicity, cultural orientations, communication skills of the researcher and the children, and cultural bias into consideration as I designed the study and interpreted the results. Qualitative methods also allow for the uniqueness of the perspectives and experiences of deaf and hard of hearing children in the context of their individual and subjective lifeworlds.

SUMMARY

The stories told in this book represent the context of time, place, and situations in these children's lives at the time in which these interviews took place. Their experiences, perceptions, and contexts will continue to develop as they grow. The children's early personal and cultural experiences are determined by the decisions made by, and cultural contexts of, their parents, families, and professionals in their lives, as well as by the historical and temporal contexts of their lives. The following chapter will present in more detail the historical, developmental, and educational contexts for studying deaf children.

2

Transcending in Time

We embrace equality and yet struggle with it in reality.
We have come so far, and yet we have not escaped the past.
—Ellis Cose, 1999

I WAS AT dinner one evening with a group of deaf friends, a mixture of young and middle-aged adults. One of the younger individuals who had grown up mainstreamed in hearing schools turned to an older person who had gone to her high school and asked about his experiences there. He responded that he had been the only deaf student at his school and that he had unpleasant memories of his social experiences. She replied that her experiences had been quite different, that she had been popular, and looked back on her high school days with fond memories. To that, the older friend said, "Things were different in those days. It wasn't easy then to be deaf in a hearing school. Attitudes are different today. There's not as much stigma."

This story is a reflection of the changes that have taken place regarding the experiences of people who are deaf. This older friend, like myself, grew up in an era quite different from today. Many deaf and hard of hearing children now have the advantage of the technology, role models, legal and educational support, and opportunities that I and many other deaf people of my generation and generations before us did not have. One of the goals of this chapter is to examine the environmental, historical, and *temporal* factors that help to explain the findings that arose from the research described in this book.[8] These factors explain, at least in part, the various

---

8. In this book I refer to the influence of time on the children's lives, and our understanding of this aspect of their lives as temporal contexts, factors, or dimensions.

aspects of these children's lives that together make up the context of their lifeworlds.

Like all research, the studies published in the literature on deaf and hard of hearing children take place at specific times. Thus, our perceptions of these children must be fluid. As environmental circumstances such as technology, laws, education, and social perceptions change, so do the experiences of children who are deaf.

An ecological perspective (Germain and Gitterman, 1996), sometimes called the person-in-environment perspective, takes these environmental and temporal factors into account when trying to understand the lifeworlds of children who are deaf. These environmental (ecological) or contextual influences on the lives of deaf and hard of hearing people have been discussed by several researchers (Glickman and Harvey, 1996; Harvey, 1989; Schlesinger and Meadow, 1972). According to the ecological perspective, we do not exist separately from our environments. People and their environments are interdependent and mutually influencing. Within this framework is the concept of "goodness of fit" between the person and various systems levels. As described by Bronfenbrenner (1979), these systems levels are called *micro-* (individual); *meso-* (small groups such as families and work groups); and *macro-*communities (sociocultural and political organizations). These systems levels are influenced by the dimension of time.

Since these systems change over time, it is important to examine the historical contexts for studying children who are deaf and hard of hearing. The critical ecological, historical, and temporal contexts influencing the lives of the children include:

- demographics
- technology
- the validation and advancement of American Sign Language
- new visions of self and others
- legislation
- changes in educational philosophies
- changing images of deaf people in the arts and media
- socioeconomic advancement
- the establishment of community services and consumer organizations
- and new approaches to research and professional practice

Deaf and hard of hearing children today experience a greater goodness of fit between themselves and their environments than did the generations before them. Deaf and hard of hearing people will continue to negotiate this goodness of fit as the world around us changes.

Perspectives and Elements of Change

Demographics

Just as the demographics of children in the United States are changing, so too are the demographics of deaf and hard of hearing children. One and two generations ago, many deaf and hard of hearing children in the schools were not identified or were not placed in appropriate educational settings. Today, a greater effort is made to identify and understand the demographics of deaf and hard of hearing school-aged children.

The Gallaudet Research Institute (GRI) at Gallaudet University has conducted annual national surveys of deaf and hard of hearing students in schools since 1968, reaching approximately 65–70 percent of students identified by the U.S. Department of Education (Allen, 1997). Between the years 1986–1996, GRI found a significant increase in the proportion of study participants with mild to moderate hearing loss and a decrease in the number of students with profound hearing loss. Conclusions from the survey indicate that this change may be due to changes in etiology, increased survey coverage, and participation among students in local public schools, and, possibly, a greater number of hard of hearing students being identified and receiving special services now than in the past.

Major causes of deafness change as environmental and medical factors change; however, the largest etiological category has been "cause unknown" for over a century (Moores, 1987). During the decade in which the most recent survey was conducted, the percentage of etiologies unknown or unreported climbed from 44 percent to 51 percent. Immunizations for measles, mumps, and meningitis, the passing of the 1960s rubella outbreak, and better prenatal care may all be contributing to lower numbers of deaf and hard of hearing children.

The number of students participating in the annual survey of deaf and hard of hearing youth who are white and non-Hispanic has decreased while the number of Hispanic students has increased. Conclusions suggest that white, non-Hispanic students may be less likely than minority students to be referred for special services in schools and that minority students are overrepresented among those receiving services.

Technology

Recently, my husband and I contacted a distant relative, Richard, about a family matter. I had not seen Richard for several years. I recalled that he was fun and pleasant to be around. As a child, I joined my siblings and cousins in laughter while we chased Richard around my grandmother's one-and-a-half acres. He jumped over bushes and lawn chairs, impressing us with his skill and stamina. When I called him, I used the Maryland Relay Service. Telephone relay services became available as recently as 1990 with the passage of the Americans with Disabilities Act. The relay service makes it possible for hearing people who do not have teletypewriter telecommunications devices for the deaf (called TTYs) to communicate with people who are deaf and who use TTYs for telephone correspondence. A communication assistant relays the call by voicing the deaf person's typed communication to the hearing party and typing the hearing party's spoken communication to the deaf caller. While I was on the phone with Richard it became apparent to me that this was probably the first time in either of our lives that we had carried on a conversation of more than a couple of sentences. It was also the first time we had ever communicated on the phone. He joked, "I see you're still pretending to be deaf," and I responded, "I see you still have your sense of humor."

Telecommunications devices for the deaf were not introduced until the 1960s. At that time, they consisted of old, large, bulky teletypewriter machines that connected to a modem and a telephone line. In the beginning, only a few deaf people had them in their homes. Telephone access was minimal. Like most other technology, the cost and size of these machines decreased as their popularity spread and production increased. Eventually, with the advocacy efforts of many deaf people and laws that supported accessibility in public places, TTYs became increasingly common in schools, health and social service programs, businesses, and places of employment. The establishment of telephone relay services mandated under the Americans with Disabilities Act further enhanced telephone access and autonomy.

Hearing aids were once bulky, obnoxious devices with wires extending from the body of the aid to the ear. This was an awkward and uncomfortably visible piece of equipment to wear. In time, hearing aids also became smaller and more comfortable, but they continue to be quite costly.

Closed captioned television made its way into the lives of people who are deaf and hard of hearing in the late 1970s. Captioning technology and legislation made it possible for deaf and hard of hearing children at home and in school to have access to television programming. In order to see the captions, consumers had to purchase a closed captioned decoder at a cost of about $200. Unfortunately, many families were unable to afford this additional expense. Schools, service agencies, and employers had to be convinced by parents and other advocates that they were necessary for their children's benefit. In 1990, the Television Decoder Circuitry Act required all newly manufactured televisions thirteen inches or larger sold in the United States to be equipped with built-in decoder circuitry.

Home computers came onto the scene a few years later, but only in a few homes. Today, E-mail is used extensively by deaf people who have computers at home, school, or work. E-mail and Internet chat capability, digital pagers, and wireless communication devices have brought a new dimension of freedom and independence in communication for deaf and hard of hearing people who have access to this technology. With all these advancements, many deaf people no longer need to rely on sign language interpreters to make telecommunications contact with others. On-line communication balances the degree of independence with the degree of privacy in our communicative interactions. Hearing people with whom we communicate on-line are often unaware that we are deaf. Thus, the prejudices that might otherwise impede our interaction are nonexistent.

Consumer advocates continue to monitor technological and telecommunications advancements to ensure access in a rapidly changing environment. The Federal Communications Commission has established a Disabilities Rights office, which regulates television, telecommunications, and Internet telephony access and works closely with deaf consumer organizations.

Computer-assisted, real-time captioning (CART) has become commonplace in meetings, classes, conferences, and presentations. This technology, which usually involves a professional stenographer, provides deaf and hard of hearing people who do not know sign language with a means of understanding spoken communication in a large group.

Validation and Advancement of American Sign Language

Breakthrough research on American Sign Language (Stokoe, 1960; Stokoe, Casterline, and Croneberg, 1965) occurred in the 1960s. Stokoe's work on American Sign Language (ASL) helped lead to the formation of new images of people who are deaf. Stokoe took a revolutionary approach by basing his analysis of ASL on linguistic principles, a break from the traditional pictorial view of ASL (Padden and Humphries, 1988).

As with many social movements, especially those that emerge in populations that have experienced decades of oppression, acceptance of ASL among both deaf and hearing people as a language in its own right did not occur overnight. Many deaf people who signed and grew up with the notion that signing was not a language, or that signing was inferior to English, required some time to accept this new idea and to experience the freedom that came with it. Padden and Humphries describe how this new freedom contributed to a change of consciousness among artists who were deaf. They were able to move from translating already developed, English-based pieces (poetry and stories, for instance) into ASL to create new works based on ASL and deaf folklore. ASL did catch on and, with it, civil rights for deaf people began to unfold.

The increase in the number of classes offered in ASL resulted in an enormous increase in the number of individuals who sign. Sign language interpreting emerged as a new profession in the 1970s, and professional interpreter training programs were established nationwide. As increasing numbers of deaf children were mainstreamed, more classes in sign language were offered in schools where deaf children were enrolled, allowing their hearing classmates to develop the skills to communicate with them. Certification of sign language instructors and increased opportunities for teaching careers in sign language interpreter training, as well as incipient ASL studies programs in colleges and universities, have advanced the credibility of the language and, with it, the viability of people who are deaf. Many states have enacted legislation including ASL among the languages offered to fulfill the foreign language requirements in high school and postsecondary programs.

New Visions of Self

Many positive changes are transpiring in the way deaf and hard of hearing people define themselves. Traditionally, there have been two major views of deaf and hard of hearing people discussed in the literature: medical and cultural (Jacobs, 1974). Theorists often call these types of views of individuals and groups *social constructions* because they are images that are created, valued, upheld, and nurtured through social interaction and are adopted by individuals through cultural transmission. The medical and cultural views of deafness reflect opposite social values.

Previously, discussions, debates, and identity issues in deafness focused on these two dichotomous social constructions. Today, in an assertive self-empowering approach, people are defining themselves as deaf, Deaf, hard of hearing, late deafened, biculturally deaf, oral deaf, Deaf of Deaf (Deaf child of Deaf Parents), or Deaf of hearing (parents).[9] The old term "hearing impaired," which connotes a deficit, is now seldom used for self-definition. All of these terms have social, developmental, cultural, and existential meanings.

The traditional medical construction of deafness has also been called the clinical or the pathological perspective. This view implies

---

9. Many authors and researchers have attempted to define and categorize their populations using the terms *deaf, Deaf, hard of hearing, oral deaf, bi-culturally deaf*, etc. I find this troubling because I value the self-determination inherent in the process of self-labeling. At the same time, a general definition of terms is useful in clarifying the author's assumptions for the reader. Therefore, it should be noted that definitions and use of these terms throughout this book represent my own application of the labels. The capitalized term *Deaf* reflects a person who identifies him- or herself as culturally Deaf, who uses ASL as his or her primary language, and who is involved with the Deaf community. The uncapitalized *deaf* is often used inclusively in this book to refer to all of these categories of individuals but is also used at times to indicate the absence of Deaf culture in the lives and selves of the children.

that deafness is a biological disorder or deficit that should be corrected. Many people who see deafness as a deficit see people who are deaf as inferior, unfortunate, and in need of help. Within this view, hearing is valued, and research to eradicate deafness is encouraged. Educational approaches consistent with this view advocate *normalizing* children who are deaf and hard of hearing through an emphasis on oral communication, auditory enhancement, and hearing culture. Speech is valued in this perspective. The term *oral deaf* is used to refer to deaf people who rely primarily on speech and speechreading for communication. A position statement prepared by Self Help for Hard of Hearing People, Inc. (SHHH), quotes the sense of hearing as a *gift* (1995, p. 1), emphasizing the value that hearing holds for members of the organization.

The cultural view has long been taken for granted by people who are Deaf. Recent studies (Lane, Hoffmeister, and Bahan, 1996; Padden and Humphries, 1988; Parasnis, 1996) have discussed the cultural aspects of being Deaf. Padden (1980) defined people who are "Deaf" (uppercase) as those who are engaged in and adopt the language, values, rules for behavior, and traditions of this culture; and those who are audiologically deaf and not living according to Deaf culture may be seen by themselves and others as "deaf" (lowercase). She tells us that people may grow up and become enculturated later in life when they come in contact with the deaf community. An audiological definition of a hard of hearing person may be a person who has enough hearing for limited speech comprehension, while a cultural definition of a hard of hearing person would be one who does not view him- or herself as culturally Deaf.

The cultural perspective advocates for the promotion and acceptance of ASL, of Deaf culture, and of people who are Deaf. People who are Deaf view themselves as an ethnic group and do not consider themselves disabled. A mainstreamed junior high school boy writes in a winning essay, "I don't think being deaf is my biggest challenge as much as it is facing other people's ideas of what deaf means . . . Being deaf is a gift from God. Here I am, proud of being deaf" (Crane, 1999).

As can be seen from the examples above, people who are deaf or hard of hearing do not always adopt identical views of themselves or identical cultural orientations. Many factors contribute to a deaf person's self-identity and, ultimately, to the being and becoming of the deaf person. Aside from type and amount of hearing loss, these factors include the following: age of onset, parental and familial hearing status and cultural orientation, educational placement, etiology, language, and communication preferences.

A very important consideration is the fact that 90 percent of children who are deaf have hearing parents. Most hearing parents do not expect to have a deaf child and begin a process of grief upon learning that their child is deaf. The experiences of hearing parents have been documented in works by Harvey (1989), Meadow-Orlans (1980), Moores (1987), and others. Today more than ever, parents are faced with a variety of controversial options regarding communication and educational placement. But in the last decade the addition of cochlear implants to this controversy has weighed heavily upon many parents.[10] Some authors contend that just as hearing parents expect to have hearing children, Deaf parents hope that their children will be Deaf (Lane et al., 1996). Contrasting with that view is a study examining the preferences for the hearing status of future children of deaf undergraduate students at Gallaudet University. The study found that the majority of students indicated no preference related to the hearing status of their children. However, 25 percent of those students mentioned a preference and almost all of this 25 percent would choose that their child be deaf (Miller, Moores, and Sicoli, forthcoming).

Because 90 percent of deaf children have hearing parents, most deaf children grow up in a hearing culture. As these children grow, they have the opportunity to choose an identity in regard to their deafness. Some may adopt a Deaf cultural identity; others may not. Many members of SHHH acknowledge they are deaf, and many

---

10. Some deaf children and adults have the option of cochlear implantation. In the last decade, there was a dramatic increase in the number of children who received implants. This growing phenomenon is rapidly adding to the diversity of the deaf community. The initial resistance of the deaf community to cochlear implants—evident throughout the last three decades—is dissipating as it becomes clear that individuals with implants are not leaving this community (Leigh and Christiansen, forthcoming). The National Association of the Deaf, which previously opposed cochlear implants, has neutralized its position. However, there is still a great deal of staunch opposition to cochlear implants, much of it aimed at the medical profession.

have been deaf from childhood, but they choose not to learn sign language and report that they identify with the hearing cultural orientation of the members of their organization (Pray, 1999).

In their struggle to establish an identity and a place in society, many deaf people have found they do not exclusively fit either the medical or the cultural model and describe themselves as living a dual existence. Glickman (1996) developed categories of deaf identity, based on points and a progression from feeling part of the hearing culture to a final stage in which Deaf culture is affirmed. Holcomb (1997) also discussed the likelihood of several identity categories based on the deaf person's exposure to and involvement in the deaf community. Glickman and Holcomb's ideas are adaptations of racial identity development models.

If we accept that bicultural identities exist among people who are deaf, then we must recognize that there is a third perspective on deafness. This third perspective, the bicultural view, includes components of both the medical and the cultural realities of being deaf. A bicultural individual lives in two or more cultures, adapts to these cultures, and blends aspects of the cultures (Grosjean, 1996). Being bicultural implies tension between cultures. Individuals who are bicultural deal with the tensions between their two cultures on a daily basis (Grosjean, 1996; Padden, 1996; Padden and Humphries, 1988).

Application of the bicultural and racial identity development perspectives runs short, however, of recognizing that 90 percent of deaf children have hearing parents and do not experience a multigenerational aspect of Deaf culture. Thus, for these deaf children, identity development models based on transcultural or transracial adoptions may be more applicable. Children who are adopted across cultures lack the benefit of multigenerational "sameness" or role models in their families. Successful transcultural and transracial adoptive parenting, which leads to a healthy identity for the child, requires that the parents/caregivers acknowledge the biological and cultural differences between themselves and their child, that they seek out role models and appropriate peers for their child, and that they be involved in the child's culture and open to learning the language of the culture from which the child is adopted (Tatum, 1997). These conditions may apply to deaf children and their hearing parents as well, but a major difference remains: orientation to sight versus sound. Thus, there is a need for a developmental model unique to the life experiences of people who are deaf, for no model based on the development of children, adolescents, or adults who are hearing can be fully adapted to deaf children.

People who are culturally Deaf face a dilemma regarding inclusion laws intended to protect the rights of children and adults with disabilities. While many deaf people, particularly those who identify themselves as culturally Deaf, do not see themselves as disabled, many others who are deaf do see themselves in that capacity. Describing oneself as disabled is consistent with the medical view. Lane et al. (1996) claim that while people who are Deaf may benefit from the laws for people with disabilities, Deaf people see themselves as a linguistic and cultural minority with an agenda that is separate from those of other disability groups, one that focuses on linguistic and cultural acceptance. These authors recognize that it would be self-defeating for Deaf people not to include themselves in these laws, but this very inclusion defeats their linguistic and cultural agenda. The term *normalize*, which was discussed earlier, has an interesting double meaning dependent upon one's view of deafness.

The *modern Deaf self* (Humphries, 1996) is a state of self that has moved from the deaf mute of olden days who was defined and controlled by hearing people to the self-empowered Deaf person of today. The modern Deaf self no longer accepts responsibility for the cultural tensions between Deaf and hearing people. Instead, the modern Deaf person coexists with hearing people while maintaining boundaries and control of the self. The underlying issue in Humphries's discussion of the modern Deaf self is survival of the self through the taking of power by a group that has been deprived of it.

This reclaiming of the Deaf self reflects earlier feminist theory that encouraged the taking back of power through "re-naming" or allowing women a voice in defining themselves (Van Den Bergh and Cooper, 1986). Culturally Deaf, deaf, and hard of hearing people are situated on a continuum representing various degrees of hearing culture, biculturalism (Glickman, 1996) and Deaf ethnicity. While there are *panethnic* (Tatum, 1997) issues that would apply to all of these groups, they also have issues that are more specific to one group than another.[11] Examples of the panethnic issues they share are civil rights legislation, accessibility factors, technology, employment, and communication. Opportunities for panethnic advocacy exist around these and other issues. While all of these groups have issues in common, the specifics of the issues are often quite varied in relation to how they apply to the specific cultural orientations, goals, values, and communication and language preferences of each group. The enactment of the Americans with Disabilities Act is a good example of how these groups have come together across ethnic lines to advocate for improvements in political, economic, and social conditions that benefit each of them.

Today, more than ever before, an increased sense of unity and harmony is felt between and among the various groups mentioned above. Tensions and boundary issues between these groups do exist and often are very heated, but tolerance for differences among the groups continues to increase. This tolerance may occur in part because of economic feasibility and the power of solidarity for political gain and partly because of a general increase in the value of harmony between and among multicultural groups in society.

Deaf and hard of hearing people are benefiting from multicultural movements and the movements to empower minority groups in America (Parasnis, 1996). Advocates and researchers in deafness have been drawn to the parallels apparent between minority groups and the deaf community. People who are culturally Deaf have been referred to as "a new ethnic group" (Dolnick, 1993). It has been said that the Deaf President Now! (DPN) protest at Gallaudet University in 1988, which resulted in the selection of Dr. I. King Jordan as the university's first deaf president, was successful because of the parallel it drew to the civil rights movement (Christensen and Barnartt, 1995). The strong and effective leadership and the worldwide support and attention drawn to DPN was a testimony to the intelligence, passion, and capabilities of deaf people as agents of social change.

---

11. *Panethnic* is used here to refer to unity and issues common to all groups of deaf and hard of hearing people.

Legislation

Legislation that has taken place in the last three decades has contributed to social progress for deaf and hard of hearing people. The four major pieces of legislation are Section 504 of the Rehabilitation Act of 1973, the Americans with Disabilities Act, the Education for all Handicapped Children Act, and the Newborn Infant Hearing Screening and Intervention Act of 1999. The Rehabilitation Act of 1973, Section 504, was the first federal legislation to prohibit discrimination against people with disabilities in employment, education, health, and social services programs. The legislation had limitations in that it covered only programs that received federal funding. Nonetheless, it provided people who were deaf with a tool for social change.

The Americans with Disabilities Act (ADA) was signed into law by President Bush in 1990. It expanded Section 504 into the private sector. This law also helped to foster greater access to public accommodation, transportation, employment, and telecommunications.

The Education for all Handicapped Children's Act, also known as Public Law 94–142, passed in 1975 and was later expanded and renamed the Individuals with Disabilities Education Act of 1990 (IDEA). It brought changes to educational programming by requiring a free appropriate public education for all children with disabilities. IDEA mandated the development of an individualized family service plan for each child, required that children with disabilities be educated with nondisabled children to the maximum extent possible, and that parents have an active role in the decisions pertaining to their children's educational plan (Heward and Orlansky, 1992).

The Newborn Infant Hearing Screening and Intervention Act of 1999 allocates funding for state grants for newborn hearing screening and intervention programs. Traditionally, hearing was not assessed until infants were eighteen to twenty months of age, and delays in speech and language development were often the first real indications to parents that their child could not hear. This federal legislation is expected to facilitate earlier detection, reverse the probable language delays, and encourage early choices in educational placement and communication.

Educational Philosophies

Educational philosophies and trends have changed dramatically over the years. Explorations into the education of children who are deaf were made by such early thinkers as Socrates, Aristotle, and St. Augustine, but efforts to establish educational programs for deaf children did not occur until the sixteenth century (Winefield, 1987). Early educators of deaf children in the United States encouraged the use of sign language, and approximately 50 percent of educators of deaf children were themselves deaf (Lane, 1984; Sacks, 1990). While debates over oral versus signed educational approaches became more heated as time passed, the infamous International Convention of Instructors of the Deaf, which took place in Milan in 1880, marked a turning point in educational philosophies, and oral education became the dominant educational approach in the United States and Europe. Between that time and the 1960s, the number of deaf teachers decreased to approximately 12 percent (Lane, 1984; Sacks, 1990).

As noted in the section above, IDEA accelerated the debate on appropriate educational settings for children who are deaf. Many concerns about IDEA emerged from members of the Deaf community. The portion of the law requiring that children with disabilities be educated with nondisabled children to the maximum extent possible is referred to in education circles as the "least restrictive environment." IDEA considers institutional settings as the most restrictive environment, and residential schools for the deaf are considered institutions under this law. Those familiar with the educational needs of deaf children believe that IDEA is beneficial for most children with disabilities but that it has a detrimental impact on children who are deaf. This negative consequence occurs because classroom success depends on free and natural communicative interactions that are not available or are extremely restricted in these "inclusive" settings. The irony of the law's outcome is that while deaf children are physically present in the classroom, they are more frequently excluded from functional communication and social relations, which are such an important part of the learning process. Therefore, opponents of IDEA see classrooms where deaf children are mainstreamed as the "most restrictive environment." They feel that these inclusive settings do not foster the free-flowing communication and natural interaction with others that facilitates learning (Ramsey, 1997).

Some people who are Deaf are concerned that the outcome of IDEA will be the decline and eventual closure of residential schools for children who are deaf. These schools play a large part in the maintenance and transmission of Deaf culture across generations. Numbers of students attending residential schools for the deaf decreased in the last two decades but have remained relatively steady in the past few years (Allen, 1999). IDEA may be only partially responsible for this decline in enrollment. Immunizations for measles, mumps, and meningitis, and improved prenatal care may be contributing to lower numbers of deaf and hard of hearing children. Despite the overall numbers of deaf and hard of hearing children, residential schools account for proportionately fewer placements (Allen, 1999). The annual survey of deaf and hard of hearing students conducted at Gallaudet University shows a strong relationship between school placement and degree of hearing loss; greater numbers of students with less than severe hearing loss experience more hours in integrated settings than do those with more severe hearing loss (Allen, 1997). This same survey also showed increasing numbers of students with mild to moderate hearing loss and fewer profoundly deaf students in the schools that were covered in the survey.

Consistent with the diversity of perspectives on deaf and hard of hearing people, some deaf people and parents of deaf children see inclusion as beneficial and embrace it. My younger friend from the dinner conversation mentioned earlier is an example of someone who has benefited positively from inclusion and the societal and temporal context in which her experiences took place. Deaf culturalists have said that parents, students, and professionals who support inclusion and regular school settings as the least restrictive environment tend to be those who have a medical view of deafness and deaf people. This is perhaps overgeneralizing. Among those who participate in inclusion are culturally Deaf children of Deaf parents, bicultural children of bicultural deaf parents, and Deaf children who use ASL in mainstream settings. For example, one mainstreamed child of Deaf parents in this study reports that she moves comfortably back and forth between Deaf and hearing people.

Many individuals believe that we need and should support both educational options. In addition, data collected in the annual survey of deaf and hard of hearing youth show increasing numbers of children with mild to moderate hearing loss receiving services in public schools.

In the last decade, bilingual/bicultural Deaf education programs have been developed. Deaf schoolchildren in these programs have the opportunity to integrate Deaf history, Deaf culture, and ASL into their curriculum. This integration aims to foster an affirming and valuable sense of self-esteem and cultural self-awareness.

Children and adolescents at Kendall Demonstration Elementary School and the Model Secondary School for the Deaf at the Laurent Clerc National Deaf Education Center (LCNDEC) also have the benefit of a multicultural curriculum that incorporates educational objectives and activities specific to minority cultures. For example, a multicultural specialist works with teachers at LCNDEC to help them identify ways of integrating diversity in the curriculum. During a visit to Kendall School, I observed student displays of famous black Deaf people studied in class.

Arts and Media

The media has traditionally been an avenue of cultural transmission and played a big part in public perception of people who are deaf and hard of hearing. As recently as 1980, deaf characters were portrayed as mute and dumb. Deaf women were often depicted as damsels in distress or helpless victims. These characterizations reflected the predominant pathological social perception of deaf people at the time.

Children of a Lesser God (Medoff, 1979), the powerful and highly successful Broadway play that was later adapted for screen, emphatically communicated cultural and linguistic differences and tensions among Deaf, hearing, and hard of hearing people in their relationships. This popular production also contributed to the changing perceptions and broader acceptance of people who are deaf that were occurring at the time. A potent message effectively communicated in the play, reflective of the American period in which it transpired, was "What about me? What I want?" (p. 68). The main Deaf character in the play makes a strong statement about wanting to speak for herself, of needing to break free of the control that hearing people had over her. Metaphorically, perhaps, this play was a way for many deaf people to acquire a voice, and it represented a step forward in the process of social change. Phyllis Frelich, who won a Tony Award in the Broadway production, and Marlee Matlin, who won an Oscar for best actress in the film, served as role models and heroes for young deaf people. Since that time, both of these actresses have portrayed strong and independent deaf professional women in television roles.

Socioeconomic Change

Another change at the sociocultural level has been the development of a middle class and a professional class of deaf people (Padden, 1996). The enactment of laws such as the Rehabilitation Act of 1973 and the Americans with Disabilities Act and advancements in technology have all helped to increase educational and career opportunities for people who are deaf. More and more deaf people have obtained postsecondary and graduate degrees and entered a variety of traditional and nontraditional professions.

Although a middle class and professional class of deaf adults has developed, barriers continue to exist across socioeconomic classes of deaf and hard of hearing people. While technology provides a wonderful avenue for independent telecommunication and access to information, it is expensive, and many deaf and hard of hearing people are unable to afford it. A computer, a TTY, and one hearing aid can cost in excess of $5,000 for a single individual. This amount doesn't include the hearing aid batteries or flashing phone and door signalers.

Community Services and Consumer Organizations

Today we have legislation that protects people who are deaf and hard of hearing against discrimination in many areas of their lives. Advocacy efforts of deaf and hard of hearing consumers have assured their civil rights. Deaf and hard of hearing people have successfully established many local and national advocacy organizations. The National Association of the Deaf (NAD) and SHHH are examples of two national consumer organizations with state and local chapters that advocate for advancement, accessibility, and the protection of their members. Consumer Action Network is a coalition of national organizations that advocates for access to telecommunications, human services, education, and other vital amenities. Groups such as NAD, SHHH, the American Association of the Deaf-Blind, National Black Deaf Advocates, Deaf Women United, Telecommunications for the Deaf, Inc., and other national organizations form the membership of the coalition. These groups and others organized out of self-identified needs for support and advancement.

Young deaf people today may be surprised to learn that it wasn't long ago that those who were deaf had to fight for the right to drive and to marry. Astrid Goodstein, president of the Maryland Association of the Deaf, spoke to my social work students one morning about the function of state NAD chapters. She gave examples of how state associations for deaf people formed as recently as the 1950s with the goal of changing laws and social practices that prohibited privileges that others took for granted.

Today more than ever before, community services are available that support the goals and activities of consumer organizations and educational programs for people who are deaf and hard of hearing. Many of these organizations are staffed by deaf professionals with graduate degrees in social work or administration. These centers offer services such as counseling, mediation services in discrimination cases, sign language interpreting, CART services, sign language classes, deaf awareness workshops, information and referral, training for other public and private agencies, and educational workshops for deaf and hard of hearing people on legal, health, financial, and social issues. They also may provide creative support for deaf and hard of hearing children through weekend activities or clubs for deaf youth. Numerous summer camp programs are also available for deaf and hard of hearing children and adolescents. Many deaf education programs offer summer family learning vacations or workshops for families with deaf children.

New Approaches to Research and Professional Practice

Another element influencing positive change in the lives of deaf and hard of hearing children today is the *strengths perspective* (Saleebey, 1992) and a push for its application among those who are engaged in research and professional practice with the deaf and hard of hearing (Sheridan, 1998; Sussman, 1992). Much of the literature on deaf children and their development has been written by psychologists and educators. Traditionally, psychologists are problem focused. They start with baselines for what is "normal" and then look for deviations from the norm. Reports on research into the development and the lives of children who are deaf have traditionally been negative because baselines established for hearing children are used as the norm. Moreover, the tests and assessments traditionally used by psychologists are primarily designed for children who can hear. Many of these evaluators and researchers do not have the skills to communicate with deaf children, a knowledge base in deafness, awareness of the diversity in the deaf population, or knowledge of appropriate evaluations to use with this population (Lane et al., 1996; Levine, 1960, 1981; Moores, 1987).

Historically, researchers have also failed to define their population (Schein and Delk, 1974). As a result, important cultural, ethnic, linguistic, and physical (i.e., neurological or disability) variables are not considered in the findings. The literature (i.e., Lane, 1992; Lane et al., 1996; Moores, 1987) reports that researchers have tended to survey the perspectives of parents, teachers, and other professionals in a deaf child's life to describe deaf children. These "others" are usually hearing people who have a different *center* (Padden and Humphries, 1988) or perspective on what constitutes a *complete* (Humphries, 1996) child. These problems cast a doubtful light on the applicability and relevance of most research results regarding studies with deaf and hard of hearing people. Predictably, accounts in the literature that attempt to describe the personality, cognitive characteristics, and social functioning of children who are deaf are often negative. Sussman calls this preoccupation with psychopathology unfortunate because "there are far more well adjusted, psychologically healthy and effective deaf people than there are not" (1992, p. 3).

While groups of deaf, Deaf, hard of hearing, late deafened individuals, and deaf people who communicate primarily through oral communication may not agree with each other's perspective on deafness, and they may experience tensions in their relations because of these differing centers, the skills and meanings that are a part of their lives add up to a larger set of strengths than pathologies. The ability of deaf and hard of hearing people to persist and survive in the midst of their ethnic tensions, to tolerate multicultural realities, and to continue to grow is in itself a reflection of the strength of both the communities and their individual members.

Viewing deaf and hard of hearing people from an ethnic stance has led to the introduction of research methods that are congruent with this new perspective. These inductive methodologies help us to understand meanings, behaviors, and experiences from the world view of the informant in the contexts in which they occur. Researchers in deafness need to be open to all dimensions of what it means to be deaf or hard of hearing, and qualitative research methods are responsive to the multiple and ever changing realities of human beings.

Special consideration needs to be given to methodological, validity, reliability, ethical, linguistic, and cultural implications when undertaking research with people who are deaf (Sheridan, 1996). One of the benefits of qualitative research for ethnic groups such as deaf and hard of hearing people is that it requires ongoing self-examination and reflection on the realities, values, and world views of the researcher. Qualitative methods help us to scrutinize the research process as well as the outcome of the research while respecting the "voice" of those we want to learn about while capturing the fullness of their experiences.

The qualitative method is a viable approach to research with deaf and hard of hearing children. This method has been applied and described in the literature on deaf children (e.g., Evans, 1998; Foster, 1996; Sheridan, 1996; Spencer, 2000). This method helps us to appreciate the uniqueness of each deaf and hard of hearing child while identifying themes common to groups of deaf and hard of hearing children in the contexts of their environments. Its utility with deaf and hard of hearing children represents a goodness of fit between research and the human experience.

WHY LISTEN TO THE CHILDREN?

Recent research and published literature have attempted to explore and describe the educational and social realities and experiences of deaf children by documenting the reflections of deaf adults on their childhood experiences (e.g., Foster, 1996, 1989; Holcomb, 1997;

Leigh, 1999). These stories are momentous in that they represent the perceptions and realities of the storytellers who have arrived at a mature perspective on their experiences. However, because of the historical and temporal context in which these stories are situated, we cannot generalize the childhood experiences of these deaf adults to those of deaf and hard of hearing children today. Policies and programs cannot be developed solely on the basis of these reflections. Consequently, it is vital that the experiences of today's children be heard.

As the preceding paragraphs illustrate, in the past, deaf and hard of hearing people have always been those whom hearing people have defined them to be. As Humphries so eloquently states, "The Deaf person's image of self was the image that the hearing person rendered" (p. 101). He continues, "A self cannot exist if it is not heard. Deaf people have had to create voices, learn to hear their own voices, and now it remains to compel others to listen" (p. 104). Like any other ethnic group, people who are deaf and hard of hearing want to control their image of self. Listening to the voices of the children allows us to move ahead in the spirit of the strengths perspective and away from a pathologizing history.

CAVEATS

The transformations in the status of deaf and hard of hearing people in America and the changes in the social perceptions that others have of people who are deaf and hard of hearing have produced a definite improvement in their quality of life. America is also a far better place to be a Black Deaf American, a Hispanic Deaf American, a Deaf woman, or an Asian Deaf American than it has ever been, but separately and collectively we are still not afforded the same privileges that hearing people take for granted. Much remains to be done.

Inequality and social injustice continue to exist across many ecological systems levels for people who are deaf. Despite the passage of the ADA, in most instances deaf people are denied equal access to medical care because the medical profession resists absorbing the cost of providing sign language interpreters or TTYs for their patients who are deaf. Thus, effective communication with our doctors has yet to transpire.

Further, there are no certification requirements for educational interpreters in many locales. As a result, many children who are mainstreamed for all or part of their education receive unregulated, substandard, and often incomprehensible interpreted classroom instruction. Even hard of hearing children in schools do not have the appropriate acoustic environments they need to benefit from classroom communication (Flexer, 1999). In many states, the public education system does not provide teachers, school social workers, or counselors who are themselves deaf or hard of hearing. As a result, deaf children have no role models.

Technology cannot replace one-to-one human communication, and therefore it should not be expected to. Children's educational computer software is chiefly inaccessible to deaf children because they cannot hear the recorded instructions or tutorials that hearing children benefit from. Many educational films and videos have not been captioned for deaf and hard of hearing schoolchildren. Rapid changes in technology should continue to be closely followed by efforts from deaf and hard of hearing advocates and national organizations such as the NAD, Consumer Action Network, and SHHH to ensure accessibility.

Although we now have a deaf middle class, this middle class status has not been accessible to all deaf and hard of hearing people. As deaf people have obtained advanced degrees and moved into professional positions, most of these positions are in professions working with people who are deaf and hard of hearing. Although Gallaudet University's president, Dr. I. King Jordan, has coined the phrase, "Deaf people can do anything except hear," it remains to be seen if hearing universities would hire such a competent, intelligent, and qualified person as Dr. Jordan to run their own schools. Although we are on the way, generally, the time is yet to come when we are called upon by others to contribute to society beyond our roles and expertise as deaf and hard of hearing people.

While models of biculturalism are now being applied to people who are deaf, most of these discussions in the literature on deafness center around the developmental and cognitive processes and capabilities of adolescents, young adults, and adults. The literature emphasizes the value in viewing deaf and hard of hearing people from a bicultural perspective, but much work remains to be done on its relationship and applicability to various age groups, including children. Scant attention has been given to the development of identity, states of being, experiences, and perceptions of children who are deaf and hard of hearing. Developmentally, children, adolescents, and adults experience the world from different cognitive, biological, and affective vantage points. We need our own developmental theories, not just adaptations of theories based on the development of hearing children. Models devised on the study of hearing children do not take the multigenerational identity gap and the visual orientation of deaf children into consideration.

I believe the state of being that Humphries (1996) calls "the modern Deaf self" is psychologically healthy and empowering; however, it is an ideal state of self that is difficult for many to achieve. This difficulty is due to the simple fact that deaf people represent multiple states of being or multiple realities influenced by variables outside of our control. These variables include the age at which a person becomes deaf, opportunities for acculturation, cultural orientation, language use, the hearing status of the family of origin, and educational placement, to name a few. These variables create other states of existence besides Deaf and hearing, with individuals falling at different points on the continuum.

Humphries discusses boundaries that Deaf individuals create to separate themselves from the influences of the hearing culture. While establishing these boundaries, modern Deaf people also impose a distance between themselves and hard of hearing, oral deaf, late deafened, and biculturally deaf individuals. The reverse is also true: people who are hard of hearing or orally deaf impose boundaries between themselves and people who are culturally Deaf in order to maintain their own autonomy in a cultural context. These boundaries are difficult to maintain, especially in light of our day-to-day transactions with the various systems in our environments. We are not separate from our environments, we interact with them, and while we can establish boundaries, we can never be truly separate.

If, as theories and perspectives discussed in this chapter suggest, we develop our identities through a lifelong process of interpreting our social and communicative experiences, and through creating meaning out of these experiences, then it is not possible for all of us to develop the same meanings or the same identities. The existential teachings of Frankl (1969) tell us that having meaning in life and finding meaning in various situations is the key to a person's happiness, motivation, and survival.[12] Due to the complex variables inherent in the development of the self, of identity, and of meaning, it can't be possible for all of us to fit into neatly organized categories or perspectives of being. Meaning is discovered in ways that are unique to each individual (Lantz, 1986). Thus, people who are deaf and hard of hearing will always represent a diverse group.

Very little attention has been devoted in the literature to the application and effects of these identity models and social transformations for people who are hard of hearing, deaf people who do not sign, and those of varying racial and ethnic heritage. These segments of the deaf population have no doubt benefited greatly from technological advancements as well as the social and legislative changes affecting the disability community. Issues of biculturalism, identity, and social being need to be explored for these groups. Do certain members of these groups also experience the kind of personal transformation, acculturation, and identity issues that the literature discusses in relation to people who are Deaf? Is there a modern self in relation to being hard of hearing, late deafened, Black Deaf, or a Deaf woman? Further research needs to address these questions.

---

12. Frankl proposed that meaning and tension exist in life and that we have the freedom and will to discover meaning in situations; he believed that we have the ability to transcend tension through our creativity, attitudes, and experiential values. For a more complete discussion of Frankl's ideas, the reader is referred to Frankl (1984).

3

Profiles and Procedures

A YOUNG GIRL with long brown hair and wide blue eyes saw me sitting in the back of her classroom as she and a friend entered the room. "Who are you?" she asked. I was at her residential school to observe and identify students for my research. I introduced myself to her, spelling out my first and last name and then telling her my name sign. (Name signs are the sign equivalents of spoken names.) I asked her name and she introduced herself to me in the same manner. A second girl arrived and we repeated the routine. While putting on their phonic ears (assistive-listening devices used in many classrooms for deaf children), the first girl asked curiously, "What are you doing here?" I explained that I was here to visit classes, to watch and learn about deaf children. As the rest of the class arrived, students began to cluster off in groups, signing with each other while their substitute teacher tried to get their attention.

Valentine's Day was near and a student approached and showed me the valentines she was making. Satisfied that she had made a connection, she put them down and walked over to join the other children as they formed a semicircle in front of their teacher. Still curious to learn more about this visitor, the first girl turned around and asked me, "Have a husband? A family? A sister?" I answered yes to each and alerted her to the fact that her teacher was trying to get her attention: "Teacher's calling you." She looked at her teacher with daring eyes and said, "I want to talk with her. You interrupted. That's not polite."

As the teacher continued to attempt to call the class to order, a final student entered the room. She sat on the chair nearest to me and turned halfway around a couple of times out of curiosity to ask me questions. "Name?" she asked me. I told her my name and she asked "Deaf?" to which I responded yes.

Prior to class the teacher and I had agreed it would be a good idea for the students and I to acquaint ourselves so I could get to know them and satisfy whatever curiosity they might have about their visitor. Once all the students were seated, the teacher allowed me to introduce myself to all of them. I went to the front of the group and told them my name. One of the three girls I had already met jumped in and said competitively, "I know!"

"I know we've already met, but I have not met most of the other students yet," I responded. Then I explained to the class that I was going to write a book about deaf children and that I was visiting their class to watch and to learn from them. Busily and competitively, they started asking for information about me, and they told me their names. Not only did they tell me their names and name signs, some of them added "nickname signs," a concept that was new to me and that they explained as "false" names. Although I was unable to confirm where this concept had come from, I assumed they had been learning about names, nicknames, and name signs in school because one of them asked me how I got my name sign and another student gave the choice of two name signs to assign to him. While nicknames are common in spoken language, "nickname signs" are not a common cultural occurrence among people who use ASL.

To an outsider, the class seemed to be a bit out of sync on this particular morning. Perhaps having a visitor was a distraction. The substitute teacher, who was hearing, seemed a bit self-conscious about her communication skills. She expressed to me before the students arrived that perhaps I could help her with her signs. She seemed to have difficulty getting the class in order. As she opened a book to read to them, the students instructed her as to where they had left off the day before. One student got up and turned on the teacher's phonic ear transmitter, which she had not activated.

As the teacher held a book in her hands, the students were eager to point to pictures, anxious to show what they knew and to gain a comfortable space physically where they could all see each other and participate. This physical struggle with space and comfort, which I call *spatial negotiation*, went on for a while, during which time the teacher was instructing them on turn taking and trying to establish some order in the learning group. One student turned to me and invited me to move up and join their circle where I could see better. I knew that this child was aware that I was deaf and that being in an appropriate "line of sight" was an important social behavior necessary for effective communication. I thanked her and said I wanted to stay where I was because I didn't want to interrupt her class. Eventually, the students became more tolerant of waiting their turn but seemed to get engrossed in side discussions with each other, talking about the assignment and collaborating on answers together until their turn came.

As I observed them, I reflected back on my own early years as a deaf child in a hearing classroom with no peers, not understanding the class discussions or teacher's instructions. I couldn't help but think about the latent learning that was happening in the classroom on this particular day. These students were all learning to interact, to work as a team, to accommodate each other, to negotiate space, and take turns. Some of them criticized each other openly, and the others shoved the criticism off with a remark back to them. The boldness and interactive learning was something I had not had access to as a child. I had grown up without the socialness, the self-confidence, the spatial and communication access that I observed in these kids. Interestingly, these thoughts started to enter my mind after one student turned to me and asked "Mother, father deaf?" "No, hearing. Brother deaf," I answered. She returned to the group discussion, and I was glad to see them have this interactive experience.

When class ended, this same girl came back to me and asked, "Time finish? Woodshop?"

She was wondering how long I would be with them and if I would be going with them to their next class, which was woodworking. "No, finish 1:09. That's all." She turned and left quickly to catch up with the others.

A few days later, I returned to the school to observe another class. When I entered this classroom, I found the children scattered throughout the room. Some of the children were sitting side by side on the carpet, some in chairs, and some at desks. Older students were paired with younger students, and they were all engaged in books. This activity was called "Reading Pals." Because I arrived after class had begun, I missed the falling into order that I had observed in the other class. The children were attentive and involved in their activity, and if any of them noticed the presence of a visitor, they did not acknowledge me.

The students continued to read for a while and then the teacher, who was deaf, gathered them at the front of the room. They formed rows in a semicircle on the carpeted floor in front of the teacher. The teacher asked them questions to see what they could remember about the *Titanic*, a story they had apparently studied earlier. One student came forward and volunteered to hold a book and turn its pages for the teacher, who performed a beautiful and captivating signed version of the story. The children sat attentively, with their eyes fixed on the teacher, squirming in their chairs in reaction to the events unfolding as she progressed. When she finished, the children had comments. One boy in particular shared some insights and added ideas. He was seated in front of the other students, and the teacher, who was standing up, repeated his comments in sign so the other students could see what was being said. I was delighted to see how the children had such an excellent role model and to see how engaged they were in their learning environment. I was impressed with the attentiveness of the teachers and teachers' aides, their alertness, skills, and responsiveness to the kids.

My purpose in making these observations was to identify students for my interviews. I also hoped to learn about their everyday activities through my visits with them. After these observations, I met with the principal and we discussed potential students. I hoped to identify students from diverse backgrounds who would be able to provide me with what researchers call "rich information." The principal and I discussed boys and girls, students who were deaf, and some who were hard of hearing, some with deaf parents, and some with hearing parents. We came up with a list of eleven students and sent information and consent letters to their parents. Three of the eleven agreed to participate. As I began interviews with these three students, I contacted parents of mainstreamed students for ideas about whom else I might want to talk to. These parents referred me to four other families.

snowball people

In the end, I had seven children between the ages of seven and ten with diverse familial, audiological, educational, and communication circumstances. Three of these children attended residential schools, and four attended mainstream educational programs. Five of the children had hearing parents. One child had one hearing and one hard of hearing parent, and one child had deaf parents. Four of the children were boys and three were girls. One child, who considered himself hard of hearing, had a severe hearing loss in the 66–85 dB range. The other six children were profoundly deaf (86 dB or greater). Five children were Caucasian, one was African American, and one was Asian. Four of the children had divorced parents.

Five of the children used primarily ASL. Two children used a combination of oral communication and Signed English, with one of these two using oral only communication at home and a combination of sign and speech at school. All of the children were prelingually deaf; five were deaf at birth. Although this was a diverse group of children in terms of their education, family, and communication experiences, if more time had been available, I would have liked to have expanded on that diversity with the addition of a child with a cochlear implant.

A sign language interpreter, Marilyn, accompanied me to all of the interviews. The interpreter was used to voice for myself and the children who signed during the interviews for the video camera, and to triangulate my interpretations of each child's communication. She later transcribed the interviews to text.

Before beginning the interview questions, I explained the purpose of our meeting to each child and confirmed their willingness to participate. I met with each child for up to three sessions of thirty to sixty minutes per session. The length and number of sessions depended on the child's attention, his or her willingness to participate, and how much information he or she volunteered. The older children in this study typically volunteered longer sessions.

To learn about the children's perspectives of themselves and others in their lives, I prepared a list of questions to ask each of them. Some of the questions were direct and some were indirect. I started by asking the children to draw a picture of a deaf boy or girl (depending on the child's gender) and then to tell me a story about the picture and the people and places they drew. To obtain further information I would ask them to tell me stories also about others who might be in the child's life, such as teachers, parents, brothers and sisters, friends, deaf or hearing people. I also included questions about how the child became deaf, how family, friends, and others in the child's life feel about the child, how the child feels about others, and what will become of the child when he or she grows up. In addition, I asked the children direct questions such as, "If you were writing a book about deaf children, what would you say in the book?" Showing the children pictures cut out from magazines, I asked them to tell me a story about what they imagined was happening in these pictures. Some of the pictures were from general family magazines such as *Parents*; others were from magazines that typically included stories or pictures about people who are deaf, such as *Gallaudet Today*. My reason for using both types of magazines was to allow the children the opportunity to relate to and create stories about pictures involving both deaf and hearing children and adults. The questions were largely uniform, but depending on factors that arose in our interviews, such as the children's attention spans, individual variables in their lives or perceptions, or the amount and type of information they volunteered, I allowed flexibility for further probing on issues that seemed to be important or needed more explanation.

Three residential students were interviewed at their school since the interviews took place during the academic year. Three of the remaining children were mainstreamed and were interviewed in their homes during the summer or fall. One of the children's parents expressed concern that there would be too much distraction at home and suggested that we find another location for the interview. I picked the child up and transported her to a local community agency that offered a conference room for our use. This arrangement allowed us to have some extra time outside of the interview and to get to know each other off video.

Early in my career as a clinical social worker, I practiced psychotherapy with deaf and hard of hearing children and their families in schools and community service agencies. Through this training and practical experience, I learned techniques for interviewing children. Some of the techniques I particularly like to use and find effective with children who are deaf are art, drama, and storytelling techniques. These approaches, which are natural and comfortable for most children, are age appropriate and allow the children to express themselves in nonthreatening ways and in their own language. Storytelling is a favorite mode of communication for children (Gardner, 1993a, 1993b). The projective techniques used for soliciting data from the children are supported by Piaget's theory of cognitive development for children under the age of ten (Piaget, 1952). Children between the ages of seven and ten are gradually becoming less egocentric in their perspectives and are progressing toward the ability to see things from another's point of view, but are not yet dealing with abstract ideas. They are still focusing on real objects and concrete issues. Thus, the stories they tell at this point in their lives reflect, for the most part, their own point of view and their own experiences and perceptions.

In psychotherapy interviews, the therapist or the child could be the storyteller, depending on the context and goals of the session. However, in the research interviews for this study, the children were the storytellers because the purpose of the research was to discover what perceptions and meanings the children ascribe to their lifeworlds and what they report their experiences to be.

At the time of this study, nothing was found in the literature on the success of these techniques with deaf children in qualitative research interviews. Some authors did discuss the practical usefulness of projective techniques such as the Draw-A-Person and House Tree Test in psychological evaluations with people who are deaf (i.e., Vernon, 1988; Zieziula, 1982). Both of these testing approaches involve art and storytelling. More recently, Isenberg (1996) has discussed the advantages of deaf people telling their stories for psychotherapeutic purposes. Art therapy was also conducted with favorable results by Glickman and Zitter (1989). A critical factor in the success of these techniques is the mutuality of language and communication between the child and the professional.

In chapters 4 through 10 of this book, readers will be introduced to each of the children who participated in this study. The children's names and other identifying information have been changed to protect their anonymity. As much as possible, contextual and background factors that contribute to the development of these children and their situations in life are explained. Such factors include the age at which the child became deaf, the hearing status and cultural orientations of their parents and the other family members, their primary language at home and school, the type of educational program the child attends, whether the child is deaf or hard of hearing, the presence of multiple disabilities, race, and ethnicity. If it appeared that stating certain of these factors would put the child's anonymity at risk, they were omitted from the profile. Thus, the chapters that follow represent excerpts from interviews with the children.

Alex, Angie, Danny, Joe, Lisa, Mary, and Pat . . . all of these children shared their perceptions of their lifeworlds through their stories, their art, and their responses to my questions. Through these interviews, readers will see that no two deaf children are the same. Yet, while the children are different in many ways, they also share many similarities. Their similarities are identified at the end of this book as the themes that emerged from this study.

"The road to the city of Emeralds
    is paved with yellow brick . . . when you
    get to Oz . . . tell your story . . . ."

                        L. FRANK BAUM, 1900

4

Danny

I ARRIVED AT the residential school where I was to conduct my first interview. As I drove slowly along the drive into the school parking lot, I thought how good it felt to have a day out of the office to get a breath of fresh air. I got out of the car, carrying my video equipment and art supplies, and took a deep breath. Drawing in the crispness of spring, I felt refreshed by the beauty of the perfect weather and the knowledge that, at long last, I was here to begin my interviews with the children.

After checking in at the principal's office, I proceeded to the classroom where I was to meet our voice interpreter. Marilyn, a certified interpreter, worked as a staff person at the school and showed me to our interview room. Then she left to get Danny while I set up the equipment. Danny, with his long blond bangs and big curious eyes, bounced into the room, obviously in good spirits. He was wearing shorts, a green T-shirt, and sneakers.

Danny was nine years old at the time of the study. He seemed mature in his language and cognitive skills but small in physical stature. I thought he looked more like a seven year old. He was a bright and very likeable little boy who responded readily to my questions. Danny was born profoundly deaf. He has one hearing sibling, his father is hard of hearing, and his mother is hearing.

Danny had excellent ASL skills. When his mother filled out the informational questionnaire I asked each parent to complete, she indicated that Danny has no additional disabilities and that family members sign with him at home. She said that she and Danny's sister use ASL and "PSE" without voicing. PSE is an abbreviation for Pidgin Signed English, a term that has been used, albeit inappropriately, to describe the way in which many people have combined

ASL with English word order. Today the term *contact sign* is used to refer to the combinations of ASL and English that are employed when users of these two languages come in contact through communication (Lane et al., 1996). Danny's mom explained that while his father has a limited sign vocabulary and expressive sign skills, and tends to sign and voice simultaneously, his receptive skills are good. Danny later confirmed this perception.

𝒫ℨ

FIRST, I ASK Danny to draw a picture of a deaf boy. Unsure if this is going to be a complicated task, he asks me if it will be "easy or hard." I tell him it is up to him and that it can be whatever he wants it to be. I lay out colored pencils and markers in front of us on the table. He asks for a peach marker, and when we see that there isn't one, he picks a blue ink pen and begins to draw a face and neck. He continues to draw for a while, pausing now and then to consider his next step. He adds a building and then a street, which he tells me is going off into the distance. When he indicates he is finished, I ask him to tell me a story about the boy and the school in his picture. He proceeds to tell me about a day in his life.

"The boy is walking along and he arrives at his school and he gets there. He hangs his coat up. He gives his bag, the boy gives his teacher, and she checks and makes sure that everything's right, and she says, 'That's good.' Then he sits down and works and works and works and works. Then when he's done with his work he plays a lot. After he plays, then he eats lunch. He has french fries and a hamburger and tomatoes. Then after that, he plays, no he goes to the library and reads. He reads a lot. And then he does some more work and then he leaves. He gets his coat and book bag, and the teacher reminds him that he's got a paper he has to take home. He walks and walks and walks and then he gets home. He's very tired, so he goes to sleep for a while. The boy wants to rest, so he lays down in his bed and then he sees a movie."

Although Danny attends a residential school, he does not sleep there. He commutes daily. I ask him if that is what the boy in the picture does and he says, "Yeah. When he gets home he likes to rest because he's very tired because he walks and it's pretty far."

"So he walks to school every day? He doesn't take a bus?"

" No. He walks . . . It's just a short way."

I want to know more about Danny's lifeworld, his relationships, activities, and his views of himself and others. Confident that the boy in the picture and in his story is Danny, I ask more questions. It turns out that Danny is an active, happy child with many friends at school. He engages in play activities that any healthy nine-year-old boy would enjoy.

"And does the boy have friends at school?"

"Yes."

"Can you tell me a story about the friends?"

"Oh, they play all the time. They play and play and play. He plays with his friends."

"Tell me a story about playing with the friends. What happens?"

"Oh, they play. They might want to borrow a toy car, and they'd play with the car and make it go . . . Oh, here." He begins drawing again. "A toy car, and it's, um . . ." He draws. "He brings it to school to share with his friends, with the other kids, so they can play with it."

"So it's to share? Sometimes do you bring toys to share?"

"Mmmhmm. I have, I brought fake bugs before . . . Fake bugs, lots of them. I have, like, seventy of them. We play with them. We play with them. It's a lot of fun."

"That boy is really busy all day at school; he has a busy day. So when he gets home, he rests, and then what does he do?"

"Well, he would play with Nintendo or watch a movie or he might go outside and play."

"And that boy's teacher, is the teacher deaf or hearing?"

"Deaf. Deaf. He has many friends, many friends."

"And tell me about his friends. Who are they?"

"Well, his friends are [here he signs several names of friends at school]. He has lots and lots of friends . . . They play 'It,' you know, where you tag somebody, and they're it, and then you run? It's also called 'tag' . . . And they go on the swing-set together."

"And is the boy happy at his school? Is he happy?"

"Yes. The boy likes to learn. He likes to learn things, lots of things."

"You like that boy?"

"Mmmhmm. And . . ." he continues drawing, "that's his book bag."

"Good. Okay."

Clearly, Danny enjoys school and is enthusiastic about learning. He appears to have a very positive sense of himself. As Danny tells me about his school, it is clear that he is very comfortable in the presence of his deaf friends at his residential school.

"Hmmm, what else do I want to know? That boy's friends, are they deaf or are they hearing or are some . . . ?"

"Oh, they're deaf. All of them. They're in Schreiber Hall, and sometimes there are hearing friends, but very few of them. But most of them are pure deaf."

"All deaf and just a few hearing. Can you tell me more about how there happen to be so many deaf friends?"

"Well, you can see," he points to his drawing, "this says you have to be deaf to go there. It's for deaf kids. That's where deaf kids need to go, to that school. Because there's a separate school for hearing people and a school for deaf people."

"And hearing kids never come to this school? Is it just deaf kids?"

"Yup."

I am curious about how Danny perceives himself and his relationships with hearing children and what he experiences in their company. He is clearly much more confident in the company of his deaf friends.

"I see. And suppose that boy would be with hearing people? What would happen if that boy was playing with hearing people? What would he do?"

"Well, his sister, who's hearing, would interpret. Just like my sister. She's hearing and she signs. And she could interpret if there are girls or boys that are hearing. He might say, 'What are they saying? What are they saying?' And if they wanted to play tag or something like that, then his sister would interpret and the brother would be fine. Because somebody would interpret . . . My sister does that."

"Oh, I see. So your sister helps you. And how does the deaf boy, with hearing people, how does that boy feel?"

"Well, he would think, 'Hmm, I don't know, hmmm.' The boy wouldn't know."

"If the deaf boy was with other deaf people playing, how would he feel?"

"Happy."

"But with hearing kids, you don't know?"

"Well some hearing people and some deaf people."

"But when he plays with hearing kids? Would he feel happy or what?"

"Well, he might be kind of nervous and . . ."

"A little bit nervous?"

"Yeah, a little unsure and awkward."

"What for? Nervous about what?"

"Cause they're hearing and they might not know . . . He might not know how to use his voice, so they might not understand."

"So he might feel a little awkward?"

"Yeah . . . Maybe not comfortable."

"And what happens with the hearing friends? How do they play?"

"Well, he has some hearing friends, but his sister interprets. That's why his sister interprets."

"How old is his sister?"

"Six. My sister's really seven."

"And how old is the boy?"

"Uh, nine."

"So the sister's six and the boy's nine?" Danny nods. "And does the sister enjoy interpreting?"

"Yup."

"She likes that? The sister is a real good signer?"

"Oh, some."

"How did she learn?"

"I forget."

"Did the boy teach her or did Mom teach her?" (Danny points to himself.) "The boy? Are you a good teacher?"

Danny appears to be proud of the fact that all of his family members know sign language.

He goes on to tell me about their skill levels. "Yeah. My mom is really good. She's a really good signer. She's hearing, but she's a really good signer. My father knows some signs, but he's not real fluent. My mother's very fluent."

"There's just the four of you at home? Mom and Dad and the boy and his sister in the story, right?"

"Really there's four in the family."

We have another fifteen minutes left in our session. I give Danny the choice of drawing whatever he wants. "Do you have an idea yourself of what you'd like to draw?"

"Mmmhmm . . ."

"What would you like to draw?"

"Well, my favorite thing . . . Is it my decision?"

"If you want."

"My decision?!" He seems surprised. I am struck by his surprise and pleasure at having this moment of self-determination.

"If you want. If you have an idea of what you'd like to draw, that's fine."

"My favorite thing is turtles." Danny proceeds to draw a picture of four Ninja Turtles standing on a roadway near a manhole with their weapons and shields. "My favorite." He continues drawing. "This is Ninja Turtles."

"Oh, you're a good artist. I already knew from your drawing what that was." He draws more, seeming to enjoy himself and adding details as he goes. I compliment his work as he proceeds, "Nice!" Like most young children, Danny enjoys entering the imaginary world of superheroes. He is able to go into great detail about these popular characters.

"Oh no. I forgot the eyes." He continues to draw, adding masks to their faces. "Let's see . . ." He draws. "The color . . . Let's see, two . . . there." He draws more. "That's his stick that he uses for fighting."

"Oh. What for?"

"I don't know." He continues drawing.

Trying to find out what he can tell me about his picture, I point to one of the turtles and ask him about it.

"Oh, this is the turtle, and he's Leo. I can't remember the rest of his name. And the other one's Don, for short. There's supposed to be an orange turtle. Oh, there's orange." Picking up an orange crayon he draws again. "And I'll do one more. There's red and orange. There's red and orange turtles."

"What's that one's name?"

"Oh, it's a real long name. It's Michael . . . I forget the rest of the name. It's a real long one."

Danny begins to explain more about his picture. He imitates moving as if using numchucks. "That's something that he moves around in his hand and it's got things on either end of it and it moves." He continues to draw. "There's one more. There's one more. They're Ninja Turtles, and they beat, uhhh . . . oh, I forget. But they beat some kind of monster kind of thing."

"Monsters, huh?"

"Yeah, you know, they're real big. I can't remember the name of them."

"Why do they want to fight with the monsters?"

"Well, they try and try to beat them. 'Cause they always steal things and they hurt people and people die and they beat 'em up. So the turtles have to beat those monsters, the bad men . . . There's one more that's red." He draws a red mask on one of the turtles. "The red one's really neat."

"Wow, that's neat. What do you think about the turtles?"

"Umm, well, I saw them on TV."

"Oh. Did you understand what you saw on TV? How did you understand it?"

"Well, I just copy the drawing from that."

"When you watch TV, do you understand what's happening?"

"Some."

"Do you have a decoder at home?"

"Oh yeah. Oh yeah."

"And so you can read what's going on?"

"Some of it. But sometimes I just watch the pictures. Then I'll look down at the words, then I'll look at the pictures again, then I'll look down."

"Is closed captioning hard for you to understand?"

"Yeah."

Although Danny is young and still developing in his reading skills, which closed captioned television requires, his following description illustrates that he clearly has no difficulty following the storyline of his favorite superhero program.

"They go looking for people. And they get in their karate stances. And the one holds his position like this, and the next one's like this, and the next one's like this. And they search for bad people and then they fight them. But, they want to kill the bad people, but there's two of them that are really dangerous; they're really dangerous. They look and they look and it's really hard to find them. And they come up out of someplace and one's looking with his eye kind of squinted like this. They go into their position and the other one jumps and leaps down. And they fight and fight and fight with the bad people, the bad men. And they do all of these karate moves and then they go 'boom' and then they hit 'em. And then there might be two dangerous guys, and one is the head guy and the next one's his assistant. And they fight and they fight and they fight and they fight, and then 'boom' they get 'em. And then the other two might be hit and they might need to rest. And they would go into . . . Wait a minute. [He draws.] They jump down into their, into the manhole. In through the manhole cover. And the turtles eat bugs and stuff. That's what turtles do, they eat 'em all up."

"Do they?"

"Yup. They eat bugs and things like that. Their favorite thing is pizza, though. These guys, they like pizza. That's what they like . . . There's this one that has clothes. They have different clothes. They have different coats and things that they can put on, and hats, when they don't want people to see them and run away. Then they put those coats and hats on and they would go and get a pizza. But they can also go into this karate stuff and they might tell somebody 'stop' and they might run away . . . Umm, there's a program that they'll watch on TV, and if they see a bad person on TV then they'll go leaping up from the underground and then they fight and then they go back down underground. And they go to bed." He continues to draw, "That's the road . . . That's so they can go down the manhole cover, remember?"

"Yes, I remember."

"If they see somebody, they can go down in there. That's what that's for, and that's where the turtles go." He shows me the manhole in his drawing and the street where cars are passing overhead.

"You're really a wonderful artist."

"And, um, there's different, um . . ." He draws.

"What's that?"

"That's the sidewalk for people to walk on."

"Oh, okay."

"And the other is for cars to go on."

It is Danny's lunch time and we have to stop. He has been very engaged in his work and seems so proud of it that he wants to take it with him to show his friends. He promises to bring it back with him next week so it can go in the book. I thank him and tell him I will see him again next week.

WHEN DANNY comes to meet with me for our second session, he proceeds to take his seat at our table and says he is hot. He seems a bit out of breath. He has been outside playing in the warm spring air. I imagine the kids' adrenaline flowing with excitement and picture them taking advantage of the opportunity to get some long overdue outdoor recreation after a cold winter.

During this session, I ask Danny what he has done since the last time I saw him. He tells me that he stayed with his grandparents over the weekend.

". . . then I came back on Sunday. I stayed over there. I wish I could stay for a month or a year! They're my favorite!"

"You really like Grandma and Grandpa. What do you do at their place?"

"Well, my grandmother gave me a gun, a big one with a target and . . . a toy, a play one. And it's got this red thing that . . ."

"A dart gun?"

"Yeah. And it's got this thing that you put on it. And there's, like, a bull's-eye."

On questioning, Danny explains for me just where his grandparents live. He had stayed with them while his sister went to a cousin's and his mother went on a business trip. Wanting to find out more about his relationship with his grandparents, I ask him how they communicate. He indicates that they can sign some, but it's clear they do not have the same level of skill that his parents and his sister have.

"And when you go and visit your grandparents, how do you communicate with them?"

"They're hearing. My grandfather signs some, he can sign some. Something, you know. Some of it gets kind of confused. My grandmother's good. Grandmother's good, but she doesn't know some of the signs. My grandfather doesn't either. He doesn't know some of the signs."

"And what do the three of you talk about?"

"Oh, nothing. Not really. I don't know what we talk about."

"So what do you do when you go and visit? What do you do when you go?"

"Uh, go to the store and buy gum and stuff."

"You just go to the store and buy gum? And you bought a dart gun?"

"No, my grandmother bought that for me."

"And you played with it? At your grandmother's house?"

"Yeah. On Friday and on Saturday and on Sunday. I played with it a lot. The whole time I kept playing with it."

"So tell me more about your grandparents and their house and so forth. What did you do?"

"Oh, um, my grandpa and I, we played basketball outside. We shot baskets. And my grandmother sat and watched. And I said, 'Grandma, would you please give me a pop? A Mountain Dew?' And she said, 'Fine,' and went in to the refrigerator and got some. And I drank it up, 'cause it was very hot . . . It was hot outside. And the pop was cold. And I drank it all up. It was good . . . Oh, that's my favorite. Mountain Dew's my favorite. I love it. My favorite. Mountain Dew and A&W Root Beer. Those are my favorites."

"Oh, I like those, too. Both of those taste really good. I agree with you. So the week before, let's see, I saw you last Monday. So Tuesday, Wednesday, and Thursday and Friday, what did you do? Before you went to visit your grandparents. Do you remember?"

"I forget. That was a long time ago. 'Cause Friday morning I went with my mother, on Friday morning. And we got there at two, to someone's [he uses a name sign] house."

"Who are they? Who are [copying name signs]?"

"My dad's mom and dad. But, um, my mom's . . . my mom's dad, um . . . My sister and I, we have race cars, and we were about two, uh, two hundred and eighty miles an hour. And my sister was two hundred twenty-seven . . . My sister was two hundred and eighteen and I was two hundred twenty-seven. I beat her. You could see 'em go by really fast, zoom. They've got these things you can put on your eye to watch them go by . . . Yeah. And it was really high up there. And we looked down and there were people down there. And we walked across and that was it."

As Danny tells me about all of his relatives, I try to decipher if the town he visited was where both of his parents were from. We labor through this for a while and then I ask if he knows if that is where his parents first met but he doesn't know.

"I was born, and I was maybe, um, five? And I was, like, 'Who's that?' But my mom and dad met and they had me I guess."

At this point I introduce magazine cutouts one by one and ask Danny to tell me what he thinks is happening in the pictures, inviting him to make up stories about the characters he sees in them. I show him the first picture of a man and a woman with a baby and he says, "Well, this is a dad. And the dad has the baby. The baby's crying and so the dad gives the baby to the mom. 'Cause the baby feels better with the mom. And the baby gets a bottle."

"Do you think that the baby is deaf or hearing?"

"Oh, hearing."

"How do you know?"

"Uh, I don't know, maybe Mom's deaf. No, I don't know, maybe because they're talking or something."

"So it looks like they're talking so it looks like they're hearing? And the parents . . ."

"Uh, I think the dad's hearing and the mom's hearing. But I don't know."

"Well, how might you know?"

"Because I think Mom and Dad are hearing. Because the baby's got its mouth open so he's probably hearing."

Although I didn't know it at the time, this was the beginning of a theme that arose from this research. Danny, like the other children, used visual indicators to make an initial assessment of who is deaf and who is hearing. Talking, mouth movement, signing, use of a voice or TTY phone were indicators of a person's hearing status. As will be seen in later chapters, some children mentioned additional indicators. Only mainstreamed children referred to hearing aids; the residential schoolchildren did not.

"Okay. That's fine. Good. Now if the baby were deaf, and the parents were hearing and the baby was deaf . . ."

Danny explains excitedly and with a sense of urgency, "The mom would start learning and learning and learning and learning and learning so, real quickly, so that she could sign. Like, that's what my mom told me, like my mom was hearing and she found out her baby was deaf, she immediately went and started learning and learned and learned real fast so that she could sign."

"That's interesting."

Danny continues, "And, because as soon as they found, as soon as the baby's deaf, Mom's always got to be learning and learning and learning and learning. They have to sign."

"Why do they have to?"

"Because the baby's deaf."

"Uh huh."

"Like I'm deaf."

"Okay. And what would the father do?"

"Well, Mom didn't tell me. I don't know."

"Does father sign?"

"Um, I think Dad's trying to learn to sign, I think. But I don't know."

"Does your father sign now?"

"Ummhmm. Yeah, he's good. But my mom is really an ace! And my sister's pretty good. She's good. Dad, Dad's good. Dad's skilled. But my mom's the best. She's the best signer."

I am intrigued with Danny's description of his parents' reaction on learning that he was deaf. Much of our literature discusses the grief process that hearing parents of deaf children experience (e.g., Harvey, 1989). Danny's expression was so positive and enthusiastic that it was clear that Danny perceived his parents' reaction to him as positive. His description of their decision to learn to sign counters the assumptions of ambivalence that we expect parents to experience and the deaf child's internalization of a parent's negative reactions toward his deafness.

I pull out another picture for Danny. In this picture a man who is deaf is sitting at a desk drawing in the midst of books, papers, and supplies. "This is picture number two. What's that? Tell me a story about that."

"Well, it's um, um, this is the father, and he works very, very hard. He's, for a test," Danny tells me. I believe he is implying that the man is studying for a test.

"A test? For what?"

"Um, I don't know."

"Where does he work?"

"I don't know."

"Is he hearing or deaf?"

"Oh, he's hearing."

"How do you know he's hearing?"

"I don't know."

Danny looks at picture for a moment and shrugs. "Well . . ." Danny doesn't find any clues in the picture that indicate if the man is deaf or hearing. He's not talking, signing, moving his lips, or using any electronic devices. He's just sitting at a desk working.

Wanting to find out what he thinks this man might be doing now, I ask, "So what does he do?"

"Ummm, he's learning and it's hard."

"He's in school? Is he learning in school?"

Danny looks at the picture again, "Can't see."

"Does it look like school or work?"

"Um, another work."

"Another work? What do you mean?"

"I don't know. No, um, it's like a town and there's houses set up there."

"And that's where he works?"

"Yeah."

"What kind of a job does he have?"

"Umm, hmm. I don't know."

"No idea?" Danny shrugs and shakes head, and I say, "If . . . okay, you're deaf. As you grow up and you're not a little boy anymore, when you're a man . . ."

Danny signs "college."

"What's your job going to be?"

"Um, well, his job is with an animal, and he might have to feed the animals."

"If you have animals, then you have to feed them? That's your job? Okay . . . I have another picture; this is picture number three, are you ready?" This is a picture of two children sitting on the floor. One is on the telephone and the other is sitting close by. They have the board game "Sorry" in front of them.

"Well, it's kids playing with games. That's it."

"Kids?"

Danny proceeds to explain further, "This kid's talking on a phone and he's [pointing to the other child] bored and he's bored and he's just kind of staring into space. And he's, like, 'Hurry up, hurry up,' this kid is. And the other kid's just yakking away on the phone. And his friend is waiting and he's bored, and he's kind of mad, and he's bored, and he's going, 'Come on, I want to play a game.' "

"Are they deaf or hearing?"

Pointing to the child on the phone, "Well, he's hearing . . ." Pointing now to the other child, "He's deaf. And he's [the one on the phone] hearing, but he can sign. 'Cause he's talking on the phone, so he must be hearing."

I point to the child who Danny indicates is deaf. "Okay. How do you know that he's deaf?"

"Um, he's deaf 'cause it means he's bored . . . Well, because this guy's hearing and he's just talking away on the phone. He's on the phone, and that means he must be hearing." Danny was the first child I interviewed, but his interpretation of the boredom that a deaf child experiences while waiting for a hearing person to finish talking (without signing) on the phone is not unique. Nearly all of the other children in the study interpreted the picture in the same way.

"Okay. Thank you."

We move on to the next picture, which includes a woman and two toddlers sitting on the floor with a book open in front of them. One child is sitting on the woman's lap. The woman is looking at the child sitting next to her, and while it is difficult to decipher from a still photo, they appear to be making the sign for either "airplane" or "I love you."

I ask Danny what he sees in this picture. "And this is picture number four. What are they doing?"

"Umm, he's got a hot dog. And mom's showing I LOVE YOU. And the baby's looking up, like, I LOVE YOU. You know, why are you learning signs?' The mom's like, you need to, you need more signs. And the baby's kind of shy, but he's trying to do I LOVE YOU. And Mom's going, 'Come on, come on. Smile. Say I LOVE YOU. And the baby's kind of smiling and going, I LOVE YOU. And that's the boy, and looking at, this is, this is [he makes up a name sign and indicates the name tag on the woman's shirt while looking down] 'cause there's a pin there. And this, um, he's hearing and she signs, and she's deaf, and he's hearing and signs."

"So the mother's deaf?"

"Uh huh."

"And the mother's got a hearing baby?"

"Yes, they're hearing but they sign."

"Okay, so the babies are hearing and they can sign and the mother's deaf?"

Danny knows that hearing children of deaf parents learn to sign; he has already begun to acquire tools that will prepare him for the possible role as a father in the future.

"Interesting. How do you know the mother's deaf?"

"Because she's signing. See? I LOVE YOU like this."

"Ah. So the mother's deaf 'cause she's signing."

"Right. And the baby's doing I LOVE YOU. He's doing it right."

"If the parents are deaf, why is it important for the children to learn to sign? What's the reason for that?"

"Huh?"

"Okay, the mother's deaf. Why do the children need to learn to sign? What for?"

"For, um, if, um, maybe if they're shy and somebody's talking or something, and they say, 'Okay,' and they see somebody signing.

And they come up and they'll talk to each other and they become friends. So you need to learn sign."

"So hearing people need to learn sign to become friends with deaf people?"

Here Danny provides us with information about how hearing children might respond to a deaf child. "Well, like if there's hearing people on a team or something like that and there's somebody that's shy, well, hearing people, they can just talk, you know. Talk with their mouths. And then they might say, 'You can . . .' and then they find out this boy's deaf and it's like, 'Oh, you can sign?' And then the boy might go, 'Yeah, I can sign. I can sign. I'm hearing but I can sign.' And then the deaf boy would, well, they would become friends. And they could be on a football team together or a baseball team together or a basketball team. 'Cause they could sign together. 'Cause they could learn."

"So how's the boy feel?"

"Oh, the boy would feel really good and be surprised, too."

"So most of the time with hearing teams nobody signs. So how does the boy feel then?"

"Kind of shy and kind of embarrassed and kind of hesitant. A little bit afraid if no one signs."

"Okay, good. That's a good story. Thank you. And this is picture number five." In this picture, cut out of *Gallaudet Today*, a group of children are gathered around their teacher in a classroom. There is a banner on the wall depicting the manual alphabet.

Danny examines the picture and begins to tell me what he sees. "Um, this is a mom, and, no, this is the boy's teacher and they're learning, doing their jobs, doing their work. And he says, 'Do you want to play a game?' And they hold hands all the way around; everybody holds hands. This boy tries to bump his way through. Everybody holds their hands together, they all hold hands, and this boy tries to bump against their hands to get out. And that's it."

"Okay, so are they deaf or hearing?"

"Hearing."

"All of them are hearing?"

"Mmhmm."

I point to the manual alphabet banner, "So what's this in the picture?"

"Uh, well they're learning fingerspelling."

I show Danny a photograph of two women sitting in chairs in front of windows. One is signing to the other. With his interpretation of this picture, we learn that Danny's positive visions for the future of deaf children include the possibility that deaf people, and in this instance, deaf women, can be medical doctors.

He looks at this picture for a moment, wondering, "Hmm. I don't know . . . I think they're deaf. I think they're deaf, both of them, they're deaf . . . It kind of looks like they might be signing. I think they're signing."

"And what do you think they're talking about?"

"Mmmm, I dunno. I dunno. Maybe a doctor."

"A doctor?"

"Yeah, I think this one's a doctor, and this one's kind of sitting back 'cause she's hurt her hand. And her hand's hurting right there. And the doctor is, I think the other one's a doctor."

"A deaf doctor?"

"Uh-huh."

Another picture that I show Danny depicts a woman sitting at a TTY. Danny tells me, "It's a mom. It's a mom, and she's calling a friend, and she's typing on the TTY. That means she's deaf . . . And she takes the phone and puts it on the TTY and there's an on-off switch. She turns it on and then she sits and waits and then she starts typing. And that's her way of chatting, of talking with a friend."

"What do they talk about?"

"Um, her friend's mother, um, her kid and her kid, there's this one boy, um, these two boys who are best friends. And the friend's mother, the boy's mother, and they're best friends. And they want to play at each other's houses and have a sleep over . . . So, um they're talking with a friend."

"And the mother's deaf. What . . . does she work?"

"She's in the home."

"Okay. She doesn't have a job?"

"No."

"No job? Why not?"

"Oh, um, I dunno . . . She's free; it's her choice . . . The mother doesn't have to have a job."

"Can deaf women have jobs?"

In addition to his perception that deaf women can become medical doctors, he foresees other opportunities as well.

"Oh, many jobs. Many jobs. There's a long list. They could do cleaning, they could get a job working with animals, oh, lots and lots of different jobs. There's a long list. Many, many different jobs."

"Okay, thank you. Last one. This is number ten." I show him a picture of a group of nine young children sitting on the floor, smiling and posing for a picture with a middle-aged man in a white shirt and tie.

"Hmm, there's a class at school. And that's the gym teacher right there. That's the gym teacher. And the class is really excited because they get free play time. And this boy says he wants a picture taken. They take a picture, and this one's grinning; the whole class is grinning. And, um, the class is having free play. And then after free play they have to do their work. And they're going to climb, they're going to climb. They're going to practice their climbing exercise."

"That's interesting. Sounds like fun. And are they hearing or deaf?"

"They're hearing."

"Okay."

"But, um, there's one boy whose favorite thing is Power Rangers . . . Right here." He holds up the picture where I can see it and points to the Power Rangers on the T-shirt of one child in the photograph.

"Do you have Power Rangers at home?"

"Oh, lots of them."

"You do?"

"Yes. I love Power Rangers. It's . . . my favorite is Tommy and Tiger."

"Well, that's good. Um, the other picture that we had before, of the woman typing on the TTY . . . Do you have one of those at home? Do you have a TTY?"

"Uh-huh."

"And do you use it every day?"

"No. Just once in a while. Just sometimes. Not very often."

Danny is young and he and his friends are still developing their language and their typing skills. Communicating effectively on the

TTY requires that both parties have sufficient English and typing skills. In addition, not all families with deaf children have TTYs. This limits the opportunities for young deaf children to communicate effectively with their friends using these devices.

"Who do you call?"

"Um, always my friends. Um, my mom calls friends and different people sometimes."

"Okay."

"But just once in a while. And then not for a long time, and then again, and then not for a long time. Not always."

"Okay. We're almost out of time. Did you want to draw a picture? Or would you rather just go back and go to lunch now? Which would you prefer?"

"I think I'll go to lunch."

"Okay. Bye-bye. See you next Tuesday, okay? One more time."

IN MY FINAL session with Danny, I ask him to tell me again what he has done since we met last week. He proceeds to tell me about visiting his grandparents and going to church on Sunday. I ask if he had an interpreter at church and how he understood what the preacher was saying. He explains that when he went to church that weekend it was with his family but not at their regular church, since they were visiting relatives. No interpreter was available at this church. Normally he attends what he calls a "deaf church," where the preacher signs and there are other families with deaf children. When I ask him if he had an interpreter at church this past weekend his response is that he does not like interpreters in church. He prefers to attend church where the preacher is signing his sermon and he has opportunities to interact with other deaf children.

"No interpreter? How do you understand what they are talking about?"

"My mom, umm, we watch and we write down. We don't need an interpreter. My mom watches and then writes down and sometimes my sister writes things down. Because I get bored watching them talk. I get bored with that . . . I don't like having an interpreter . . . I don't like that . . . it's better with the kids . . . Well, in my church, it's a deaf church. My church, there's some deaf and some hearing. And there's the deaf and hearing groups. There's the deaf group and the hearing group and I join the deaf group. And that's better. And the preacher's deaf."

Going back to our magazine cutouts, I show him another photograph of five children leaning on a fence, smiling as if posing for a picture. He looks at the picture and imagines there is a mother taking this picture of the children, "There's a mom . . ." Pointing to children in the picture he says, "This is their friends."

"Tell me about those kids. Who are they, what are they doing?"

"They're all hearing."

"And tell me a little story about those hearing children."

"Well, they're playing outside, and the mom's saying, 'Come on, come on. I've got something special for you.' And they're all watching and they're smiling. And Mom is ready to take their picture. They're posing for the picture. Then when they're done they're going to play. And in the evening they'll have supper—some kind of supper or snack, I don't know. And then they'll go to bed." Danny points to each boy in the picture as he says, "And this boy will go home, this boy will go home, this boy will go home, this boy will go home. This is the boy whose mom is taking the picture."

Wanting to know more about Danny's relations with hearing children, how they communicate, and how he feels in their presence, I pose some more questions for him. Danny tells us initially that the deaf child might be rejected by hearing children and may feel sad. He says he doesn't know how the child's mom would feel, and imagines the mom doesn't sign and he would have no one to talk to about his experience. Later, he seems to recall his coping strategies in those situations and decides that type of incident wouldn't happen anyway because there would be other deaf children around, and the mom could help interpret and everything would turn out okay.

"Okay, now if they're all hearing, suppose a deaf child came along and wanted to join and play with them. What would they do? What would those children do?"

"What do you mean?"

"Okay, they're all hearing, right? If a deaf boy should happen along and say, 'I want to play with you,' what would they do? How would they react?"

"Well, they'd be puzzled and they'd say, 'Go away, go away.' "

"So they'd kind of shoo him away?"

"Yeah, 'cause they're hearing."

"Well, that's not very nice. How does the deaf boy feel?"

"Kind of sad. 'Cause they don't want him around. And he might be kind of mad and kind of lonely. That's how he might feel."

"Would that happen very often?"

"Mmhmm."

"What would the deaf boy's mother say about that?"

"I dunno. I dunno."

"Would his mom try to help the deaf boy?"

"No. Mom's hearing and doesn't know sign."

"Who does the deaf boy talk with to explain what happened to him?"

"I don't know . . . He might just say nothing."

"Does that happen to that one deaf boy only or does it happen to many deaf boys?"

"None . . . Umm, 'cause there'd be other deaf. There'd be some other deaf, some other hearing."

"Well, if that happened, what would he do if he wanted to feel better?"

"Ask his mom to interpret."

"Then Mom could help, and that would make the boy feel better?"

"Mmmhmm."

"Okay. And what else can that boy do?"

"They could all get together and, umm, if the deaf kid joined them there'd be six of them. They could play 'It' or something."

We are ready to move on to the next picture. Danny becomes concerned and asks me what time it is. He says he thought we had only five minutes left because his teacher told him he'd only be here for twenty minutes. I sense that he is anxious to go back and get involved in his regular activities. So we agree to work for only five more minutes. I show him the next picture. In this picture, a woman is talking on the phone and there are children playing nearby. I ask him to tell me what he thinks is happening.

". . . Well, mom's on the phone talking, so mom's hearing. And he's hearing too. And she's hearing and she's talking to a friend. And, um, maybe the friend and, umm, no, umm, hmm . . . They're working, that's the teacher . . . And, um, the kid's playing with the sister and they're not allowed to do that. They're breaking the rules in that room . . ."

"The kids are at mom's work and they can't play there? Is that what you mean? Is the child deaf or hearing?"

"Hearing. They're supposed to be quiet. 'Shhh,' they're supposed to 'Shhh' be quiet."

"Oh, they can play in mom's work if they're quiet?"

"Well, they have to be quiet. They can't play rough."

I tell Danny that I have learned a lot from his stories. ". . . And when I was watching your story, I learned something from you. That sometimes deaf children aren't comfortable with hearing children, right?" Danny nods. "So what do you prefer? If you're not comfortable with hearing children, what do you do?"

"I stay and play with my sister, with her."

"Okay."

"And play by myself. My sister's hearing, but she can sign. And, my sister's hearing, but she can sign, my sister can. And Mom, too, she's hearing, but she can sign. My Mom's a really good signer. And my dad, he's hearing and he can sign."

"Yes, that was another thing I understood from your story. That you really appreciate it if hearing people learn to sign. You really like that, right?" Danny nods in agreement. "That helps you to play and to understand better."

"Yes."

"And so you like that, if hearing people learn to sign, right?"

"Yes."

"Your mom is a very fluent signer; you're proud about that, right?"

"Yes."

"And your sister signs and interprets and you're proud of that, too?"

"Mmmhmm. Yep."

". . . and in the story, some of the information that I learned about is that when deaf children play with hearing children, that the deaf children might feel bored sometimes and left out?"

"What do you mean?"

"Feel bored sometimes when they're playing with hearing children? They feel left out, kind of alone? Do they feel that?"

"Like, like, um, they might be kind of scared . . . Uh huh, with hearing kids in a group if they're talking and stuff. Like if they're not talking with me, if they're just talking with each other, then I feel alone and I just kind of play on my own if they're talking. If the other boys and girls are hearing, you know, I'm just alone and playing."

"Okay. And also last week, when we were looking at the pictures, I learned something from you. You said, 'That woman is deaf,' and you said that woman's a doctor, right? So does that mean deaf people can become doctors?" Danny nods. "When they grow up . . ."

"Yes."

"Right? They can?"

"Yes."

"Oh, I like that. Okay, good. I learned a lot from you!"

"The last one, um, next week, um . . . Do we have an interview next week, or not? When's the last one?"

I explain to Danny that this is our last session and thank him for his help and contributions to the book.

"I really enjoyed meeting you and chatting with you. You have taught me a lot! And thank you for that. I appreciate your taking the time from lunch and play time and school time to come here and see me. That was very nice of you." Danny smiles and nods. "Okay, well thank you very much . . . Is there anything else that you wanted to share with me? Anything else that you think I need to learn?"

"No, nothing."

While Danny has always seemed eager to return to his usual school activities, and has always appeared very engaged in his day-to-day routines at school, he seems a bit reluctant to end today's session.

"Nothing? Okay. Thank you."

I give Danny a hand-drawn thank you note that I prepared in advance for each of the children. He gets up to leave and we say our good-byes.

ℰఢ

LIKE ANY nine-year-old boy, Danny enjoys superheroes and a variety of group and individual play activities. He is an imaginative, creative, and articulate child. He readily participated in these interviews. He was able to describe his feelings and how he communicates in relationships with both deaf and hearing peers and family members. Danny reports that he feels a bit nervous and unsure of communication in the presence of hearing peers. Danny is happy, active and, like the majority of the children interviewed, he takes being deaf for granted. He is aware of resources that are available to him. He is involved in his milieu and anticipates going to college and having a career. He has Deaf adult role models and peers who are Deaf at his residential school. He has a very positive perception of his relationship with his parents and sister and a strong assurance of their love for him. His family is involved in activities that support his development, language, and resource needs. He is aware of differences between deaf and hearing people and has constructive means of dealing with communication barriers.

5

Angie

ON A GORGEOUS autumn day, I drove out to meet Angie and her family at their home. Angie and her parents came out of their house as the interpreter and I pulled into the driveway. Angie was a bubbly, outgoing child whose red hair was pulled up in a ponytail. She walked ahead of her parents and greeted me as I was getting out of the car. She carried her favorite stuffed animal with her, a long-haired white dog on a leash. She introduced me to her dog, told me it was her favorite, and walked with the interpreter and me back to the house to meet her parents.

Marilyn, our interpreter and camera operator, helped me set up the camera in the living room, and Angie and I sat comfortably on the floor so we could use the coffee table for drawing. The multi-colored trees outside the living room window made a picturesque backdrop and seemed to match the vibrant mood of this happy ten-year-old child.

Before I had set up the interview, Angie's hearing parents had shared information with me about her background. They explained in our written correspondence that Angie was profoundly deaf and was mainstreamed in a total communication program for deaf children. The family was encouraging Angie to communicate in Signed English, the approach used at her school. They stated they were considering having her learn ASL. In our interview, Angie appeared already adept at ASL.

Because Angie was adopted as an infant, her parents did not have information on how or when she became deaf, but they knew she was ill in infancy. They were able to confirm that she was deaf by the age of three. They shared with me that Angie has attention deficit disorder. Angie was so enthusiastic in our sessions that she answered many of my questions in connection with other topics or she responded to direct questions without my needing to use projective techniques. A few times I had to redirect our focus as Angie sometimes quickly shifted to new ideas and topics. This restlessness may have been due to her attention disorder.

ॐ

To BEGIN the interview, I open the box of colored pencils and markers for her and lay them out with some drawing paper. Angie rapidly goes through the markers to find what she needs and eagerly begins to draw.

"Very nice. That's your home, with Mom and Dad. Tell me more about your family."

"My family likes to work with me."

I think it is interesting that Angie chooses the word *work*. Does she see herself as a child who needs *working with*?

"Your family likes to work with you? Well, what kinds of things do you do?"

"We play."

This doesn't confirm my question about her self-perception, but does tell me that they play together.

"What kinds of things do you play?"

"Games."

"What games?"

"I have a Nintendo game. That's my favorite."

She shows me her hand, which by now has some marker smudges.

"Oh, the color, yeah, it'll wash off."

She returns to her drawing and asks for my assistance. She signs GAME. "Game? I don't know how to spell that."

I spell it out for her, G-A-M-E.

She continues to draw and then links two F handshapes. I'm not sure what she is saying, "F?"

"I have . . . wait a minute." She gets up, goes into another room, and returns with a board game called "Connect Four."

"Oh, 'Connect Four.' I've never heard of that before. Is it a fun game?"

"Yes. My mom gave it to me." She writes the name of the game onto her picture, copying the letters from the box.

Wanting to learn more about Angie and her family, I say, "You like that game? And there's three people in your family, right? Mom and Dad and you? Can you tell me more about your family and yourself?" But Angie is busy drawing and doesn't answer my question.

She changes the subject, "My favorite movie."

Unable to see what she is referring to, I try to clarify, "Your favorite?" but there is no response.

I change the subject, "Where do you go to school?"

"At Oakland."

"Can you tell me something about your school? What do you do there?"

"The kids in the class, let's see, there's three . . . We're in third grade and fourth grade and maybe fifth grade, I don't know." She continues drawing. "Kids. Kids. How do you spell 'kids'?"

K-I-D-S.

"You spell so fast. I can't understand."

"Okay, I'll do it slower. K — I — D — S." She indicates she understands and writes the word on her drawing then tells me there are seven children in her class.

"Seven kids in your class, are they all deaf? And did you always go to Oakland or did you go to another school before that?"

"It was kindergarten on up. It's for deaf kids."

"Okay, so you went to kindergarten at Oakland too? And first, second, third, fourth? You're now in fourth?"

"Fifth."

"Okay, kindergarten through fifth grade you were at Oakland?"

"There was another school. Preschool, Greendale." Then she changes the subject once again, "I have a bike."

"You have a bike?"

In her drawings, Angie has been writing topic words, which she tells me about and draws pictures of. "I don't know how to spell it."

"Bike?"

"Yes."

"It's B-I-K-E." She writes "b-i-k-e" on her drawing. "That's good."

"Can I show my parents?"

"Sure. Okay."

Angie gets up and leaves the room with her picture. She returns in a moment. I had told her at the start of our session that we would

draw pictures and she could tell me stories about herself. In this drawing, she started with a picture of her house, which included many windows. She added sunshine and clouds and two birds flying nearby in the sky. She also wrote topics of her conversation on her drawing: that she and her parents live in the house, and they like to play the game "Connect Four." She likes movies, there are seven kids in her class, and she has a bicycle. This picture shows that she has been telling me many things about herself and her life. For a while I didn't think that things were following a logical order, but this picture brings it all together. While she hasn't gone into detail about her family, her play activities, her school, or her bike, she has told me many things about herself that she believes to be important.

"Good. Now, can you draw a picture of yourself?"

"Me?"

"Yes."

She draws, then stops and vocalizes and shows me that the tip of her pencil has broken off.

"Oh, let me see if I can find another one." We look through the box for another identical color. Angie finds one and continues to draw. Her drawing of herself shows a little girl in brightly colored clothes with a smile on her face.

"That's good. Okay. Tell me a story about that girl." Angie picks up a pencil again and begins to write a story. "Do you prefer to write, or do you want to just sign a story?" She continues writing.

Angie reads the positive message she has written, "I love you and I like cats and dogs. My name is Angie and I'm ten."

"That's nice."

"Can I show my mom?" We remove the sheet of paper from the art pad. Once again, she hurries off, eager to show her mother the drawing and returns to join me.

"Wonderful. Now can you tell me a story about how you became deaf?"

"I forgot." She continues drawing throughout the conversation.

"Do you know how old you were when you became deaf?"

"I don't know."

"Were you born deaf or did you later become deaf?"

"Older."

"About how old?"

"I don't know . . ." Angie doesn't know how old she was when she became deaf, and this is not surprising because that information was not available to her parents either. Since she was adopted, it is difficult to ascertain the details of her early development. She changes the subject.

"I'm going to go to a hearing college."

"You're going to go to a hearing college?"

"And learn to understand."

"You'll learn to understand? Learn to understand who?"

"People. Learn to understand."

I'm not quite sure how to interpret the comment about learning to understand. Does this reflect a responsibility she feels as a deaf child to change and become more like hearing people, or is this just her way of explaining what happens in college: you learn and you understand and you grow. That aside, the following passages reflect a very positive perception of herself as being well behaved and as having a bright future that includes college and work.

She continues drawing her picture of a star and includes the phrase, "I am good at school." Connecting her comments about college with career choices, I ask her, "When you grow up, what do you want to do?"

"Work."

"Where do you want to work?"

"Maybe with food. I don't know."

"Oh, maybe selling food? Uh huh."

"You work?"

"Oh, where do I work? Where I work I do counseling with deaf people."

Angie persists in her drawing.

"A star."

"That's a pretty star."

She continues to draw, and as she draws she tells me bits and pieces about herself.

"I am good at school."

"Do you get good grades at school?"

She nods and continues drawing. Then she distinguishes her behavior from that of another child and tells me, "One boy in my class isn't good . . . He gets in trouble all the time when he plays . . . He acts funny. He's in kindergarten."

"In kindergarten?"

"And first grade. I don't know. But he's bad and the teacher gets mad."

As Angie begins to talk about her peers I am curious to find out more about who these children are, how they relate to each other, and what it all means to her. She tells me that she has both deaf and hearing friends and adds that her hearing cousins sign with her. She may consider her hearing cousins to be friends.

"Do you have many hearing friends or deaf friends?"

"Deaf. Deaf and hearing."

"Deaf friends. And where are your hearing friends? Where do you see them?"

"Signing."

"Here at home or at school?"

"At home."

"At home. And how do they learn to sign?"

"They learn to sign. My cousins. They know what I say."

"That's good. So they understand what you say. And at school are the teachers deaf or hearing?"

"They're hearing."

"And do they sign?" She nods. "And what do you do on Sunday?"

"We go to church."

"Does your church have interpreters?" She shakes her head. "No? How do you understand what's going on there?"

"I have a friend in church who's an interpreter, but I don't understand, so Mom interprets for me."

"So your mom tries to interpret for you so you can understand." Angie was not the only child in this study who said that her mother assists in communication outside of the family. "And what else do you do on Saturday and Sunday with your family?"

"Rain."

"Rain?" I'm not sure what she means by this.

"Yesterday after breakfast, I had four cookies."

"Four cookies."

"Mom and Dad were mad that they didn't get any."

"So you didn't share with Mom and Dad."

"I got in trouble."

"Did you get in trouble?" I ask. She nods.

"Is Mom mad?" She shakes her head. "No?"

"No. She just said stop and laughed." Clearly, Angie and her parents have fun together.

"What else do you like to do?"

"Um, I like to go places with my parents in the car."

"You like the car?"

"I'd like to drive it, but my dad says no, I have to wait 'til I'm bigger."

"Right. When you're sixteen you can learn to drive. What else do you do?"

Here Angie asks me about my son, if he likes to climb, and then she says her dog with floppy ears and the cat climb. I am unsure what she means. I ask her if she has any pets and she says none, but says there are birds outside. Then I refocus back to her friends, and she tells me a bit more about how she communicates with hearing children.

"You have some hearing friends. Do all your hearing friends know sign language? Or some of them don't?"

"My friends don't know how to do football. Football passes. And one bad kid played and stole, the team, said safe."

"Your hearing friends—if they don't sign, what do you do?"

"My mom can help if I sign and they don't understand."

"Your mother helps . . . When you're with hearing children, if they don't know any signs, how do you feel?"

"Ask to write, speech, hearing people . . . Hearing people talk, and kids understand, and you have to ask them to play, the kids, the hearing kids, and then we can go."

"And when they talk to you, can you talk? What do you do when they talk to you? What do you do?"

"We just play."

"And they play with you?"

"Yes."

"And what kind of games do you play?"

Angie shrugs. Regardless of whether or not hearing children sign, Angie indicates that they are still able to play together, and she seems to take this for granted and doesn't indicate discomfort in this situation.

"Where do you play?"

"Over there, there's lots of toys. Big ones. That's my favorite. It's near. With a helmet and gloves. Because there's no cars I can ride my bike . . . Because there's a fence over there, it's safe over there at the park . . . It's level."

Angie is talking about a playground in a park not far from her home.

"Near the park. If you go over there, and there's some hearing children who come there to play, what do you do?"

"I ask them if they want to play, and if they don't they just say no . . ." When Angie gets to this point, she begins to tell me about a new deaf friend who doesn't live nearby. "There's a new girl who's a friend who's deaf. Her name is Jenny. She's in fifth grade. Friend, house, job, mom and dad."

"Does she live near you?"

"No. In Davidsonville . . . and last Wednesday, she kicked the glass window, like that over there, and the glass broke. And her parents were mad and she can't come anymore . . . Uh huh. She got in trouble. They got mad and said that she had to pay. She'd have to pay at my school."

"Are there any deaf children near your home? . . . What do you do during the summer?"

"I swim . . . And I have no brothers or sisters to play basketball. I get bored . . . and it's hard. Sometimes I watch TV and I get kind of tired." Summer boredom isn't unusual for hearing children either.

"Uh huh. TV makes you tired. Do you have closed captions on your TV? You have that?"

"Right there, that one doesn't have it." She indicates they have two televisions. One has closed captioning and the other doesn't.

"So you have another TV? What's your favorite TV show?"

"Kids."

"Kids? Is that the title of the show?"

"It's funny."

"It's a funny show? What's the name of it, do you know?"

"They have animals in the water, and there's this boy and a bear who's really funny and they have bats and a girl and Taz and this man X and I like Batman and seven, I love that. And I think there's this movie about this little kid."

Like Danny, Angie is still young and probably doesn't understand all that is captioned on TV.

"Not big kids like you, huh? You said before that when you grow up you want to work in a store. What do you want to do?"

"Sell food."

"Oh, sell food, uh huh."

Angie holds up her drawing for me to see and says, "I'm done." She shows me a picture of a star.

"Oh, I like that. That's nice."

"It's a star."

"It's pretty."

"You can take it home . . . I love doing art . . . At school, every day on Wednesday, I have art. It's really hard for me to understand."

"Art's hard for you to understand? Why?"

"Because of the interpreter. And music."

"Oh, you have an interpreter for that at school."

Angie, once again, gets up and proudly takes her picture to show her parents. She returns with a videotape of a Walt Disney movie called *Goofy*.

"Oh, you like that? *Goofy* . . . What happens in that story?"

"His teeth grow. And his feet grow."

"Oh, his teeth get real long?"

"Yeah, and his feet. And his ears on his head. It's funny."

"Oh, it sounds like a bad dream."

"And he gets in a lot of trouble at school. He gets in trouble."

"In trouble at school?"

"Yeah, with the principal."

"I see." Angie has mentioned getting in trouble at school or home on a few occasions already. This seems to be an important issue for her. She seems concerned about behaving—as if this is a challenge for her.

"And there are some kids that are bored in school and they get kind of wild."

I am curious how she thinks hearing adults might perceive her. "Tell me, if there are adults, hearing adults, and they see you, a deaf girl, what do they think?"

Angie doesn't answer this question. She seems to have other things on her mind and changes the subject.

"I don't live in Davidsonville. I like Davidsonville. It's far." Angie lives in the suburbs south of Davidsonville.

"What do you like about it?"

"Cause I could go to my friends."

"Oh, your friends are there." Angie begins drawing again. She is working on a pink and purple cat. She asks me about my twenty-one-month-old son who rode with me today and is at the park with his babysitter while Angie and I meet.

"Does your son sleep in the car?"

"My son? This morning, yes, but this afternoon while I was driving here he was awake. And he was playing and he talked to Marilyn [our interpreter]. He talked to her and signed to her both. When you grow up, will you have children do you think? Do you want to have children when you grow up?"

"Sometimes hearing, sometimes deaf."

"Sometimes hearing?" I am uncertain what she means by this, perhaps that sometimes babies are born hearing and sometimes they are deaf.

"Sometimes deaf people are born and they can't understand . . . When you're a kid parents have to take care of you. They're stuck. Kids can't stay home alone."

This may be Angie's way of communicating her own desire to be protected. Angie is adopted, and her protection issues may be related to unanswered questions about separation from her birth family. These comments could also indicate some level of awareness that parenting has responsibilities that include protecting the child, or might allude to her perceptions of her own hearing parents protecting her.

"So when you grow up and become a mother, will your children be deaf or hearing?"

"I don't know."

"What do you hope for? Do you hope your children will be deaf or hearing?"

"I'd prefer deaf."

"You'd prefer deaf? Why? Why would you prefer deaf?"

Angie continues drawing.

"If they were hearing, what would you do?"

"Deaf or hearing. Sometimes you have to work hard for homework to read and practice speech. If you don't understand."

"For homework. Do you practice speech? With who?"

"Mom."

"With your mom?"

"I practice speech. I practice a lot. It's hard. And I have to keep practicing all the time."

"It's hard for you to do speech? In school every day, do you have speech?"

Changing the subject, she shows me the picture she has been drawing to which I respond, "A purple cat!"

"It's my favorite." She holds up the drawing to the camera. "It's a purple cat. I made it up." She continues drawing, and writes the word "c-a-t" on her picture. "I write in colors."

"Your other friends in school who are deaf, when they grow up, what do they want to do?"

"I have some friends at church who will get a TTY."

"A TTY?"

"So that I can understand. 'Cause I can't understand talking on the phone. I can't understand what's going on. If Mom's not here. So if something happened, I need to have a TTY." Once again, Angie conveys personal safety and protection concerns.

"So you don't have a TTY yet? But you'll get one? I have a TTY at home."

"It's kind of boring."

"You'll get one and then what would you do?"

"There might be, a deaf robber might sneak in and might steal it . . . They might put him in handcuffs and take him off to jail."

"A deaf robber?"

"Mmmhmm. It could happen. When parents travel, kids might have a party and make a mess, and the parents get mad and say, 'That, outside.' Does your son make a mess?"

"Sometimes. If that happened, what would I do?"

Angie is finishing up her picture. She doesn't answer my questions, but she holds up her picture for me to see.

"That's very pretty. Okay, that's good. Great. I want to try something different, okay? We don't need those markers; I'm going to put them away." At this point, I decide to move on to the next phase of our interviewing. We put the markers away and I take out my folder of cutout magazine photographs.

"The brown one." She hands me the brown marker.

"Oh, there's the brown one, thank you." I ask if I can keep her drawings for my book. Angie nods. "Thank you."

"My mom? My mom? Can I show my mom this one?"

"Sure."

Angie leaves the room once again to check in with her mom and returns carrying her stuffed dog. Playfully, she says, "My dog, my dog, my dog. It'll bite." She brings the dog toward me as if it is going to bite.

"It'll bite me? Oh, I'm scared!"

Angie laughs, "Are you going to run away?"

"Yeah, I'd better run away!"

Angie puts her stuffed dog on the coffee table. "Very pretty." She shows me the dog's ear; a piece has been torn off. "Cat got the ear. A cat got it by the tail and flung it."

"Oh, did it hurt?" She laughs and shakes her head no.

"Oh, okay. Now we're going to do something different. I'm going to show you a picture, and I want you to tell me what's going on in the picture. This is the first one. What's happening? Who are they?"

"Baby. Is that your son?"

"My son? No, it's not my son."

"Is that you?"

When Angie first looked at this magazine cutout she seems to have thought it was a picture of me with my son and husband. It's a picture of a man and a woman standing up holding a baby. I tell her it is not my son but don't want to spoil her imaginative speculation regarding the picture, so I try to avoid answering further questions about the identity of people in the pictures.

"I would like you to tell me a story. Can you make up a story about that?"

"That's the husband. They're deaf." Like other children in this study, Angie begins to ascribe identities to the characters in the pictures by telling me if they are deaf or hearing.

"How do you know?"

"They're sick."

"They're sick? How do you know they're sick?"

"He's looking up; they know sign. The mother knows sign."

"So they know how to sign? How . . ."

Angie looks at the picture, notices it has been cut out of a magazine, and says, "This is cut out."

I explain to her that I cut them out for us. "I cut them out and pasted them on paper. I did that."

"At school, we do it this way, so you can take it off. Can I show this at church?" She is relating our activity to things she does at school.

"Oh, I need to show it to other children to ask them, so I use them again and again."

"Deaf children? To deaf children? Are you going to my friend's house?"

"Just a lot of different deaf children."

"In Davidsonville? They have a lot of children."

"Yes, they do."

"It's far."

"It's pretty far, yes . . ." I want to bring our focus back to her statement about the parents in the picture being deaf. "Anyway, how do you know they're deaf?"

"He's sick. He can't hear."

"Sick?"

"He can't hear." Angie may know that she was ill in her infancy and that may be the reason why she is deaf. She appears to be projecting images of her own infancy.

"And are the mother and father deaf or hearing?"

"I think they're deaf."

"The mother and father both are deaf?"

"Maybe."

"And how do you know?"

"I think they were born that way. Maybe my mother's deaf. I don't know."

"Whose mom, your mom? Your mom may be deaf? Or may be hearing?"

"Yeah, I don't know." Here I suspect she is imagining her birth mother.

Angie indicates to the camera that she's wrapped the dog's leash around the table leg. Trying to keep our focus, I show her the next picture, "What's going on there? Who is that?"

"He's deaf."

"He's deaf? What is he doing?"

"Working."

"Working? And what kind of work?"

"Making something for deaf people."

"How do you know he's deaf?"

Once again, Angie tells me that the person in the picture who she identifies as deaf may have been sick. "Maybe he was sick and couldn't be born and grew up and knew sign, not talking."

"Sick and couldn't be born? What do you mean, he couldn't be born?" I wonder if this is a fantasy about how she became deaf. Or does it represent her understanding of why her parents decided to adopt? Does she think her adoptive parents could not conceive because one of them was sick? My hunch is that her comment represents her explanation of her own birth and the reason for her being deaf.

"I don't know . . . The dog's going to bite, dog's going to bite . . . I like to tease." She has changed the subject.

"You like to tease. Okay. What's going on in this?" I show her a picture of two children sitting on the floor. One is talking on a cell phone, and the other has his eyes closed with his head in his hands.

"He can't hear."

"Can't hear?" I ask.

"This person's deaf."

"Who is deaf?" I ask, and Angie points to someone in the picture.

"This person's deaf? What about this person?"

"That person's hearing."

"That person's hearing? How do you know?"

"Talking on the phone. And this person's getting really bored. And waiting and waiting. The friend's chatting on the phone. He wants to play a game with him. But he's bored; his friend's bored. And he's making faces maybe at his friend or something. And the other one's just ignoring him." The person she indicated was hearing is the one on the phone. Angie had the same reaction to this picture that the other children had, which indicates that they all feel bored in situations of communication inaccessibility.

"Okay."

She looks at the next picture. This picture shows two toddlers sitting on the floor with a woman. One of the children is signing along with the woman. It appears that the sign signifies either "airplane" or "I love you." Like Danny, she quickly decides it means "I love you."

"He's deaf . . . Oh, I know. Signing I LOVE YOU. This one's deaf and this one's hearing."

"How do you know? How do you know which one?" Like the other children, Angie identified visual indicators in the photographs, such as signing and talking, as revealing the hearing status of the person in the photo.

"The I LOVE YOU is deaf. Sometimes they're together and sometimes separate."

"Sometimes deaf and hearing are separate? Why are they separate?"

"When you're born, if you can't hear, when you grow up, you can be separate deaf . . . You go to a hearing aid doctor, and then you're fine."

"You're fine? With a hearing aid they're fine? Are they still deaf?" I am reminded here of Schlesinger's (Schlesinger and Meadow, 1972) poignant description of the images that deaf children may have of their futures when they have no deaf adult role models to help them foresee what possibilities exist for them. Schlesinger states that without deaf adult role models, deaf children may wonder if they will become hearing, disappear, or die. Angie has had the opportunity to meet deaf adults, but they are not a part of her daily life. She has told us that she envisions going to college, having a career, and having children. She has also told us that she knows she will grow up, that she will still be deaf, and that she will be fine.

"But they can't hear anything. And they can't hear, and you say, 'My name is Angie,' but they couldn't hear. But a hearing aid, it can help you with talking. And the baby girls [hearing babies in a family she is acquainted with] they say 'Mom' and 'Dad.' "

"When your mom and dad found out you were deaf, what did they do?"

Angie responds with an explanation of her own educational history. "Went to school and to kindergarten, first, second, third, fourth. And then fifth. And then I'll go to middle school, and then I'll go to college for hearing people, and I'll understand."

"When mother and father find out their baby is born deaf, how do the parents feel?"

"I don't know." Here Angie reports she doesn't know how they feel, but in other places she has indicated that her parents worry over her and work hard with her. She seems to carry a sense of responsibility to *overcome* what she may perceive as her challenges. Alternatively, perhaps she is expressing the values and pressures that others project onto her to achieve.

"If your baby was born deaf, when you're married and have children, if you should have a deaf baby, how would you feel?"

"I'd feel fine, maybe confused if the baby couldn't hear."

I want to learn more about what she would be confused about. Angie's parents didn't know that she was deaf when she was adopted. I wonder if confusion was a theme in her adoption story. "You would feel confused?"

"You know a flashing alarm clock? I have one to wake me up, but I wake up, but then I sleep, and then the light flashes. And that way

you can know if the baby cries, if my son was crying, at night. And
I would say, 'Stop,' to his brothers and sisters, if it was kind of scary
. . ." She knows that there are electronic devices that flash lights to
alert deaf parents to their child's cries as well as lighted alarm
clocks. Angie is discussing parental protection of her children. Perhaps by "confused" she means that as a *deaf* parent she would need
devices such as a baby-cry alert to know what is happening with her
son.

"Scary, why?"

"There was this movie, a story, about, these parents got really
mad, and they wouldn't let them."

"Parents wouldn't let them watch the movie?"

"Not a scary movie because kids get scared and they cry and parents get mad. And some movies they can't go, I couldn't let my son
go to watch. I'd say no until he's grown up in the future. If it was a
funny movie he might laugh, like this." She points to her *Goofy*
videotape.

"But if your baby were deaf, how would you feel about your baby
being deaf?"

"I couldn't hear."

"Uh huh, you can't hear. Happy or sad, confused, worried,
what?"

"Worried."

"Worried, why?"

"Because I can't hear. When I got big, I know my parents were
worried, they were worried about me."

"Okay. This is number five."

"I think . . . I think, a, b, c, d, e, f . . ." She is pointing to the manual alphabet banner on a classroom wall in one of the pictures.

"The ABCs, yes."

"That's a deaf class deaf book. Deaf, a deaf book . . ."

"Deaf books? What do you mean by deaf books?"

"That you pay. My parents have deaf books that they read and
understand."

"Oh, a sign language book." Hearing parents of deaf children
who attend deaf education programs often have opportunities to attend sign language classes or parent-teacher meetings where they
network and learn about parenting a deaf child. She knows that her

parents have worked hard to learn to sign and to meet her educational and communication needs.

"Deaf kids go to school and have deaf friends and they're not shy." Angie seems to think the picture depicts a class of deaf children. Her response indicates her comfort in the presence of deaf peers.

"Deaf friends are not shy? With hearing friends are they shy?"

"Sometimes kids are shy and they don't talk to bigger kids or adults or parents. They're shy."

"Okay, good. And how do you know they're deaf?"

"Born."

"They were born deaf? But when you look at them, how do you know they're deaf? How can you tell?"

"Everyone wants to work with deaf people."

"Oh."

"Big, little, babies, nurses, doctors. If you're sick they give you medicine to make you feel better." Angie has mentioned being sick on several occasions. This seems to be significant to her.

Going back to her comment that everyone wants to work with deaf people, I ask, "Do you want to work with deaf people?" Angie mentions several professionals in her life—teachers, doctors, nurses. Harvey (1989) tells us that typically deaf children have more professionals in their lives than hearing children do. I imagine that in addition to the professionals that Angie has mentioned, there are others: interpreters, audiologists, speech therapists, and community resource personnel.

"I might work with little children to be safe and teach them, and might watch them so they could be safe. Like if there's a fire or something like that. You have to be safe and you can't play."

"So, to teach little children to be safe? Safe from what?"

"From bad things with their parents. And if kids, if there's a sister and brother and a baby gets into make-up and stuff like that."

"Oh, you have to be protective sometimes. Tell them 'no' and take something away and give them something else to play with."

Angie pretends to write on her face with a green marker.

"That happens, yes. Okay. This is number six." I introduce the next picture, but Angie has more to tell me about mischief.

"Your son might take markers and mark all over himself. He might draw on his teeth. You'd have to wash it off."

"Have you done that before?" She nods. "With green or what color?"

"Blue. It smells good . . . It's not food, you can't eat it. Your son might write on the wall . . . Sometimes kids write on the wall." Satisfied that she has made her point, she looks at the next picture. In this photo, two women are sitting opposite each other, signing. One is middle aged and the other is a young adult. Angie explains, "They're helping adults and older kids who are deaf." Once again Angie indicates the presence of helpers in the lives of people who are deaf.

"Are both of them deaf?" Angie nods. "How do you know?"

"It's the son and daughter, born deaf, grown up." She appears to see the gender of one of the individuals differently from me.

"A son and daughter born deaf who have grown up, become adults? What are they doing? What's this person doing?"

"Talking to that person."

"About what?"

"I don't know . . . I don't know their story."

We change pictures. "Okay. So what are they doing? This is number seven."

"Talking about a crazy dog." This is also a picture of two women chatting. One is signing, and the handshape, caught in the photo out of the context of their actual conversation, leaves one to guess what they might be discussing. Although there are a number of possibilities, it appears to Angie that she is signing DOG.

"Oh, they're talking about a dog? How do you know they're talking about a dog?"

"Maybe a deaf or a hearing dog."

I am unsure if she is referring to the dog not being able to hear or being a certified support dog for deaf people, which are commonly referred to as *hearing dogs* or *hearing ear dogs*. I attempt to clarify but am still uncertain of what she means. "A hearing dog?"

"I think deaf."

"Hearing or deaf, you don't know?"

"The dog barks. They're deaf, all of them."

"All of them are deaf?"

She quickly moves on to the next picture, where she sees two young children conversing on a playground. One of them is visibly wearing a hearing aid. "Oh, he's got a hearing aid. I know."

"You know he's got a hearing aid."

Angie shows me her hearing aids and tells me she has two of them. "Two . . . It's shaped like this. It goes in here. It hurts sometimes."

"It hurts?"

"Yeah, it's awful." She looks at the picture. "This is the friend."

"Friends?"

"These kids are friends, and there's a bad kid who's hurting a person. They should keep with good kids. Some bad kids, you know. They might not know not to talk to strangers, that you should run away. It's awful. My dog . . . He might want to run away, and he might break the camera. And the camera would go flying and we'd have to catch it. He might break the window and a turkey out there."

"A turkey?"

"I'm teasing." She looks at the next picture. "That's a deaf woman typing."

"On TTY?"

"Type on the phone. At Oakland, at Oakland school, my class."

"Oh, you type on the TTY?" Angie is imitating talking on the phone. "Have you called on the TTY before?"

"No, I haven't. You talk on the phone, you type, you talk on the phone, you type. I will. I will."

"You will. Okay."

"I know . . . More, more." She is looking for more pictures.

"No, this is the last one."

"Oh, a lion." She is referring to a picture of Simba from Walt Disney's *Lion King*, which is on the T-shirt of a girl in the photo we are looking at. This is a photograph of several children and one adult sitting on the floor posing for a group picture.

"A lion?"

"Deaf, at school, and they help. They can't hear. And you don't know what to do, the children's names and stuff. And he's really tired . . . This person's parents." She indicates the little girl sitting on a man's lap in the front of the picture.

"The parents are tired?"

"Yeah. 'Cause the name, name, name."

"Name?"

"Yeah. It's hard to get the names, 'cause you don't speak. It's better to talk."

"Oh, so you practice talking? Is it hard for parents to help children talk?" Angie nods.

We conclude our interview and Angie runs outside to play.

ᆥᎧ

ALL OF ANGIE'S brightly colored drawings match the happy, bubbly child she appears to be. The house she drew for me included sunshine, windows, and birds flying in the sky. She reflected a positive image of herself as a well-behaved child who does well in school and who has a bright future. She did seem to worry about making mistakes, and indicated that she works hard to maintain good behavior and to master speech. She communicated that she is aware of rules for self-protection such as not talking with strangers, and she also communicated a desire to be protected, a concern that may be related to Angie's unanswered questions about her adoption.

Like the other children in this study, Angie knows that she is deaf, she knows where other deaf children are, and she knows that many resources are available to her, such as lighted alarm clocks, TTYs, closed captioned television, hearing aids, and baby-cry signalers. Her parents told me during our visit that Angie attends organized recreational activities with other deaf children outside of school, and she indicates that she is comfortable in their presence and struggles more in the company of hearing children who do not sign.

Angie seems to see her parents as worrying about her and working hard to help her. She sees them getting books about deafness and learning to sign. She also mentioned that they work with her on her speech, and she sees this process as somewhat laborious for them as well as for herself. Aside from this difficulty, Angie reports that she and her parents also have fun together, laugh, play games, joke, and love each other.

Regarding her future, Angie mentioned parenthood frequently and anticipated how she will respond to her children as a deaf parent. She seemed to prefer deaf children. Angie considers the responsibilities of parenting, and she applies her own experiences in her family to her future role as a mother. She needs protection and her parents protect her; therefore as a mother, she would protect her own child. She is also anticipating what it means to be a deaf parent.

Angie predicted that she will learn to drive, go to college, work in the food industry, and live separately from her parents. She knows that she will still be deaf when she grows up and has already begun to collect a repertoire of images of herself in the future and resources for success.

Because Angie was adopted, she does not know how or when she became deaf, but she is aware that she may have become deaf from illness. It appears that she may be trying to fit some pieces of her adoption puzzle together. For example, she talked about how her birth mother might have been deaf. There is a huge gap in research on issues related to deaf adoptive children. More research into the experiences of these children and their families is encouraged.

Angie reported playing with both deaf and hearing friends. If she runs into communication difficulties with hearing peers, she has strategies ready: writing, using her speech, and relying on her mother's help. She suggested she may need to take the initiative to ask hearing kids to play with her and then added, "We just play." She has a number of activities she enjoys—playing games and going places with her family, riding her bike, playing soccer and basketball, and playing with her stuffed animals. She appears to miss the company of her deaf schoolmates who live in Davidsonville. Angie took pride in the work she was doing for me, and she eagerly went to show each completed picture to her mother. She worked diligently on her drawings throughout our interview.

6

Joe

W HEN MARILYN and I arrived at Joe's home, his mother answered the door and introduced us to a friend of hers who was visiting. She called upstairs for Joe, who she said was working on his computer. When Joe didn't come downstairs, she went up to find him. A few moments later, Joe came down the stairs, wearing a warm smile on his face. He was a tall, ten-year-old boy who initially seemed slightly shy. Joe was nicely dressed, well behaved, friendly, and mature. He stayed a bit behind his mom, not making eye contact until I began signing. He quickly warmed and opened up his heart in our interview.

Joe was mainstreamed in his local school district at a total communication program. His previous educational programs were a combination of oral and total communication. Joe has a severe hearing loss and considers himself hard of hearing. He became deaf at approximately five months of age from an unknown cause. Joe's parents are divorced. He lives with his mother and visits his father. All of Joe's family members are hearing. He has no additional disabilities. He and his family communicate primarily through speech, but some of them also know sign language. He is African American and had the most residual hearing of the seven children in this study.

We chatted a bit as Joe's mom showed us to the family room. Joe communicated with me through speech and sign. He seemed to be more comfortable if he could just talk without also signing.

Looking back on my initial meeting with Joe, I see that my own realities framed the way in which I explained the purpose of our meetings and asked him questions. When I told him I was writing a book about deaf children, I did not mention hard of hearing children. When I asked if he considers himself deaf or hard of hearing, he told me he is hard of hearing but also later referred to himself as deaf. For example, he talked about a friend who is "deaf like me, he talks." Although I erred in this omission, it became clear in these interviews with Joe that he sees that there are similarities and differences among deaf and hard of hearing children. Joe was so open about his feelings, so articulate and willing to relate, that I didn't need to ask him to draw many pictures to help facilitate our interview. He was very inquisitive and was able to directly share much of what was on his mind.

ℰ∂

WHEN JOE, seems ready to begin, I ask him to draw a picture for me. He draws a picture of a boy wearing a Dallas Cowboys football uniform and says that the Cowboys are his favorite team. He confides that he has many drawings hanging on the walls in his room. I ask him to tell me a story about the deaf boy in the picture. It becomes apparent that Joe sees himself as a boy who has "trouble hearing." He tells me about the difficulties he encounters with hearing children who tease him at school and in his neighborhood. He explains that he hasn't been able to get the support he and his deaf friends need from school personnel to put a stop to the teasing. He is angry about the situation and fearful that he or other children will get hurt.

"I think maybe," he looks at the picture for a moment and then back at me, "he has trouble with hearing and people tease him. You know, um, he, um, he doesn't hear. He hears less."

"Who teases him?"

"Brian."

"Brian? Is that somebody from school?"

"Yeah."

"Is that a hearing person or a deaf person?"

"A hearing . . . no, um, hearing . . . he talks, but he's always teasing and . . ." Joe's stories about the teasing he experiences with hearing children are much more painful than anything the other children in this study expressed. The children typically have both comfortable and uncomfortable experiences with hearing peers, but Joe's distress over the negative experiences stands out from all the others. He seems to need to talk about this situation.

"Do hearing people give you trouble and tease you?"

"Mmhmm. And then, um, I ask them to stop it. But they still tease and call names and get friends in fights and stuff like that. And we tell the teacher but the teacher says just ignore it."

"And how do you feel about that? When that happens?"

"I feel angry."

"And does that happen to other deaf kids in your school?"

"Yeah. And then, um, me and this other person sometimes get sick or get hurt. And sometimes people are in the hospital. And many times it happens that people are hurt or they're in the hospital. Then you try to tell the teacher about what to do and the teacher just says, 'Ignore it,' or 'Stop' . . . One day, umm . . ."

Joe is clearly dealing with some troubling issues. I can empathize with his hurt, because as a deaf person who grew up in hearing schools, I had similar experiences. "You're in the fourth grade now? And you're ten years old? In January? You know when I was ten . . . I was a deaf girl in a hearing school and the kids made fun of me too. It was hard. I can remember that. But it got better."

Joe goes on to tell me more stories about situations where he and other deaf students are teased at school. He is clearly uncomfortable with these situations and the lack of resolution. "One day, um, I have a new friend named Nancy, and there's another person whose name starts with a 'B,' and there are people who will try and help us by, when people tease and other things, and they tell the teacher, but the kids don't pay attention. They don't pay attention. Those people pick on me because, because I didn't hear very well for the low sounds and loud voices. I can hear the lighter sounds. And sometimes they'll call my name."

"And that makes you feel what?"

"Upset."

"Upset. I understand. When a teacher sees that happening, how do the teachers feel?"

"They feel like, they feel like, some of those people, um, they might feel upset and not know what to do, my teachers might not know what to do. Because, um, well and if you're upset the teachers might not know what to do." Joe's strategies for coping with this teasing include telling his teacher and the school counselor, but this isn't working well for him right now. "Okay, when that happens, you try to talk to the teacher. What else do you do?"

"I tell my counselor and try to get some information. But they just won't, they won't."

"That's really hard for you." Joe nods in agreement. Moving on, I indicate the boy in the picture Joe has drawn and say, "Tell me some more stories about that boy."

Joe goes on to tell me about another deaf boy at school. He says this boy is also made fun of, but he doesn't let the hearing children off easy.

"He fights . . . but my friends help us." Joe names some friends, including two hearing children and another deaf student. "Then, my other friend, my other friend's name is Mark. Mark. He's in middle school. Yeah. 'Cause he had to go to a different school because there was too much trouble in that school."

"What kind of trouble?"

"Too many fights because, get mad and get in fights too much." He tells me about a hearing boy at school who starts fights and lies. "That boy . . . he lies."

"Oh, he lies? That's really, sounds like a really sad situation. And Mark's not there anymore? Some of your friends have moved? That's really sad that he moved. Do you have other friends, deaf friends? Katie is deaf?" I am referring to names of students he mentioned earlier.

"No."

"Oh, so Katie is hearing?"

"Yes. And Emily is hearing."

"Oh. So do the two of them sign?"

"A little bit. And they're learning from me." While Joe has encountered some very hurtful relationships with hearing peers at school, he is also developing some positive relationships with hearing children. One of his coping strategies is to teach hearing children to sign. He takes pride in his contribution to their friendships and sees that he has something positive to offer them, which gives him a sense of mastery.

"So you're teaching them? That's wonderful. Do the other kids sign?"

"Um, some of them. Named, um Robbie. And there's some hearing . . . he's a hearing kid, but he knows a lot of sign language."

I wonder if Joe has an overall feeling about school. When I ask if he likes school his response is, "Yeah, it's fun. I like gym and art, but not music. That's boring . . . It's boring. They just talk and sing."

"Music is hard for you?"

"Yeah. I only sing in rap."

"Rap, oh. Do you like that?"

"Mmhmm."

"Where did you learn rap? Who taught you?"

"My sister."

"How old is your sister?"

"Twelve."

Here Joe tells me about his brothers and sisters, their ages, and where they live. Some of them live with his father. Joe is not certain of all of their ages. He tells me that his parents are divorced and that he thinks he was five or six when that happened. He says he doesn't know why the divorce occurred.

"When you visit with your brother and sister . . . Do your brother and sister sign?"

"Only my sister. My brother doesn't. He just talks to me."

"How much can you hear? Are you hard of hearing or really deaf?"

"I'm hard of hearing."

"So you can hear some?"

"Yeah."

"Do you understand people's voices?"

"Not all people's voices. I understand people with light voices, not deep voices or low voices." Joe identifies himself as hard of hearing based on the fact that he has residual hearing, which he finds useful. It will also become clear later in our sessions that Joe sees other communicative, linguistic, behavioral, and cultural differences between himself and deaf children.

"And if they're louder can you understand?"

"No. Light voices."

By this, I assume he means high frequency voices, "Oh, light voices. Okay. And can you hear on the telephone?"

"No. But I'm going to get a TDD. To type for . . . for Christmas."

Joe also talks about things he does with his family. "Well, I, um, I play with my family sometimes and sometimes I don't want to play . . . Sometimes I play, you know, blind, um, it's a race . . . It's, you put a blindfold on so you can't see, and then you have to try and find the bones . . . yeah. The bones, and you reach in and try and find them . . . And then me and my brother play soldier sometimes. And I have one cousin who comes and we like to play football." Even though there are inconsistencies in communication with his family members, he appears to feel safe with them and reports a variety of recreational activities they enjoy together. Joe's perception is that he understands a lot of their communication. He seems to see family communication difficulties as minimal compared to those he experiences with hearing children.

Picking up on what he said about playing football with his cousin, I ask, "You like football? Are you good at football?"

"Yeah. Yeah, I'm a good receiver. You know, the, uh, what do they call it? Um, um . . . You know when you throw it and you catch it?"

"Oh, you're good at that, huh? Do you play football on a team?"

"No, not yet . . . Next year."

"You will? In school? Well, that's good, that sounds like fun." He seems to look forward to this. "So how does your family communicate with you?"

"They talk."

"And everybody talks with you? No one signs?"

"Well, my sister signs a little bit. Sometimes my mom."

"And how much do you understand?"

"A lot."

"You understand a lot?"

"Yeah."

"Do you lipread?"

"Mmhmm."

"And when you have dinner with your family, do they talk to you? And do you lipread and get what they're saying? Do you know what they're talking about?"

"Yeah."

"And when you get together with your relatives, how do you communicate?"

"Um, we talk and I read lips."

"Uh huh. Talk and read lips? And how does that work out?"

"You have to go slow, make it clear."

"So they help you to understand, okay. And do you ever get frustrated?"

"With my uncle."

"With your uncle. Why?"

"Because he talks real fast. And my Uncle Robin talks too fast."

"And what do you do when he talks fast?"

"I tell him to slow down, and he'll say, 'Okay.' " Here Joe imitates his uncle's deep voice. "But then he talks fast again." Joe knows what his communication needs are. One of his strengths is that he asserts them and feels entitled to have his communication needs met.

"Okay. And what about playing with your friends? Do you have friends around here?"

"Mmhmm."

"How do you understand them?"

"Well, because I'll tell them, if I don't understand them I'll tell them, 'Will you move your mouth so I can understand you clearly.' And they'll say 'okay' and then they'll say it so that I understand. Um, my friend over there, Shelly talks real fast and sometimes I don't understand."

"Yeah, I have to do that, too. I'll have to tell people to please slow down. I agree, yeah. So you have a lot of friends around here?"

"Uh huh."

"What kinds of things do you do with your friends?"

Like the other children, Joe enjoys a number of recreational activities. "Well, football, soccer, and tag, and kind of like a race, but you try to run real fast and then you get the football, and play baseball and . . ."

"You seem to like sports a lot. You play a lot of different sports. Football and softball . . ."

"And soccer and hockey and softball, hmm, and football."

"That's great. You're a good athlete, hmm? I bet you are. What about religion? Does your family go to church?"

"Yeah, we do."

"What kind of church do you go to?"

"We go to Christ Church, and the Faith Church."

"And do you have an interpreter there when you go?"

"Not at Christ Church, only at Faith Church. And I go to Faith many times. I just go to Christ Church for now 'cause Faith starts at nine o'clock."

Wanting to know more about other people in Joe's life, I ask about his teacher. "Well, my teacher, my mainstream teacher's funny. And he's funny and is very friendly with other people and bites his fingers and makes faces and we don't have to work a lot."

"You don't have to work a lot? Do you like that?"

"Yeah. But in my deaf class we work and sometimes, um, my teacher is named [Joe gives two name signs on the chin] and one is real funny. But sometimes this other teacher acts crazy, makes funny gestures and stuff. Like that. And we do hangman, do you know what that is? Hangman? That's a game. And sometimes we play on the computer." Joe tells me how much he enjoys playing on his home computer. "I play friendly computer. That teaches you how to use the computer. And there's a rabbit writer . . . You have to re-member the carrot and these other words in order and there's a card that it flips over and if it's the same." Joe smiles while he tells me about the academic side of his school experience. He has both pleasant and unpleasant experiences with school.

"So it teaches you new words, vocabulary, and is that fun?" He nods. "Let's go back to your teachers at school. Do your teachers sign?"

"Yes. But my mainstream teacher doesn't sign. But we have an in-terpreter there."

"So this interpreter interprets for you in the mainstream classes?"

"And she and, um, me and . . ." Joe signs many name signs. I was not aware that Joe's mother was observing from the next room, but Joe sees her stop him to remind him that the interpreter and I do not know the name signs of the people he is talking about. He then proceeds to spell out their names. He says many of these people sign.

"And do you prefer to have a teacher who signs or do you prefer to use an interpreter?"

"I like the interpreter 'cause the interpreter's funny. Sometimes when my teacher's reading a book sometimes it's pretty funny."

"So your interpreter does that?"

"And it sounds funny, yeah."

"And if you could choose for yourself, which would you rather have? A teacher who signs or do you prefer to have an interpreter?"

"I prefer to have an interpreter . . . because there's a hard time with the mainstream teachers. I have a hard time to teach . . . Umm, with my teacher in, the mainstream teachers . . . I teach them sign language."

One of the challenges of inclusive education for deaf children is that many of their teachers do not have a good understanding of what it means to be a deaf child in a hearing classroom. In addition, many of these teachers are unable to communicate with the deaf children. This gap can lead to misunderstandings of the deaf child's behavior, needs, relationships, and communication. Whereas deaf adults expect to educate hearing others to facilitate successful communication, friendships, and work relationships, this is an additional burden for a deaf child in a hearing school. Yet Joe seems to take upon himself the responsibility of teaching sign language to hearing peers and teachers. This is a pressure that hearing children do not experience. I interpret Joe's preference for an interpreter as being related to the comfort Joe feels in their relationship due to the interpreter's expertise, understanding of, and ability to communicate with him.

"Oh, I see. So you teach them signs. They didn't know any signs before?"

"No. They never knew any signs before."

"So, until they met you, so you're the first deaf student there?"

"Yeah."

"Do you like all of your teachers?"

"Mmm, not all."

"Some of them you don't like? Why?" Joe doesn't answer. "Okay, some of them you don't like? Some of your teachers?" He nods in agreement.

"Do all of your teachers, do you think, understand what it's like to be deaf in a hearing school?"

"Um, I like to teach the other kids sign language and I like to play games with language."

"So you're teaching a lot of people signing?"

"Not all of them, but my girlfriend and other girls and, and some boys."

"Tell me about your girlfriend."

"She likes sign language and soccer and sometimes football."

"Is your girlfriend deaf or hearing?"

"Hearing."

"And so you're teaching her signing, too?"

"Mmhmm."

"Does that help the two of you communicate?"

"Mmhmm. And I can understand when she speaks."

Joe was not the only child in this study who reported teaching other children to sign. This appears to be a common strategy among them.

"Okay. And you said that sometimes the hearing children make fun of the deaf children?"

"Mmhmm."

"Do deaf children . . . What do they do with each other? Do they make fun of each other? Do they like each other? Do they play together? Or do they fight? Or what?"

"Sometimes me and my friend, this other boy named Christopher. He's deaf like me and he talks, too. And sometimes we fight and sometimes we play together. Sometimes we argue."

Joe identifies with Christopher, another *deaf* child who *talks*. He relates this in a relaxed manner. Joe is comfortable enough in relationships like this that he can discuss their arguments as if they are just taken for granted.

I want to find out more about Joe's history. It becomes clear that he doesn't have complete information about how he became deaf. "How long have you been signing? Have you always known sign language? How old were you when you started learning sign?"

"One."

"One. Oh, you've been signing for a long time."

"And I've signed for nine years."

"You've been . . . yes, that's right . . . How did you become deaf?"

"I don't know. My mom would know."

"Have you ever asked your mom?"

"No."

"Do you know what you're going to do when you grow up?"

"Uh huh."

"What are you going to do?"

"I would like to go to, um . . . You know, where . . . Have you heard of where deaf kids go for college? I want to go to that school."

"Yeah, I know that school. Gallaudet." I am surprised that Joe has heard about Gallaudet and pleased that he has mentioned it and sees that as a possibility for his future. After all, I attended Gallaudet and had a very positive experience there.

"Yeah, that's it."

"I went there. That's where I went to college."

"And, um, I would like to play football. And I would like to live in Dallas city."

"In Dallas? So you'd like to play football there? For the Dallas Cowboys?"

"I want to."

"Ooh, that sounds like fun. That sounds like a good goal. Okay. Do you know of any football players who are deaf?"

"Yeah . . . Yeah, from another high school. His name is K, um, K. I don't know his last name . . . One kid who is, who got hurt . . . There's this one deaf kid. Um, he had to go to the hospital for three years . . . I don't know why. When they were winning, and they're losing, and they're playing . . . You know you have first down. The team had a first down and they came together and the one team, the player got knocked over."

"That's really sad. Hopefully that won't happen to you."

"Me, too."

"Okay . . . When I write my book, about deaf children, what do you think I should put in there?"

"That some kids, some kids were born with hearing. They could hear. And sometimes, sometimes, um, kids have a disease, and it makes them lose their hearing. And some, um, something gets broken in their ear or there's a problem. My friend Theresa, um, who's deaf, she could hear when she was born. And then when she was three years old she got sick. And then she couldn't hear anymore and she became deaf . . . And some kids can get the wrong kind of shots and that could make them, um, not able to hear. And some could be born with no hearing. And sometimes people get sick, sometimes it's from shots, sometimes they're born that way."

Earlier, Joe had said that he didn't know how he became deaf. His mother had indicated to me on the information form I asked parents to complete that the cause of Joe's deafness was unknown, but that they believed it could have been a side effect from one of his immunizations. It appears that he does have some unconfirmed information about how he became deaf.

"So every deaf kid is different?"

"Yep."

Joe's responses to my questions about what I should put in my book about deaf children show that he understands the diversity among children who are deaf and hard of hearing. He knows that he and other deaf and hard of hearing children share some commonalities, but also have their individual stories to tell about communication, their families, their relationships, and how they became deaf. "What about communication? What should I put down in my book about communication?"

"Some kids read lips or hear some or watch signs."

"And what should I put down about deaf children's families?"

"Some, some can sign and some can talk and some can talk and sign both."

"Okay. Good. And what about friends?"

"Well, some people communicate by, by . . . If they can communicate by, if you can teach them how to sign, or they can read lips, or they might be able to hear well."

"Okay."

Joe tells me a story about a Deaf family he knows. His wide eyes, surprised expression, and rapid signing show his amazement that an entire family can be deaf. "And I have this one friend . . ." He signs the names of his friends and voices, "Thomas and Catherine. They're all from the same family. And all of his family, their whole family, their whole family, the parents and everybody is deaf. They're all deaf. And they have a lot of deaf kids in their family. This one family, they're all deaf. I was really surprised when, when Thomas's mom had the baby, and then Catherine was born deaf."

"So it's a big family and they're all deaf. What do you think about that?"

"Well, when they all came one time, and I said, when I talked they didn't understand. I tried talking and I had to sign. And then they signed back to me and I thought, 'Whoa!' "

"So the kids sign?"

"Yeah, but when I talked, um, I just thought they were hearing, but they looked at me funny and then I started signing and then they signed back."

"So you found out they were deaf. Was that a big surprise?"

"Yeah." Anecdotal evidence suggests that there are fewer black deaf than white deaf families (Redding, 1999). Statistics from the Annual Survey of Deaf and Hard of Hearing Youth (Graduate Research Institute, 2000) suggest that hereditary deafness occurs more frequently among white schoolchildren (21.9 percent) than black/African American schoolchildren (11.5 percent), while black/African American children have more postbirth causes of deafness, such as meningitis. The increase in postbirth cause for black/African American children may be related to fewer opportunities for health care and less access to immunizations.

"That's interesting. When you grow up, do you think you will have deaf children or hearing children?"

"I never thought about it."

"What about when you get married? Do you think you'll marry a deaf lady or a hearing lady?"

"Hearing. A hearing lady."

"A hearing woman? Why?"

"I don't know." He laughs. "I don't know . . . Um, because my girlfriend is hearing and so I guess I'd like to marry her."

"Okay. You've got a head start, right? Okay. Well, that's all. And I'd like to come one more time to see you. It doesn't have to be at two o'clock. We can change the time. I'll talk to your mom and see when's a good time, okay?"

As we are closing our interview that afternoon, I ask Joe if there is anything else he wants to tell me.

"Um, some kids get cancer from their ears."

"Get what?"

"Cancer."

"Cancer? From what?"

"From their ears."

"How can you get cancer from your ear?" I'm not sure I understand what he is saying. I'm concerned that such a frightening perception for a child came up at the end of our session.

"Yeah."

"Are you asking me that or . . .?"

"No. No. My friend, my friend Emily. She got cancer from her ear."

"Really. How old is she?"

"Um, eight . . . nine."

"And do you know how she got cancer?" He nods. "How?"

"From my friend, you know my friend Theresa." He is telling me he heard this story from another friend.

"Have you asked your mom about that?"

"I, for, my interpreter, her husband was going to ask about that and tell me about that."

"So is it true that this person has cancer in her ear?"

"No, um, from her ear and it came down here." Joe is pointing to his clavicle. "Because, because, she had water in her ear and, when, and they put more water in and gave her a little bit of cancer. And then it moved down."

With Joe's mother close by, I bring her into this conversation, asking her if she can clarify for Joe and me what was happening with Emily. She is aware that the child has cancer but says she doesn't know anything about a relationship between that and the child being deaf. Joe appears to have concerns that if this can happen to one deaf child it can happen to him. I encourage him to talk more with his mother about it.

As Marilyn and I leave that day, Joe accompanies us out to the car. He picks up his basketball and, with a wide, warm grin on his face, he waves good-bye as he begins shooting hoops. His mother waves from the door as we pull out.

AT OUR NEXT interview, which we have on a mid-December evening, Joe has been watching *The Wiz* on TV. I explain to him that we are going to do something a little different this evening, that we'll be looking at pictures and he can tell me stories about what he thinks is happening in the pictures. I show him a photograph of two adults, a male and female with a baby.

"It's a new baby."

"Uh, a new baby, okay. And can you tell me something more about that picture? Can you make up a story to go with it?"

"Well, the baby might have just been born, and then maybe the baby became deaf after a while." Like many of the other children in this study, Joe begins to indicate what he perceives as the hearing status of the people in the photographs.

"Okay, so the baby was hearing and became deaf? How would that happen?"

"Um, the baby might have gotten sick or there might have been an accident."

"Okay. And if that happened how would the parents feel?"

"Worried. They'd be more worried."

"What would they be worried about?"

"About the baby. If the baby had an accident or was sick, and then became deaf."

"Are the parents hearing or deaf?"

"They're hearing."

"They are? Okay. How can you tell? How do you know that? How do you know that the parents are hearing and the baby's deaf?"

"Because I can see them talking, but the baby . . . looks like the baby's deaf."

"Okay. The baby looks like he's deaf. Okay. What does a deaf baby look like?"

"Um, they look like they're not hearing things. They're not looking around and paying attention to sounds."

"Okay. So because of the way that baby is looking. And the parents would worry about the baby? They might be afraid the baby would have an accident? How could an accident happen?"

"Well, um, there might be an accident that would cause a problem with the baby's ear or something. Or the baby might be sick. And they might need to do something. The baby might put something in his ear or might have taken some poison or something."

"Okay, so the parents want to protect the baby?" Joe nods in agreement.

Joe, like Angie, has no certain information about how he became deaf. He, Angie, and their parents only have ideas to speculate on. Thus, these two children ascribe the possibilities they have identified for themselves onto the characters they see in the photographs.

The next picture I show Joe is a picture of a man who is actually deaf. Joe views the picture and explains, "That's a guy who might be drawing something. He might be a deaf person . . . Might be drawing a cartoon . . . Uh huh. Maybe a deaf cartoon."

"A deaf cartoon. I've never seen a deaf cartoon. What would that look like?"

"I saw one yesterday night."

"Did you see one on TV? What was the title of it?"

Joe voiced without signing, "The Teenager." Not understanding him, I look to Marilyn, who interprets for me what Joe has just voiced.

"Oh, 'The Teenager.' That was the cartoon?"

"And there's this guy who's deaf. This deaf boy, and he's real dumb, and this deaf boy was, like, he was acting real crazy and stuff and banging into stuff."

"Crazy, what do you mean by that?"

"Well, because he couldn't hear and there was this car that came and crashed and, you know . . . Well, then, there's this one man who asks this question, he's, like, 'What?' and 'Do you want dessert?' And he had some ice cream . . . and then he said, 'What did you say?' Not knowing what was going on and stuff. It was very funny." Joe didn't seem immediately affected by or critical of the negative stereotypical image of deaf people that this program presented, or at least in his interpretation of it. At the same time, programs such as this certainly don't help him or other deaf children in their quest for self-concept. Nor does it make the world a friendlier place for them. Joe's response to the program was typical of most ten year olds in their uncritical attraction to the entertainment side of television.

"And is the person who's doing the drawing deaf or hearing?" I ask. Earlier, Joe had indicated that he thought the man in the picture we were examining was deaf. Now he changes his mind.

"I think hearing."

"You think he's hearing. How do you know he's hearing?"

"'Cause he doesn't have a hearing aid on." Joe and two other mainstreamed children in this study indicated the presence of hearing aids as clues to a person's hearing status. None of the children from residential placements identified hearing aids as indicators of a person's identity.

"Okay. Do all deaf people wear hearing aids?"

"Well, no, not that many deaf people wear hearing aids. Sometimes my friends, Thomas and Catherine, they don't have hearing aids because in their family everybody's deaf. All of them."

"So they don't wear hearing aids. At school do they wear them?"

"Well they use these things, the phonic ears . . . I think it's weird." Phonic ears are assistive-listening devices that deaf children in many school settings wear for acoustic amplification.

"You think that's weird?"

"They sign all the time. They just sign. You know, they don't yell or anything except the dad sometimes will yell. But if they want to get their attention they flash the lights." Joe is referring to the manner in which deaf family members get each other's attention. Since the family members are deaf, visual and tactile rather than vocal means of summoning are utilized.

Joe is able to distinguish between the behaviors in his hearing family and those in Thomas's family. At school, however, he notes that his teacher uses some of the methods that are used in his friend's family.

"Uh huh."

"They flash them on and off and then that gets their attention."

"You don't do that here in your house?"

"No, I hear well enough . . . And hearing people sometimes, if there's a group of all deaf they might flash the lights to get people's attention. But sometimes people ignore it."

"Does your teacher do that?"

"Sometimes the teacher will flash the light a bunch of times. And sometimes we just ignore her."

"Okay. And here at home things are different with your family than with the deaf family?" Joe nods in agreement. "How else are things different?"

"Well, because if you yell they can't hear and, um, they might throw something."

"Throw something?"

"Yeah, something soft, not something hard. And sometimes if I have my phonic ear or my hearing aid with me, there's this like microphone. And you call my name in the microphone and I'll notice it, even if I'm upstairs. You know, I can't hear that far, but with the phonic ear you can hear things even at a distance with the person who has the microphone."

Looking at a new picture now, Joe tells me, "I think that this guy's hearing and this guy is deaf."

"How do you know that?"

"Because this guy's talking on the phone . . . and this other guy is not." He is referring to the photograph of the two children sitting on the floor with a board game in front of them. One is on the phone and the other is waiting next to him.

"And how do those two guys feel?"

"Well, the hearing guy's happy. But the deaf guy's bored, and he's upset."

"That's what he looks like. Yeah. Why would he be upset? What about?"

"Because he wants to talk on the phone. Or . . ." Here I was unable to decipher Joe's signs. He struggled with his fingerspelling. "Or he might want to order something. You know?"

"Order? Oh, okay, order something. On the phone. Okay. What do you think will happen to the hearing boy when he gets done with the phone?"

"Well, maybe the deaf boy will try and talk, but he can't."

"The deaf boy will try to call someone and he can't? And then how would he feel?"

"Sad."

"Sad?"

"And he might be kind of upset and he might not like that. He might be bored." Joe, like the other children, suggests that the deaf child in this communicatively inaccessible situation may be bored. He adds, however, that the child may also be upset and sad about not being able to use the phone. In chapter 4, Danny also reported feeling sad and mad in this type of situation.

"So, sad and upset and not liking it and being bored."

"Mmhmm. He might want to do something to help, but he can't."

"Want to do what?"

"He might want to talk on the phone by himself. To order something or whatever."

Joe appears to hold a lot of his emotions inside. His reaction to many of my questions so far in these interviews has been similar to what the literature suggests might be expected from a person who became deaf and is grieving the loss of hearing. Becoming curious if I had missed out on background information, I ask Joe, "And has your hearing always been the same? All the while that you were growing up? Has it declined? Has it stayed the same?"

"It's been the same."

"It has been? Okay. You know, when I was a little girl, I could talk on the phone. Some. Not a lot. But with certain people. And now I can't. But how do you think that makes me feel?"

"Well, you might feel, um, you might feel upset and sad, if you want to call someone yourself and not have to ask another person to talk on the phone. You might want to do it yourself."

I don't want to bias Joe's answers, so I decide to hold off until the end of our interviews to share my experiences with him. "Okay. I don't want to give you the answers now because I want to know what you're thinking. Okay? But later, when we finish, would you like me to explain more to you?" Joe nods. I wonder if Joe knows deaf adults who might model positive behaviors and perceptions of being deaf. I wonder where his sad perceptions are coming from. What is missing in his life that the other children have access to? What about African-American Deaf adults? Where are his models? Does he have a tougher time with teasing in his school environment than the other children have? Is this what is affecting him? Has he begun to incorporate the perceptions of his peers into his self-concept?

We go on to the next picture. "Okay. Number four." This is the photo of the toddlers sitting on the floor with a young woman holding a book and signing something.

"I think that these two are both, um, they are deaf, um, because . . . Pam and, the teacher, and it's teaching them how to sign."

"Pam? How did you get that name?"

Joe points to the name "Pam" on a name tag in the picture. "From here. That looks like maybe a Y and this boy is learning how to sign and this boy's just looking at the names."

"Okay. So who do you think the two children are?"

"They're deaf."

"They're deaf. And is the teacher . . ."

"The teacher's hearing."

"Okay. Teacher's hearing. And I wonder what's in that book?"

"Uh, stories. Or something, um, it might have signs in it. Or maybe the ABCs, the manual alphabet."

"Okay. And another question for you. Why would the teacher be hearing? Why not a deaf teacher? I'm just curious. Do you know any deaf teachers?"

"No. But, um, I forget. Oh, it might be because, maybe if that teacher's deaf then they can't talk to the other teachers or they can't talk on the phone. That kind of thing. So maybe it would be just wanting to learn how to sign."

"I'm not sure that I'm understanding. You're saying if a teacher can't talk, then . . . Could you repeat that?"

"If a teacher is deaf, then she can't talk to the other teachers, or if she can't talk she won't know what to do. If the other teachers don't sign, they won't understand her." Clearly, Joe doesn't have deaf teachers who can set an example of the capabilities of deaf adults.

"Oh, okay. Thank you. This is number five."

"I think that all of them, the kids, are deaf. Except for the teacher, and the teacher's hearing . . . Well, maybe they're trying to teach, um, teach them how to sign. Or, um, they're going around and they're connected to each other . . . And you can see the alphabet in sign all around the wall there. So that's why I think they're deaf."

In another picture, Joe identifies children that he thinks are deaf. "I think that they're deaf because I can see this is going around and sign . . . I think they're both deaf."

"Okay. And I wonder what they're talking about?"

"Well, maybe a job or school . . . Well, um, maybe some trouble."

"They might be . . . What kind of trouble? Who would be in trouble?"

"This person."

"And what did that person do?"

"Um, he killed someone, or hurt someone, or . . ."

"Hurt someone? Why would she hurt someone?"

"Well, maybe she was mad."

"About what?"

"Um, about some words or something. Might hurt her feelings."

"Okay. So someone has said something and hurt her feelings? Okay. Who might have hurt her feelings?"

"Well, maybe some guy. Or maybe somebody who plays football."

"And where would that be? After school or at home or . . ."

"At school." Joe's stories continue to depict the discomfort and intense feelings he experiences in his school environment. I am concerned for him.

"Okay. Number eight."

"Um, let's see." In this picture of two children conversing on a playground, one wears a hearing aid. "This one is, um, I think this one on the end is deaf because there's a hearing aid. And this other boy is hearing but signing. He's hearing but he's learning how to sign. And they're talking. He's talking to the deaf boy." Joe does imagine and experience positive communication and relationships with some hearing children despite the pain he feels from the negative interactions he has at school.

"Okay, good. And number nine."

"That woman is deaf because, um, I've seen . . . Well, I think she's deaf because she's using a TDD, and that's for deaf people who can't talk on the phone. And she's got a new TDD." Like the other children, Joe is aware of the technology and electronic devices that are available to him and what purpose they serve.

"And who's she talking to?"

"Maybe to a friend."

"A hearing or a deaf friend?"

"A deaf friend."

"A deaf friend, okay. And I wonder what they're talking about?"

"Well, they might be talking about what happened to her."

"And what could have happened?"

"Well, maybe she got a divorce, or maybe she has a boyfriend that liked her who doesn't like her anymore."

"Does that happen sometimes?" Joe nods. "Has that happened to you?"

"No. And I'm going to get one of these." He points to the TTY in the picture. "For Christmas."

"That's great. And then you can call your friends."

"Yes."

"I'm going to have a TDD." Joe does not yet have a TTY at home. It has been my experience that many families with hearing parents and one deaf child acquire TTYs when their child's reading and typing skills have progressed to a point where the child can begin to use them. Joe seems excited about obtaining a TTY.

"Well, that's neat. I'm happy you're getting a TTY. Great. Okay, number ten." We move on to the next picture.

"I think maybe, um, they are, um . . . They're deaf. Except for this girl, and . . . I think she's hearing and she has a deaf sister." He is looking at a picture of several children sitting on the floor posed for a photograph.

"How do you know that?"

"Um, because, um, I don't know the name of it but if you're deaf or somebody else in your family's deaf you might . . . when you're little you're deaf, then you might start to hear better. You might be able to hear well, but you would still be deaf."

"So you can hear better?"

"Yes."

"So your hearing would improve as you get older?"

"Uh huh."

"Oh, okay. That's interesting. I've never seen that happen before. Do you know of deaf adults who when they were little they're deaf, then they became hearing as they got older? Do you know someone like that?" He nodded. "Who?"

"I can't remember the name."

"Do you think when you grow older that you'll be able to hear better?"

"I think so. I hope."

"You hope so. I get the feeling from you that . . . you tell me if I'm right or wrong, okay, but I get the feeling that you would rather be able to hear than to be deaf. Is that right?" Joe shrugs. "Would you rather be able to hear or is it okay to be deaf?"

"Both."

"Both? Tell me more about your feelings about being deaf."

"Well, I like to be deaf because I like signing. And compared to other kids I like two ways, I like signing and speaking both." While much of Joe's projective storytelling as well as his responses to my direct inquiries have told me that he has had some very painful peer experiences, he still experiences some positive meaning in being deaf. This gives me a sense of relief for him.

"I see."

"And I like that."

"Okay. I think that's all the questions that I have for you, but I'd like to share some things. Is that okay?" Joe nods. I am concerned about the issues that Joe has raised during this interview. From what he expressed in these sessions, he seems to face a lot of teasing at school. He also appears to have concerns about becoming ill in the future. He has both positive and negative perceptions of his school experience. I wonder if he has any role models and I think it might be important for Joe to know that I experienced some of the same kinds of teasing when I was a child, but that I'm very happy now and that there are things you can do to stop the teasing.

"Do you know many deaf adults?" Joe nods. "You know many? How many deaf adults do you know?"

"About twelve or thirteen."

"And do you talk with them a lot?"

"Mmmhmm."

"And where do you meet them?"

"In . . . school and . . . sometimes at school and church."

"Okay. The reason I was asking you was because sometimes when deaf children are little they're not sure what's going to happen to them when they get older. What kind of work they're going to do and if they can work because they can't hear and so forth. And you were talking a little bit ago about how maybe when you get older your hearing might get better. And your stories about some of those pictures showed me that you thought that deaf children might feel sad sometimes because they can't hear. And I just wanted to share with you that when I was little I could hear a lot better than I can now. But it doesn't bother me. I'm very happy. I like my work. I have a nice husband that I love very much. I'm a very happy person, and I'm not sad because I'm deaf. I think it's important for you to know that. That deaf children, when they grow up, they can be happy. Okay?"

"Maybe sometimes deaf people can, um, can get wild and sometimes . . . And sometimes, um, when you get fourteen or fifteen, um, and they might have to go to a hospital for . . ."

"Have to go to the hospital for what?"

"Um, if when you're say fourteen years old, they might be, um . . ." Joe signs "Feb." We struggle a little here as I try to put what he is saying into context. I spelled out the word "February?" Joe and I look at the interpreter to confirm that we are understanding each other. He continues, "It's called, let's see, Emily and, and . . . There's this new, um, Emily, she's had a lot of problems and she's acting real crazy and she made a lot of mistakes in school and she's improving now but she's twenty-five now."

"Okay, well I think it's important for you to know that Emily is only one person, okay? And one deaf person who has, what did you say she has?"

"It's almost like cancer."

"Are you worried that will happen to you?"

"Yeah."

"Well, I wish I knew what that was called, but not everybody gets sick."

"Well, no, I didn't say she became sick, but it just happened. Like, on her birthday when she became nine, then she started getting really wild and acting really wild. And then, um, she stole something and, um, it was at school at two, two in the afternoon."

"Okay, well, she's only one person, right? . . . Did you talk with your mom about that?"

Joe shook his head no.

"Well, maybe that would be a good idea. Talk with your mom. And maybe you can learn more about Emily and what happened to her and why that happened. And then you can learn to protect yourself so you can be sure that will not happen to you."

"I hope so. But I don't know how it happened, but maybe she, um . . ." Here Joe uses his voice without signing. Not understanding, I look to the interpreter, who asks, "Operation or hyperactive?" Joe clarifies, "Hyperactive. And she got really wild . . . I think I'd like to go to a deaf school. What's the one that starts with a G?"

"Gallaudet?"

"You know, where everybody's deaf? It's where people go to college."

"Yeah, that's Gallaudet. I went there. I loved it there. It's a neat school."

"And I want to . . . I wish, um, I wish I could become a cartoonist, and an actor."

"You'd like to be an actor?"

"Yeah."

"That's great. And you like to draw?"

"Mmhmm."

"Great. Well, Gallaudet has, you could major in art. You could study art at Gallaudet. And they also have a theater department. So you could major in theater. You could study theater and become an actor or an artist."

"I like to act . . . and, I do, um, I've acted, I've acted in plays. But the play's done, and I'd like to become an actor."

"What play were you in?"

"At school . . . and there's the joker for the king. I played the joker. And it was a real funny part. And the other people laughed. And, um, then after the play was over I, um, did stories for everybody. It was really hard to change back and use my voice again."

JOE IS A well-mannered, kind, and talented child with many interests. Being mainstreamed, Joe doesn't seem to have many deaf adult role models, and he appears to have many questions about what being deaf means for him now and in the future. He is aware of resources that are available to him. He feels safe and loved at home and enjoys many recreational activities with his family and friends. He also recognizes and asserts his communication needs. He has very good skills in negotiating his world.

Joe expresses the desire to go to college, to be a good athlete, and to become a cartoonist or an actor. At the same time, he has many concerns about the quality of his relationships with his hearing peers and sees himself as different from more culturally Deaf individuals. The pain he experiences in his relationships with hearing peers at school who tease him weighs heavily on him. It is unfortunate that intervention for the teasing he experiences is not forthcoming from school personnel, who should be doing more to prevent the harassment he reports. I am relieved to see that he also has many positive relationships with deaf peers and looks to the future with optimism as he envisions going to Gallaudet, and becoming an athlete, actor, or artist.

But being deaf is not the only identity issue that Joe is probably dealing with. He is a minority child in a mostly white school and neighborhood. Joe doesn't raise this as an issue, perhaps because I am white. Wanting to respect wherever Joe may be in his racial identity, I asked his mother in a follow-up telephone conversation if she thought racism might be part of the reason for the teasing that Joe reports. She responded that his teachers say they don't see it happening, "so it's all relative."

I wondered had I been a black researcher if Joe might have discussed racism with me, or if I would have been more attuned to the implications of racial relations and racial identity on his perspectives. Perhaps this perception is akin to his developmental level, in that he is not yet consciously aware of the racism that may affect many of his experiences. It is possible that Joe is not dealing with racial identity issues on the same conscious level with which he is dealing with deaf identity issues. Being African American and deaf, Joe experiences a sameness at home where everyone is black but a difference between himself and his family members because he is the only deaf individual. Joe also sees himself as different from other deaf children because he talks and considers himself hard of hearing even though he has a severe hearing loss.

Rosenberg (1990) and Hughes and Demo (1989) state that shields exist in families of color to protect the developing sense of self-esteem in their members. This same dynamic may occur in Deaf families. Redding (1999) explains that this buffer does not exist in relation to deafness in black hearing families with a child who is deaf. Gallaudet Research Institute (2000) states that the numbers of black deaf families (11.5 percent) are small compared to white deaf families (21.5 percent) due to the lower incidence of hereditary deafness among African Americans.

The number of minority professionals and teachers in deaf education programs throughout the country is as low as 10 percent and only 11 percent of these minority professionals are deaf (Andrews and Jordan, 1993). Recent literature has begun to assert the needs of minority students in the deaf education system and expose the extent of oversight and racism that exists (Cohen, 1993, 1997; Cohen, Fishgrund, and Redding, 1990; Redding, 1995, 1997; Parasnis, 1996, 1997). These authors urge us to examine and respond to the needs of minority students through a variety of means, including increasing the number of deaf minority professionals and teachers (Redding, 1997), changing educational policy and programs (Parasnis, 1997), recruiting and retaining deaf minority graduate students (Redding, 1997), recognizing the need for minority role models, linking schools with community agencies, and providing opportunities for Deaf students of color to develop leadership skills and participate in school governance and support for family involvement (Cohen, 1997). Research that looks at the perspectives and experiences of deaf children of color in various educational settings would be of great value in helping us understand what these children experience and in helping us develop programs that are responsive to their needs.

7

Alex

SEVEN-YEAR-OLD Alex arrived for our interview wearing blue jeans and sneakers. He sported a short-sleeved, white T-shirt, which highlighted his dark tan, black curly hair, and long-lashed dark brown eyes. Alex seemed enthusiastically absorbed in his school environment but somewhat detached from me in our sessions. He participated in the interviews somewhat reluctantly, and I imagined he didn't appreciate having his classroom activity interrupted. He appeared to be very comfortable in his residential school with other deaf students.

Alex was born profoundly deaf and his mother reported the cause to be unknown. His parents are both hearing. He has one sister who is hard of hearing and another who is hearing. Alex uses ASL, his mother is a proficient ASL user, and other family members use mostly Signed English. Alex's parents are divorced. Alex has no reported additional disabilities.

❦

AT THE START of our first session, I want to confirm Alex's willingness to participate. He reports he was not made aware previously that our sessions would take place. I go through my scripted explanation of the purpose of our sessions, and he gives his verbal consent to the videotaped interview. I also introduce the idea of his drawing pictures and telling me stories about them. I look down for a moment at my notes to see if I have forgotten anything. While I am looking away from him, Alex is ready to get to work and he begins looking for the colored pencil of his choice, "There's no pink. There's no pink." He has finished signing this by the time I look up at him.

(As I write this now, I am reminded of a drawing I observed displayed in the hallway of Kendall Demonstration Elementary School. The teachers there, and in many deaf education programs today, incorporate deaf culture into their curriculum. The students at Kendall had the opportunity to create art that demonstrates what they learn. One student drew a picture of an eye with the caption, "eye contact is important to Deaf people." A glance in the other direction can mean lost information.)

I continue my introduction, completely unaware that Alex had said anything, "Later on, after I've written my book, then I might give some presentations to audiences who don't know about deaf children. And, um, . . . I'll use the stories from the children in the book to tell them how deaf children feel and that'll help them learn something. Okay?"

"Uh huh. Uh, you don't have no pink."

"What?" I have been so busy following the rules of consent to participate that I am out of context with Alex. He has been far more interested in drawing than in listening to my introduction.

"Pink. There's no pink."

"Oh, there's no pink. Mmm, you're right. I don't have any pink. Maybe next week I'll buy more. We'll have more colors, okay? Well, anyway, if you decide later that you don't want to help me write my book, that's fine. You just have to let me know, okay? And today, I would like for you to draw a picture of a deaf boy. Okay? Would you do that for me?"

"Deaf? A deaf boy?"

"Yeah. You want to draw a picture?"

"Uhh." He seems a little stuck. He clearly is eager to draw, but perhaps drawing a deaf boy is not what he has in mind.

"Well, what do you want to draw?"

"Umm." He thinks about it for a moment, then says, "I've got an idea."

Alex draws a picture of a flower. He tells me a story about how the flower will grow as a plant and then with enough rain it will open up and continue to grow. I am uncertain how well metaphors will work with Alex. I decide to introduce a deaf boy into the picture and see what will come from that.

"That flower gets really big, and then imagine that a deaf boy, a person, a deaf boy would come, and what would he do . . . what would happen?"

"Well, it rains and rains and rains."

"But what about that boy . . . ?"

"Well, he'd water it and put the seeds in and water it and it would grow . . . It's started to open up, and it gets bigger and bigger."

I ask him to include a drawing of "a little boy who's deaf in that one. Could you draw that?"

"Why?"

"Well, I'd like to know about deaf children, and if you draw that then I can understand about deaf children."

"Oh. I need . . . uh . . . yup." Alex starts drawing and explains, "This is a friend. It's a friend . . . I need tan." Once again I don't have the color Alex desires for his drawing. I know I need to add variety to my supplies.

"Yeah, you're right, I don't have any . . . Next week I'll bring more colors."

Alex picks a different color and continues to draw, changing his mind here and there as he proceeds. "Mmm . . . no . . . forgot."

"Mmhmm? Are you done? Okay, is that a deaf boy?"

"Mmhmm."

"Can you tell me a story about him?"

"Uh, why?"

"Because in order to write this book I need some information. I need you to teach me about deaf children. So could you tell me a story about this deaf boy?"

Alex tells us this deaf boy is his best friend. Choosing someone as a best friend implies a level of comfort with that person. Comfort in relationships with others that the children consider to be like them is one of the themes in this study.

"A deaf, deaf boy. And sometimes, um, he goes to my house and we play. And sometimes he sleeps over at my house and sometimes, um, I go to his house. And, um, so we go back and forth to each other's houses. And, he's my best friend. That's it."

"So when you play, what do you do?"

"Well, we play with my Nintendo, I have . . . Yeah, you, you play it on the TV."

"Okay, and you're both deaf."

"He's my best friend."

"Okay, wonderful. And where does he go to school?"

Alex uses a name sign. "Um, over at, at, um, I don't know the name of it. It's a new, it's a new one, it's a new one." At first I think he is talking about a new school. But I soon realize he means a different teacher in the same school that Alex attends. "There's a new teacher there. It's a new, he's in a new teacher's room . . . Um, he's, he wants to learn a lot . . ." Learning is important to Alex.

When I ask Alex to draw a picture of a deaf boy and his family, an interesting thing happens. After Alex draws the family picture, I ask him about the family members, whether they are deaf or hearing and Alex says they are both deaf and hearing because they can sign and speak both. In the use of projective interview techniques, it is assumed that the qualities ascribed to the characters in the children's stories may actually be qualities that the children might otherwise identify about themselves. Thus, when Alex describes this deaf boy's family and how he determines who is deaf or hearing, he may actually be discussing his own family.

"This is Dad. Dad, um . . ." He continues drawing.

"Great. Okay. And this is the deaf boy. Who's this?"

"His sister."

"Who's this?"

"His mom and his dad."

"Okay. Are they deaf or hearing?"

"Um, she signs, and talks both. She can sign and she can speak . . . the sister. And the mom can sign and speak both, and the dad can sign and speak. All of . . ."

"So are they hearing?"

"Well, hearing and deaf both, 'cause they, they sign and speak. Both."

"Oh, okay. So can she hear or is she deaf?"

"She can hear."

"And mom?"

"Can hear."

"And dad?"

"Can hear."

The children in this study show a pattern of acceptance and comfort in relationships with people with whom they can communicate. Here it appears that Alex considers these family members to be like himself because they can sign. How they communicate appears to be more of a focal point for Alex than whether they are deaf or hearing. Alex sees communication as the basis of his relationships with others as well as the determining factor in the identity that he ascribes to them.

Next Alex tells me about his grandparents and what is important in his perception of them. When I ask if his grandparents are deaf or hearing, Alex says they are hearing and quickly follows that with a statement about their inability to sign. This distinction contrasts with his description of his immediate family members as deaf and hearing both because they sign *and* speak.

"Okay. And that family, when they go on, do they go on vacation sometimes?"

"Yeah. They would fly. They'd fly. Or . . ."

"They'd what?"

"Well, they'd go to North Carolina. They'd go to North Carolina. And they would, they would drive and they would swim and swim and swim and swim. I met my grandmother. My grandmother lives in North Carolina, you know that?"

"Okay."

"And, um, come and play and swim and swim and swim and stay for three days. In North Carolina for three days swimming."

"Ooh, sounds nice. Your grandmother and grandfather live there?"

"Mmhmm."

"Are your grandparents hearing or deaf?"

"They're hearing. They don't know sign."

"They don't."

"Oh, they know some. They know a little bit."

"And this deaf boy, how would he communicate with his grandparents?"

"They'd write."

"They'd write?"

"Yeah, or, or, um, I'd ask my parents to help and to tell them what, what I said. Both those things. Uh, um, sometimes I need my mom's help, um, if I can't write it."

Writing is a strategy that several of the children in this study identified in situations where communication is inaccessible. In addition, several of the children also identified mothers or sisters as helping them communicate with hearing people.

The following passage illustrates the positive regard that Alex must feel from his family.

"Oh, okay. So, how does the boy happen to be deaf?"

"He was born that way."

"Born deaf, uh huh." Wanting to understand Alex's perception of his parents' reactions to his deafness, I ask how the parents feel when the baby is born deaf.

"They're excited."

"Excited when the baby is born deaf? Is that how the parents felt?"

"Mmhmm. Yeah, they, they felt excited, you know."

This response might come as a surprise to some people. We read so much in the literature on deafness about how parents of deaf children grieve when they learn that their child is deaf and expect that the children will introject what they perceive as negative parental regard for them and develop poor self-esteem. It turns out that Alex wasn't the only child who had such a positive response.

"Great. Great. Okay. And the sister? How does she feel? That the brother's deaf."

"Well she, she's not born yet. She . . . the, the boy is born first, and she was born second."

"Oh, okay."

"So it was just the boy and the parents."

"Okay, so the boy is older than the sister. The sister is younger, okay. So his sister is hearing, and, um, when they look at him, at the deaf child, what do they think?"

"Well, they know sign." Clearly, the sign language abilities of his family members is an important part of Alex's perception of them and his comfort level.

"Okay. And the boy's school is a deaf school?"

"Yeah, it's here."

"Okay, here. And is, are his friends deaf or hearing?"

Alex responds that he has both deaf and hearing friends. His friends at his school are all deaf since it is a school for deaf children, but he does play with hearing children at home, and he tells us how he approaches communication with hearing children.

"They're deaf."

"All of them?"

"Well, all of them here."

"Okay, and what about his friends at home?

"Well, he has friends."

"Are they deaf?"

"Well, let's see. One, two . . . two, that are near. Two that are near my home. Right there and right there." He points to places in the picture he has drawn. "Just around the corner. But I, I, I, I forget the names. Um, see there's um . . ." (He uses several name signs here.)

"And, um, he plays with other children near his home? The deaf boy does?"

"Yeah. He runs and plays with his friends."

"So they run, and what else do they do?"

"Um, they play basketball and they play 'It' and, um, I forget the name of the other game. Um, where you throw something up and you run and then you've gotta stop and um, there's like three people and uh, they, it's like . . . You have to freeze and then if they, they touch you and you move . . . It's, it's a game."

"Okay."

"And, um, then, um, there's this one that you . . . the other person would have to take a, a turn, you know, there's this thing that you roll, and if, if it goes . . . that you throw and it goes and it comes . . ."

"And it comes back to you?"

"Yeah. Yeah. Um, and I got hit with one of those once, really hard. This thing's really hard, you know. Somebody threw it and it hit me."

"All right. And that boy who is deaf, if he's going somewhere by himself, someplace like to the store, the grocery store, and he's deaf, and everyone else around him is hearing, when they look at him, what do they think of him?"

"Umm, I think, um, um, something, um . . ."

"If he's all by himself? Mmhmm? When they see him, and he's deaf, how do they feel about him being deaf?"

"They might talk."

Here once again, while asking Alex what hearing people would think or feel in the company of a deaf child, Alex responds in relation to the method of communication that would be used. Communication methods are important to Alex as he evaluates his relationships with others.

"They would talk to him?"

"Mmhmm. And, and you just kind of shrug and go, 'I don't know. I'm deaf.' You could write, 'I'm deaf.' And then they would understand. Then they'd understand, they'd say, 'Oh, excuse me.' And then you could write things and read things and write things."

"Okay. Would they like the deaf boy? What?"

"Yeah."

"Yeah? They would like him?"

"Uh huh."

"Well, that's good. And, um, deaf children, if there's a group of deaf children, and they see a group of hearing children, what do the deaf children think of the hearing children?"

"Well, they'd know they're hearing, and they could, they could write to each other, they could write."

"So deaf or hearing, it doesn't matter, they can play together?"

"Uh huh."

"Okay. As that deaf boy grows up, what's he gonna do?"

"Oh, he hasn't grown up yet."

"But he will. He's going to grow up. What's he going to do in his, in his future?"

"I don't know. I don't know."

"Will he work?"

"Um, he won't be with his parents. He'll, he'll be somewhere else. He might work or he might have a house." Alex, like the other children in this study, has a positive image of his future.

"What kind of work would he do, what kind of job?"

"Oh, I don't know . . . Well, um, he might want to work, um, with the police."

"The police?"

"Uh huh."

"Deaf policeman?"

"Yeah. Maybe when I get big, I want to be a policeman."

"Okay. That's interesting. Why do you want to be a policeman?"

" 'Cause I'd like it."

"Have you seen policemen on TV?" Alex nods. "What do they do? What do the police do?"

"Get the bad guy."

I want to learn more from Alex. I gave him a hypothetical scenario where he is on television and has the opportunity to tell hearing children about deaf children. Alex has pictures in his mind from real-life experiences in front of audiences that he has told me about.

"Okay. Now, um, we've got the TV . . ." I point to the camcorder. "Imagine that the TV, um, sometimes there might be a whole audience full of people, and people would be sitting there and explaining, teaching about something like you might have seen before on TV. Now, if we had an audience of childr . . ."

Alex quickly and excitedly interrupts me. "Like dancing and, and music var . . . various instruments, and piano and guitar and things like that and, um, and, um, well . . ."

"Okay, um, you would perform?"

"Right, yup, and there'd, there would be people lined up and they would see it on TV."

"Okay. If we had an audience of hearing people, hearing children, watching this TV, and you had to give them information, tell them a story about how different deaf children feel . . ."

Excitedly, Alex responds, "Have a deaf person, a deaf person can stand up there and sign, they can sign for the TV. Hearing people can talk, and deaf people can sign."

I am not sure exactly what Alex means by this. I think he is saying that a deaf person would sign and a hearing person would interpret for him.

"You mean that there would be an interpreter there?"

"Like my friend, my friend's an interpreter."

"Your friend's an interpreter, okay. Well, if there was an audience of hearing people, and you were on TV, and the camera was on you, when you wanted to tell those boys and girls some information or a story about deaf children, what would you teach them?"

"But, but, but, you know before, um, they taught me with, with, um, with my friend, we went and we, and we taught, my best friend and I, and, let's see, when . . . with, um, let's see . . . I can't remember the name of the store. Um . . . um, it was, like, at the mall, at the mall, it was Christmas." Alex was describing being in a Christmas performance at the mall with his classmates.

"You did signing? You signed a song?"

"Uh huh, yeah. And we had, um, it was, it was at Christmas, it was an 'I Love Christmas' song."

"Oh, and there was an audience of hearing people there? Oh, and they all looked at you, and they learned something about deaf children, right?"

"Uh huh."

"Okay. Well, if it was the same thing again, um, not a song, though, not a song, but if you were telling a story about deaf children, could you do that?"

"Christmas. Mmm, like that. I, I, just a Christmas and, um, Santa Claus went to visit, and they had, um, things that he gave out, and, um, some cards, you know, with, um, with the reindeer and stuff, know, these li . . . these little, um, badges."

This performance lingers as an important memory for Alex. While he doesn't make up a story he would share with hearing children, he obviously is sharing a message with me, one that says, "Deaf kids can be performers too, I enjoy performing, and audiences enjoy us. Christmas is an important holiday to me."

"Okay. Hmm, let me try and think. Umm, what do we need to do? Oh, okay. If, remember, um, what I just told you about writing a book about deaf children, that I'm going to write a book? If you were writing that book, what would you write?"

"Uh, about the mall and Santa Claus?"

"No, no. Not about the mall and Santa Claus. Um, this is different now. If, um, you were writing a book to teach about deaf children."

"Oh, I know." Alex picks up a marker and begins to draw. "I know." He shakes his head and puts the cap back on the marker. "No, not th . . ." He opens the marker again, "Yeah," and continues to draw.

"D . . . hmm . . . Pigs."

"Oh, pigs in the house?"

Alex continues drawing and begins to tell me the story about the Three Little Pigs. "They're . . . they're gonna eat, the, the wolf's gonna eat them."

"What's that?"

"The wolf. He's gonna try and eat the pigs."

"Oh."

"He's gonna try and eat 'em."

"And what happens?"

"Well, the pig peeks out, and, and then he runs and he runs and he runs. And the wolf climbs up, um, up on the chimney, you know? He goes up there, and he gets this idea of going down the chimney. And he, uh, he rolls along 'n' along 'n' along 'n' along the, in . . . And, um, drops over the end, into the water. He comes down, splash! And there's water in there. And he goes and he drowns him in the water."

"And is the pig safe?"

"Yep. He's safe."

"Well, that's good. And is the wolf, um . . .?"

"He's dead."

"Oh."

" 'Cause he goes in the water. Boom in the water and he's dead."

"Okay. That's good. Well let me see, then . . . Another story. Umm, would you like that information to go in the book?"

"It's the three pigs, the three pigs."

"The three pigs, hmm?"

"And the wolf."

"Mmhmm."

"And there's one, um, the one pig makes this house, the first one makes it out of, of straw. And um . . . ." Alex proceeds to tell me a very involved account of *The Three Little Pigs*.

"So the pigs are safe, and . . ." I attempt to summarize.

"The . . . the wolf jumps up out of the water and he runs away and he, and he doesn't come back."

"So in that one the, the wolves are safe and the pigs are safe, both. Okay, well thank you very much."

I learn later that this is a story Alex is reading in school. His comprehension of the story is so good that he can repeat it back to me with great detail. My intention when I ask what he thinks should go in a book about deaf children is to find things he thinks are important for hearing people to learn. Indirectly, Alex tells me here that he enjoys and understands children's stories and he is a competent storyteller. This is an important lesson in our understanding of the literacy of deaf children—a message well worth noting.

"I'll see you again next Monday, okay? And can I keep your pictures, for my book?

"Uh huh."

"Okay, thank you."

AT OUR SECOND interview, Alex has been taken out of his computer class. He is disappointed at having to leave his class to come to our meeting and he stays somewhat reluctantly. When I ask him about his week, he tells me about reading *101 Dalmatians*, drawing, and playing Nintendo. Today we look at the photographs. I ask him to tell me a story about the first picture.

"It's a baby and a dad looking at the baby."

"What are they doing?"

"They've got clothes."

"Uh huh. Are the mother and father and baby hearing or deaf?"

"They're deaf."

"Who's deaf?"

"All of them."

"All three of them. Can you tell me more about that family?"

"I don't know." Alex seems a bit reluctant to participate this morning. He moves the picture away.

"It's pretty hard, huh? Okay, let's try another picture, okay? Let me put that one back. This is number two." It is the picture of the deaf man at his desk.

"Um, writing, drawing . . . drawing something."

"Drawing what?"

"Uh, for a movie."

"Drawing for a movie?"

"Uh huh. Right there. He's doing a story."

"Oh, that's interesting. Is that man deaf or hearing?"

"Hearing."

"How do you know?"

" 'Cause that's my favorite. I've seen it before, and he talks." I imagine that perhaps Alex thinks this is a picture of Walt Disney at his drawing board.

"Okay. Why don't you think he's deaf?"

" 'Cause I saw him on TV, and he's hearing."

Television is a big part of contemporary society, and its effect on children is the subject of much debate. By now, we are seeing that television is a big part of the lives of the children in this study too. Even though closed captioning is available, television presents the verbal aspects of television in a written mode for deaf children, a format different from the auditory mode that hearing children receive. Although the children in this study are developing their reading skills, it is clear that television plays a part in their perceptions of things around them.

"Okay . . ." I show Alex a picture of two boys on the floor, one talking on the phone and the other sitting close by. They have a game of "Sorry" in front of them.

"That's a game. Right there." He points to the game in the picture. "With little pieces that you move around. I have it at home."

"You have it? Do you know the name of it?"

"Umm, it starts with an 'S' but I can't remember the name of it. I can't really see it."

"Those two boys, are they deaf or hearing?"

"I think they're deaf."

"How do you know they're deaf?"

"I think, I saw, he must be hearing."

Alex is slouching over. I'm unsure what the context of his day presented before he came to our session. Is he tired? Does he want to return to class? Because he is slouching with his arms and head on the table in front of us, I'm unable to see his signs or his face clearly.

"I can't see you. Could you sit up so I can see you better? So I can see you sign?"

He sits up. "I'm tired."

"You're tired today, okay. Could you tell me again, how do you know that they're deaf?"

"One's talking on the phone so he must be hearing. But maybe he . . . No, he's making it up, he's pretending to be hearing, he's playing. He's not really on the phone."

Regardless of whether or not he thinks this child is hearing or just pretending to be hearing, for Alex, the act of "talking on the phone" is an indication that the person is hearing.

"Oh, okay."

"He's making it up. He's playing."

"So that boy's just pretending. He's not really on the phone. He's pretending to talk . . . Okay. This is number four."

The characters in the next picture are signing, and Alex interprets the act of signing as an indication that they are all deaf.

"It's a girl and a baby and they're signing about an airplane flying . . . They're deaf."

"Who's deaf?"

"Both. Both of them." He points at the picture three times. There are three people in the picture.

"All three of them are deaf? And are they learning sign? Did they see an airplane, did they go on an airplane?" Alex nods. "Okay, good."

We move on. He continues to indicate whether or not characters in the pictures are deaf or hearing. Alex is detached today, and he has told me he is tired. I think he is also disappointed to have to leave his computer class. His responses are briefer and less informative than they were last week. We look at a new picture, and he tells me the children in the picture are playing. "They're playing a game on swings and it's a real big, big, big playground all around them."

"And what are they playing?"

"They're playing a game . . . They're climbing; there's climbing equipment."

"Oh, and what's this boy doing?"

"Um, he's signing AMERICA."

"Oh, yes it does look like AMERICA. All right." We go on to the next picture. "Number nine."

"She's typing on the phone . . . She's deaf. She's a deaf woman . . . She's a mom."

"She's a mom? Does she work or does she stay home? What's the mom do? What's that mom do?"

"I don't know."

Sensing Alex's restlessness, I ask if he would prefer to draw pictures than to tell me stories about these. He hands me the picture, and I put it in my folder and close it. When I view the tape later, I see that while I am doing this, Alex signs to himself, "I want to leave now," but I do not catch what he said because I'm looking elsewhere.

"What? Did you say something? I missed what you said."

"No."

I get out more crayons and paper. Alex looks at them and indicates the one he wants. "That's better."

We both take out colors and arrange them on the table in front of us. He draws for awhile, pausing to make decisions about colors, sighing here and there, and commenting on how difficult this is. When he finishes, I ask him about his drawing.

"That's it? That's great. Who is that?"

"It's me."

"It's you. What are you doing?"

"You know, it's for a drama, you know. For pretend. It's not real, it's for a play. It's just pretend. It fools people. It's for a play. And I forgot."

He draws some more. I ask him where he saw the play, and he tells me it was at a different school and the school also has a lot of computers . . . "They have a, a, umm, fifteen in a row, um, they've got fifteen computers."

"You really like computers, right? You really like computers."

"They've got lots of them. They've got like fifteen computers."

"Fifteen kids you mean? At their own computers?"

"Like, this one would be mine, and it would say 'Alex' and then another would say 'Mark,' and another would be somebody else's name. And that would be my name and my seat and it would be up above there. And we would all sit in a row."

"And what would you do on the computer?"

"Um, games and drama like this." He points to his drawing. Alex continues to draw what is either an image from a computer game or a scene from a play. He stops for a moment, trying to recall the image, and says, "I forgot . . . It's a play. It's just make-believe. Um, there's a girl and a cow and they go walking along. And there's a man who's chopping away with an axe. And the cow gets mad and starts charging. It's pretty funny. He fights with it, with the bull or with the cow. Then he gets a rope and he lassos him and he's hanging on behind 'cause he's caught in the rope. It's pretty funny. And he can't stop. He can't stop. There's a tree and he gets wrapped around the tree bunches and bunches of times. Then he booms into the tree, and the tree kind of starts to fall over, and he's going 'ahhhh' . . . It's not true. It's made up. And there's this guy and he's hiding, and he's got a mask like on Halloween, but it's not real."

"Did you make it up?"

"It's a play."

"What's the name of the play?"

"Umm, it's *The Farmer and the Cow.*"

"Oh, okay. Do you have another story you want to tell me today?"

"No."

"That's it?"

"I want to go to computer."

We end our session and Alex returns to his computer class. I thank him and remind him that we have one more session, and say I look forward to seeing him next week. I am confused about Alex's story. Is this story a recollection of a play he was in, from his imagination, or was it a computer game?

ALEX ARRIVES today for our final interview, saying he'd rather stay in his art class. Last week he told me he wanted to return to his computer class. I acknowledge his enjoyment of those classes and ask if we can have a short meeting today. He agrees to that, a bit reluctantly. I ask what he did in the week since our last meeting.

"Nothing. Nothing. Boring. Reading. And money . . . Playing Nintendo at home."

"So who do you play with?"

"My sisters. We have three, no we have four of these, uh, the things for Nintendo. My sisters."

"Sounds like fun. And what did you do with the long weekend? You were off Friday, Saturday, Sunday, and Monday. What did you do?"

"Vacation time so I got to sleep late . . . I didn't wake up. So I got to sleep."

"So you rested a lot. Did you go out and play?"

"Nope. I slept and slept and slept."

Alex then relates an involved story of how he catches bugs, bees, and bats near his home.

"You're really smart. So your home's near a farm. Are there other children who live near you? Are there many children out there?"

"There's some friends near my house."

"People you play with around there?"

"Yeah. There's W and R and . . ." He gives several name signs, "and um, I can't remember . . . a blond kid."

"Are they hearing or deaf?"

"I can't remember their names," he says. "They're all hearing. They're hearing. But some of them know how to sign."

"How?"

"I taught them." Like many of the children in this study, Alex takes the responsibility upon himself to teach hearing children how to sign so they can communicate.

"You did? Oh, that's wonderful . . . So they didn't know how to sign and you taught them."

I intend to keep my word and keep this session short. Alex has the same intention and he beats me to it.

"I want art. I want to go now."

I tell Alex we can finish now. I share with him some things I learned from him and ask him if I have understood all of that right. Alex is too eager to get back to his art class to confirm this for me. I thank Alex for his patience and his help and give him one of the handmade thank-you cards that I made for all the children. He gets up enthusiastically and returns to his art class.

෴

Like Danny and Pat, Alex was very engaged in the classes and activities at his residential school. He was absorbed in his art and computer classes and expressed a preference to be there rather than interviewing with me. He also seemed to take his deafness for granted. He had a variety of play activities that he engaged in, alone, with his sisters, or with his deaf friends. His stories indicated close relationships with deaf friends.

He didn't say a lot about hearing children but, on being asked, stated that they could play together and communicate with some adaptations. Those adaptations included his teaching them to sign, writing, or asking his mother to interpret for him. He and the other children in this study all play with hearing children and have developed strategies for coping with communication challenges this situation presents. Alex seems to take his play relationships with deaf and hearing children for granted. Regardless of communication, play occurs.

Alex perceived hearing members of his family who can sign as deaf and those who cannot as hearing. Interestingly, he indicated that hearing parents love and respond positively to their child upon learning that the child is deaf: "They're excited." He was imaginative and could relay both real and imagined stories very easily. Although I didn't have much information about his reading ability, Alex was only seven years old, and it was clear that he had a strong comprehension of *The Three Little Pigs*, a story he was learning in class. Alex also sees a bright future for himself and anticipates growing up to become a policeman.

8

Lisa

Everything was all set for our first visit to Lisa's home. I called her mother earlier in the day to confirm our appointment. I arrived at Lisa's house with my camcorder, tripod, felt markers, colored pencils, and paper. Lisa had been expecting us but did not accompany her mom to the door to greet us when we arrived. Lisa's mother showed us to the dining room, where she thought we could most comfortably conduct our interview. Since Lisa had not joined us yet, her mom went to fetch her while we set up the equipment. Marilyn, the interpreter, could hear Lisa and her mother talking in the background, although she could not quite understand Lisa's responses.

Lisa's mother returned and explained that although she was encouraging her daughter to come in and meet us, Lisa was not quite ready to do so. She explained that Lisa was afraid of the camera and afraid to communicate with people she did not know because she was concerned they will not understand her. I explained that I had met Lisa a couple of years earlier at a theater workshop and wondered if Lisa might remember me from that. Her mother went back to again encourage Lisa to come join us, as Marilyn and I continued to set up the room.

When we had finished, we went with Lisa's mother to meet Lisa. As we turned around a corner from the dining room into the hall, Lisa just as quickly disappeared behind the wall in the den. We waited to give her some time to come out from hiding by herself while her mom encouraged her. Then we started through the kitchen into the den, and she slipped behind the walls in the next room, peeking around only occasionally to get a glimpse of us. Lisa has large brown eyes and long, curly, auburn hair. She is of average height, and her tanned complexion and strong physique give the impression that she is an active summer athlete. Her mother invited us to be seated, thinking Lisa would warm up and come out to meet us. I explained that Lisa did not have to do the interview if she didn't want to, but her mother decided to give it some more effort, thinking that Lisa just needed a little time to warm up.

Lisa was profoundly deaf at birth from an unknown cause. At the time of the study, she was ten years old, was mainstreamed in a public school total communication program, and had Signed English skills. She later transferred to an oral-only program. Although Lisa's family communicated orally with her, the mother shared with us that Lisa needed more help with her speech. She has no additional disabilities. Lisa's mother and father and two sisters are hearing.

ℱ

I PROCEED to tell Lisa's mother about the theater class where I first met Lisa and how we had done a scene from a play. As we are talking, Lisa peeks around the corner at her mom, trying to stay out of our sight. Lisa tells her mother that she doesn't remember me. Mom asks me what were the signs from the play. While her mother repeats the words for Lisa to see, Lisa laughs at her.

Soon afterward she makes up her mind to come into the room, but she stays a bit out of sight by hiding behind the coffee table on the floor. Although Lisa doesn't remember me, or the theater workshop, she is slowly beginning to warm up and make eye contact with us. She still needs her mom there for a little while as she gains confidence in our ability to communicate and begins to trust me. I ask Lisa about her summer experiences, and she turns to her mother on several occasions for help in answering questions or reassurance that she can make herself understood.

As Lisa's eye contact and comfort level increase, I suggest that perhaps we not use the camera just yet, and then she agrees to sit at the table with me. I let her see me put the lens cover on the camcorder and turn the power off, pointing the camera away from us. Then Lisa, her mother, the interpreter, and I all sit down at the table. Lisa's mom is seated opposite her and the interpreter is seated opposite me, with Lisa and I sitting next to each other at a thirty-degree angle on connecting sides of the table.

When I ask Lisa if she can draw a picture for me of a deaf girl, she hesitates, saying she doesn't know if she can. I think that she might not be comfortable drawing and tell her she doesn't have to if she doesn't want to. I ask if she wants to tell me a story about a deaf girl, or one about herself. She is still hesitant, so I just start asking her questions about school, friends, and home. She says she goes to gymnastics twice a week and to soccer twice a week. Her gymnastics class is composed of other deaf and hard of hearing students. When I ask her how she understands what she is supposed to do on the soccer team and who explains to her, she says she doesn't know and looks again at her mother for help in answering the questions. I ask her if the other girls help her and she gestures "so-so" with her hands. Voicing, she tells me her soccer team won the championship, but the interpreter and I do not understand her at first. When we do understand, I ask her if she knows that I am deaf too and that I don't understand all the time because I can't hear either.

I go on to tell her that I grew up in a hearing school and didn't always understand what was happening, and that sometimes kids were nice and helped and sometimes they weren't. Her mom tells her to tell me about her trophy. When her mother leaves the room to get the trophy and pictures, Lisa begins to use her signs with me, telling me about her soccer schedule. When her mom returns, though, she stops signing.

I ask Lisa more questions about her friends, and if she has any brothers and sisters. She mentions a friend, a boy, but says she does not know where they met. Her sisters are twelve and thirteen and are both at swimming practice.

Her father comes home from work and we say hello. Lisa and I resume our interview, and when I ask her how long she has been playing soccer, she responds that she does not know and asks her mom.

I return our discussion back to the subject of the video camera and ask if she has one at home. She says she does. I tell her why I need it, explaining how my voice and her voice might not be picked up well by the camera, and that the interpreter is there to voice for us so we will not have to worry about our voices. Then, after we are finished with the interview, the interpreter will take the tape home and type the interview for me, so I won't forget anything that we say. Then I can use that information for the book I'm writing. I tell her that no one will see the tape except her, myself, and the interpreter, and that when I am finished with it, I can even give it to her if she wants so she can be sure no one else will see it.

I ask if it will be okay if we start over again when I come back on Thursday. She says, "I guess," but I am not convinced she is comfortable with that idea, so I ask if she'd like her mom and the interpreter and me to do a pretend interview so she can see how it is done. She agrees.

The three of us conduct a mini-interview, and Lisa watches intermittently as she attempts to pull the box of markers off the table yet stay hidden from the camera. We proceed for a few minutes with our mock interview. Her mom is telling me about Lisa in response to my request for a story about a deaf child. Mom tells me how talented Lisa is. It is clear that her mother recognizes her daughter's talents and strengths.

"A story about a little deaf girl. I know this wonderful little girl. Her name is Lisa . . . Lisa. And she is so talented and can do many things. She can play soccer and basketball and gymnastics and baseball, and she tries real hard at school. She is doing a real good job at getting along with people, and she is a wonderful person to be around and she's so much fun."

I ask if the little girl is deaf and Mom nods.

I say, "Sounds like a nice girl. One that I would like to know."

"I think you would. I think you would. She's a very nice little girl."

"Where does Lisa go to school?"

"Lisa goes to school at Norwood. She is mainstreamed for half of the day and . . ."

"I missed that," I interrupt. "She goes to school . . ."

". . . at Norwood. She is in the hearing impaired classroom for the morning and with the normal class, the hearing class, in the afternoon."

After our mock interview the interpreter tells me that, unbeknownst to me, Lisa had dropped the box of markers on the floor while we were talking, making a very loud "boom" in the middle of our conversation. Lisa giggles as Marilyn explained this.

I turn to Lisa and tell her that what she just saw Mom and me doing is what she and I will do. I ask her if it is okay if we do that on Thursday and she agrees. Her mom suggests that maybe Lisa can draw some pictures before I come back, and then she can tell me about them when I return. I add that I will leave all the art paper, markers, and pencils here for her. By this time Lisa seems much more comfortable. We pack up the camera and say good-bye to her mother, but Lisa is not in sight. As we are loading the car, the interpreter informs me that Lisa had called my name from the house next door. I look and wave good-bye, signing that I will see her on Thursday.

As AGREED, Marilyn and I return on Thursday to see Lisa. She and her mother greet us at the door, but Lisa stays back about six feet, close to the wall. She smiles at us as we enter, and the interpreter and I proceed to set up the camcorder. Lisa sticks close to her mom as her mom encourages her to come in and sit with us. When we are ready to begin, her mom leaves the room, which encourages Lisa to talk to me on her own now.

From where she is situated, the interpreter is having a difficult time understanding Lisa's speech. I am sitting next to Lisa at the table and have less difficulty understanding her. I rely on speechreading her, often asking her to repeat what she has said. Although Lisa usually communicates orally at home, she gradually begins to sign with me as her comfort level increases.

Initially, when Lisa does sign, her gestures are below table level near her lap. I'm unsure if this reflects her own discomfort with signing, or if sign is just not the language she and her parents use at home.

In the process of transcribing these interviews, the interpreter/transcriptionist left many of Lisa's comments and responses blank in the transcripts, particularly at the beginning of our interview. These omissions were due to the difficulty she experienced in understanding Lisa's voice and her inability to see Lisa's signs from where she was positioned. Thus, after this interview was transcribed, I went back over the transcripts and videotapes and was able to fill in many of Lisa's responses. However, where neither of us understood a word or phrase, a question mark (?) is entered to indicate missing data.

Once we get started, Lisa tells me about school, family, friends, activities, and church. She has prepared a picture of her school for me and tells me the name of her school. She has not brought the rest of the paper with her that I had left last week because she does not want to draw more pictures.

Lisa begins to tell me about the picture she has drawn of her school. She is voicing here without using any signs. "Norwood is my school . . . in fourth grade."

Because I am speechreading Lisa and want to be sure that I am understanding her correctly, I often repeat back to her by simultaneously speaking and signing what I have understood her to say, and then I follow up with other questions.

"Good, you're in fourth grade now. And this is your school? Tell me more about your school."

She continues voicing. "It's hard work."

"It's hard work. What kind of work do you do?"

Lisa responds but I don't understand. Thinking she has said something about being in the third grade now and not the fourth I say, "You're in third grade, and you do what?" Still speechreading her, I think she says "butterfly," and I repeat that back to her as a question, "Butterfly?"

Lisa brings her hands to the table and signs X. With this she voices, "Multiply."

Understanding her, I repeat, "Oh, multiplication."

"And divide."

At this point, I am still speechreading her, but she is beginning to use some signs at lap level when we run into difficulty. I also continue to repeat after her to verify I have understood her.

"And division. Multiplication and division. I remember that. That was hard for me, too. Are there deaf children? Last year in the third grade, were there any deaf children in your class? In your math class?"

Lisa responds but at first I don't understand, so once again I repeat, "In math?" Then realizing she was naming a classmate, I repeat the name and then add, "Oh, just one other deaf child?"

She signs "Me," and speaks, "Mac . . ."

"You and Mac?"

As this dialogue progresses, it becomes clear that Lisa is explaining that she is placed in a self-contained class but then is mainstreamed with hearing children for math, gym, physical education, art, and music. She says that in one of her classes, her teacher signs, but in the regular classes, she uses an interpreter. Lisa does not use the term *interpreter*; she explains she has someone go with her from room to room and sign for her what the teacher is saying. I ask if it was an *interpreter* like the one we have with us and she smiles and says yes. Our communication has a feeling of effort. It seems that I am focusing so much on trying to understand and be understood by Lisa that the content is suffering.

"David." She speaks and then she fingerspells, "D-A-V-E-D." Then again she fingerspells "D-A-V-I-D," then voices "is in my" and under the table signs the last word, "class."

"So that was last year. What about second grade? How many deaf children were in your class?"

"Mac was in my class. Addition and subtraction."

I don't completely understand. "Mac was in your class and what?"

She signs "plus" and "minus" under the table while voicing, "add and subtract."

"Addition and subtraction. Addition and subtraction. Okay. That was easier. But then third grade was a little harder. Do you know what you're going to learn this year?" Lisa shrugs.

"Have to wait and see?" I ask. She nods. "So in second grade it was just Mac and you? Two deaf children?"

Lisa tilts her head a bit to the right, voicing "Other," which is also signed at her lap level.

To clarify, I ask, "One other boy?"

"More."

Wanting more details from Lisa, I ask, "Four? Or five?"

"Ten. Maybe ten."

"Oh, okay. Any hearing children?"

Both the interpreter and I have some difficulty understanding Lisa's response here.

"?? . . . In class, there was only [she signs three name signs] one person in class name was ? another one that was ?"

Thinking that she is including the teacher's name here I ask her, "Oh, that was a name? Can you spell the teacher's name?"

"Mrs. Henry and then there's Mrs. Douglas."

"Oh, Mrs. Douglas. And that was second grade?"

"That was first and second, third, fourth, fifth grade." She is still signing at lap level, and my position at the corner of the table allows me to see her signs below table level.

"So you had the same teacher for four years? So this will be the fourth year with the same teacher?"

"And math teacher."

"And a math teacher. So do you have those two teachers for all your classes?" Lisa nods. "Yes? . . . You don't have to worry about changing teachers every year. You know who your teacher will be."

"? paper with math?" she signs.

"A lot of paper work?" I ask, unsure.

"? a paper ? Which class I need to go to math, math teacher."

Now I understand that she is talking about a printout of her class schedule. "You have to look at the paper to see which class you have? So there were fewer deaf children in your class last year and more hearing children, right?"

"Last year it was all ? Mrs. Henry and other people who were hearing."

I'm not certain that I understand her here, so I ask, "All the deaf children were with Mrs. Douglas? Is that what you mean? But some of them go to a hearing class? Is that what you mean?" Here Lisa looks confused. "Say that again for me. What did you say?" Lisa smiles. "How many children in your class were deaf last year? Three?"

"Maybe ten. A few."

"Ten last year. Any hearing children?"

"Only deaf. In Douglas's class it's always deaf."

"So sometimes you're in an all deaf class and sometimes you're in a hearing class?" Lisa nods in agreement. "I see. So you change teachers?"

"Sometimes I go to math, I go to another teacher, a math teacher. And then after that I come back."

"Oh, back to the deaf class?"

"Yes."

"With Mrs. Douglas? Okay, I see. I understand now. I remember I visited a class one time where all of the children were deaf. Some of them stayed there all day, and some of them went to other classes with other teachers and then came back. Is that like yours?"

"Yes."

"Uh huh? At school, how do you communicate?" Lisa doesn't respond; she looks away, thinking. "Do you sign, or do you talk, or both, or what?"

"Both."

"Both?"

"All the time sign and talk? Does the teacher sign or just talk?"

"Both."

"The teacher signs and talks. So are you in what they call a total communication class, do you know what that means?"[13] Lisa doesn't respond. "That program? Total communication is kind of like when the teacher and children sign and talk at the same time."

Lisa shrugs, "I don't know."

"Or an oral program is when the teacher and children only talk."

"The teacher always talks."

"Only or always?"

"She's hearing. Teacher."

"And doesn't sign?"

Lisa helps me understand how communication is handled in her school with the following description: "All the people from other class, they help people, the hearing teachers. Tell the teacher what the hearing people said, so they know." Lisa is now signing above the table.

I'm not quite sure yet what she means. "Who are the other people? The boys and girls?"

"Other adults to ? class sign. They tell me what she said."

Now it becomes clear to me. "An interpreter? Like Marilyn?"

"Yes."

To summarize, Lisa has told me earlier that she is mainstreamed for some of her classes with hearing children and that other classes are *self-contained*, consisting of deaf children only. When she is

---

13. In reality, this is not an accurate definition of *total communication*. Signing and talking at the same time is actually called *simultaneous communication*. Total communication is an educational philosophy and instructional method that incorporates a variety of visual and auditory methods including sign language, speechreading, fingerspelling, and amplification. What I was trying to communicate to Lisa in this context was that in her present educational program the emphasis is not on speech alone, but that both speech and sign language are utilized.

mainstreamed with hearing children, she has a sign language interpreter accompanying her in the classroom.

"I see. How many classes do you have an interpreter for?"

Lisa shrugs and voices, "About five or ten or I don't know."

"Five? Or ten? I see. Do you like school?"

"I don't know."

"You haven't decided if you like school or not? Is that right? Some days do you like it and some days not?"

"It's okay."

"It's okay? What do you like about school?"

"Math." Here Lisa is signing at lap level again.

"Really? You like math?"

"Learn something."

"Learning something? What else do you like?"

"Art. Art."

"You like art? Are you good at art?"

"And music."

"Music, you like music?"

"Like that. I have music and art and gym."

"Are those your three favorites?" (During the interview, I thought she was saying that she liked music. But later, reading the transcripts, I decide she probably said that she "didn't like that" when I asked about music.)

"Two. Art and gym."

"I see. What do you like to do in gym class?"

"Run. And games."

"I bet you're good. And you like art? What kind of art?"

Lisa voices, "Weaving" and then signs, "Weaving."

I understand her sign, which described the activity, but I do not have an English name for it and struggle to understand what she was calling it.

"What's that called? I forget." Knowing that Lisa knew the word but that I was having difficulty speechreading her, I look to the interpreter who fingerspells, "W-E-A-V-I-N-G."

"Oh, weaving, okay. Do you use one of those frames that has the little points on it?" I'm thinking of a rug-making instrument.

"No. ?? and you bring it through and back and through. Wait, I'll show you." Lisa leaves the room and returns with her art project. She proudly displays a small, colorful, woven wall hanging.

"Oh, that's beautiful. And did you make that?" Lisa nods. "That's beautiful. Do you hang it in your room?"

"Bathroom."

"In the bathroom. It's real pretty. How did you do that?"

I think it is interesting that Lisa says she enjoys her music class at school. She sings with the other students. When I ask her what they sing she becomes rather shy and says she doesn't know. After this she seems to change her mind about liking music.

"And you said that you like music class too, right?

"Makes me so tired."

"It makes you so tired? Why does music make you tired?"

"Because sing, sing, sing, sing."

"And do you sing?" Lisa nods. "What kind of things do you sing?"

"I don't know."

"Do you know the names of the songs?"

"Maybe in fourth grade I'll do the recorder. I don't know."

"You'll do the recorder?"

"I don't know."

"Would you like to learn to use the recorder?"

"I guess. Some people like music. I don't."

"Some people like music, but you don't?"

"I like other things better. I like gym better."

"Mmmhmm. I think that a lot of deaf people enjoy gym and sports."

"Maybe more . . . there may be more new deaf in school."

Here I think Lisa is saying she may go to a new deaf school. "You think you might go to a new deaf school?"

"No, maybe more new deaf . . . in our class. Deaf class."

"In your class, mmhmm. Do you hope maybe there's some new deaf people there?" I am not sure if she considers this a good thing or not.

"I don't know."

"You have to wait and see. Are you nervous about school starting or are you excited or what?"

"Excited."

"Excited? When I was leaving last Tuesday I saw you have a friend next door. You have a friend that lives next door to you?"

Lisa tells me her friend's name. "Over there. Heather . . . H-E-A-T-H-E-R."

"Tell me about Heather."

"We play down in the basement."

"You do? I played in the basement when I was your age. What do you play?"

"I don't know."

"Games?"

"Ping-Pong."

"Oh, Ping-Pong. Really? You have a Ping-Pong table?"

"My aunt."

"So your aunt has a Ping-Pong table?"

"But she gave it to us."

"Oh, she gave it to you. Did she?" Lisa nods. "Do you like to play Ping-Pong?"

"Yes."

"It's probably cool down there in the summertime."

Lisa hasn't talked a lot about friends yet. I find myself asking her about them. When asking her more about how she gets along with other hearing children at school, at soccer, and at her other activities, she doesn't volunteer much information about the quality of their relationships. She also doesn't discuss communication issues in relationships with hearing and deaf children.

"What else do you do? What else do you and your friends do? You and your friends, when you get together, what do you do?"

"Today I go to Kristen's house."

"Kristen?" I ask.

"Do you know Kristen?"

"I'm not sure. What's her last name?"

"It starts with a B. I don't know her last name." Lisa gets up, goes to the desk, checks for something, and returns to our table. "I don't know." I think she was checking to see if she had Kirsten's last name written down somewhere.

"Okay. Is she in your class in school?"

"In fifth grade. She will be sixth grade, so she's going to middle school. Do you know [name sign]?"

"Jenny? No."

"She's my best friend."

"Really? Is Jenny deaf or hearing?"

"Deaf."

Lisa, a mainstreamed child in a total communication program, indicates that she has a best friend who is deaf, just as Alex, a child in a residential program, does. Both of these children met their best friends at school.

"Deaf? How did you meet Jenny?"

"? school ? We were fourth grade and fifth grade. She will be in sixth grade so she's going to middle school."

"So Kristen and Jenny, are they in the same class? The same age?"

"I don't know."

"Do Kristen and Jenny go to the same school?"

"I don't know."

"Did they go to your school last year?" Lisa says they did. "Will they go to your school again this year?" She shakes her head.

"? to middle school."

"Oh, middle school. That's why you don't know if they're in the same class. It's a different school."

"At Kristen's house I watch movies, funny movies, and Kristen has a new dog. They have three dogs. Kristen's got three. I knew they had two, and then I went over and they got a new dog, a white dog with such soft hair."

"Three dogs is a lot of dogs. You have a dog, right?"

"One."

"Is your dog, does your dog tell you when somebody's at the door?"

"I don't know."

"Is your dog a hearing dog?"

"No."

"No? Do you know about hearing dogs?"

"My dog's not deaf."

"Okay, you know, you see sometimes when you see blind people and they have a dog, and it helps them across the street? Have you seen that before? Well, deaf people have dogs, too, that you can train, and the dog will tell you when somebody's at the door, or they will tell you when the phone rings, or they will tell you when the alarm clock is ringing in the morning. They will tell you if the fire alarm is ringing. Did you know that?"

"My mom and I got a Frisbee, and my dog will jump and catch it."

"That sounds like fun. But your dog's not a hearing dog? A trained hearing dog to help you know if somebody's at the door?"

"My dog always barks and barks and barks. I don't know ??"

"You don't know what?"

"When ?? growing and growing up."

"Growing up fast. How old is your dog?"

"One and a half."

"One and a half. So still a puppy. Yeah. Does she chew on things?"

"She puppy chews ?? . . ." Lisa gets up and goes to stand near the hall. "Here." She points to an object that the dog chewed on and returns to our table.

"Oh. My dog did that, too."

"And my dog chewed the chair."

I am still curious about Lisa's dog and if they are going to train her to become a hearing dog. I decide to tell her about my dog and how she alerts me to the doorbell and other sounds.

"My dog is a hearing dog. I had her trained before I got married. My dog and I lived alone. And my dog tells me when somebody comes to the door. When somebody goes to the door and knocks on the door, then my dog will run to the door and bark, then she runs and gets me. It's called a hearing dog."

"Mine just barks and barks and lunges and scratches if people come near. If somebody comes in the house, my dog pulls and she scratches." Lisa's dog is still a puppy and will need to be a bit older before support dog training can begin. I am not sure from our dialogue if she is aware of the concept of a *hearing dog.*

"She wags her tail very hard when she sees people."

This visit takes place during the summer months while Lisa is out of school. I am curious about other aspects of Lisa's life and her summer activities. I inquire, "So what else did you do today?"

"My mom picked me up at Kristen's house. And then we came home."

"Did you stay at Kristen's all day?"

"Mom . . . we left at twelve thirty, and then Mom picked me up at four o'clock and we came home." Here she is half signing and half talking.

"I see. So, do you visit many of your deaf friends during the day?"

"Steven and Kristen."

"Steven and Kristen during the summer?" Since many deaf children do not live near their deaf classmates, I ask her, "Do they live close to you? Do you have to drive?"

"Steven's mom called me, 'Would you like to go swimming at Steven's house?' And my mom asked me, 'Do you want to go swimming?' and I said, 'Yeah.' Then I put my bathing suit on and we went to Steven's house and went swimming."

"Sounds like fun."

"That was yesterday . . . Cold water."

"I saw your towel out there. Your towel. On the porch out in the front. I thought maybe you went swimming today."

We also talk about church. Lisa's family is Catholic and attends mass on Sundays. I ask Lisa how she knows what they are saying in church and she looks perplexed. I wonder if she has not understood me or if she has not thought about it before. I ask if anyone helps her understand what they are saying in church and she says sometimes her mom does.

"Does your family go to church on Sunday?"

"Twelve, twelve, my mom is always telling me twelve, twelve, twelve."

"Every Sunday? Where do you go to church?"

"I go to communion."

"You go to communion? And did you make your first communion already? When did you do that?"

"At church school you have to practice. Then you take communion. They have a white dress and curl my hair. My mom ? Kathleen ??"

"And you go to CCD class to study religion?" Knowing that Lisa attends a public school, I assume she attends religion classes offered by her church to prepare for her first communion.

"C, C, church, aaaah. Church school. I have to practice communion around two I think."

"Church school? What night do you go to church school?"

"At seven o'clock. I go to church school at seven o'clock."

"On Sunday?"

"No, on Monday."

"Every Monday? Every week?"

"I don't know."

"Well, you're a busy girl. You have gymnastics, soccer, church school, homework. Busy, busy." While we are on the subject of activities and her busy schedule, she tells me that she also has speech lessons. She asks me, "Do you know Mrs. Cameron? For speech."

"Oh, she's your speech teacher."

"And we talk about the dog."

"You go to Mrs. Cameron's house for speech? When do you do that? What night do you do that?"

"We leave about . . ." Lisa gets up and goes to the desk again to check a schedule . . . "Eleven in the morning."

"Eleven in the morning during the summer?"

"On Tuesday and on Thursday, I think." She gets up again to check the schedule once more . . . "Tuesday and Thursday."

"Tuesday and Thursday. You're very busy." Later I realize that I had an opportunity here to talk more with Lisa about her perceptions of speech lessons since this seems to be a significant issue in her life. But, mentally, I am still with her at her Sunday school classes and church. I remember that the other children have talked about accessibility issues in their family's religious practices, and I am curious about what more Lisa can tell me here and if her experiences have been similar.

"So you told me about church. Do you have an interpreter in church? Do you know what they're talking about in church? How do you know what they're talking about?"

"I don't know."

"Do you follow the book? Do you read the book?"

"Some people help me by writing." Lisa reveals here that writing comes in handy for her from time to time, just as it does for the other children in the study during periods of communication inaccessibility.

"When you go to church on Sunday with your family, does someone help you to follow and understand what they're saying?"

"My mom." Here again is a child whose mother also helps with communication when the environment is not accessible.

"Your mom does. You have two older sisters, right? Do they go to church with you?"

"Sometimes they sleep a long time. My mom and me go to church or my dad and me go to church. My sisters stay home and sleep."

"Let me think what else I wanted to ask you about. Can you think of anything else you wanted to tell me?"

"My school starts September fifth."

"September fifth. That's about two weeks. How do you feel about that? Are you going to get new clothes for school?"

"??"

"What?"

"I think few."

"A few? When does gymnastics start again?"

"I don't know ??"

"Hmmm?"

"I point my toes."

"Does your gymnastics teacher sign?"

"Last year the interpreter interpreted what she said."

(Upon reviewing the transcript from this interview, I saw that the transcriptionist noted that a dog started to bark in the background. She also noted that airplanes were flying overhead. I wasn't aware of this during the interview and do not know if it was distracting for the interpreter.)

"Remember you were telling me about your soccer team? You said sometimes the other girls don't help you?" I'm trying to learn more about how she communicates in different situations.

"On August 31 I'll have soccer practice. At six o'clock. On Thursday."

"How do you understand what you're supposed to do?"

"??"

"What?"

"My coach tells me what to do."

"Your coach tells you what to do." She nods. "Do you like the other girls on the team?" Lisa nods. "Do you get along with the other girls on the team? Are they your friends?" Lisa nods.

"? back." I don't understand the first part of this.

I repeat the part of her response I think I understand, "You'll go back?"

"I remember them again, from last year's team. I remember who. We played and played and played, and then . . ."

"I didn't understand, last year what?"

"I don't remember who the people were, the hearing people, I remember who, and then I know them. Same coach, same team."

"Same team this year?"

"I don't know. Different coach I think . . . All my friends."

"Could you explain?" Lisa is not telling me much about the quality of her relationships with her peers. I'm uncertain if she finds it uncomfortable to talk about, if she really doesn't consider her experiences uncomfortable and therefore not significant enough to discuss, or if she isn't sure how to communicate something so complex. My hunch is that on a conscious level she doesn't feel she has any difficulties or experiences anything unusual in her relationships with hearing children. Perhaps she just takes her relationships for granted as many of the other children in the study do. The difference is that the other children more readily point out communication challenges and problems with fitting in than Lisa does, and they are able to tell me how they approach those difficulties. Lisa has friendships with both deaf and hearing children and talks about their play activities, but she does not volunteer information about communication or her feelings about it.

Lisa seems to be the most challenged in her communication, and one might think that this would be bothersome, if not traumatic, for her on an unconscious level. She does tell us that, of all these children, her best friend is deaf, and that statement in itself implies that she may feel more comfortable and able to achieve a bond with this deaf child more readily than she can with the hearing children she mentioned.

In our next session, we will use the magazine cutouts as a projective technique and in closing our interview this evening, I am hopeful that I can learn more about Lisa's perceptions of herself and others through this method.

"Okay, well, why don't we stop for tonight, and I'll come back again next Tuesday, okay?"

Lisa gets up and goes to the desk and brings a schedule back with her. "Tuesday."

"Next Tuesday, August 29. Okay? Do you want to see yourself on TV?" She smiles and nods in agreement. "You want to. Do you have a VCR?"

"In the family room."

We go into the family room where her mom is and put the tape on. Lisa shows me her dog as her mom tries to keep him from jumping on us. Lisa takes a strong interest in the tape and is encouraging her mom to watch it and stop talking with us. Her mom has been explaining to me that they know about hearing dogs and got their dog to have him trained, but that the support dog organization said they would not train a dog that was not obtained through the organization. Lisa and her sisters became attached to the dog, so they decided to keep him but have been unable to get the dog trained.

Her mom also confirms Lisa's explanation of her total communication program and how it works, but says she is not happy with it. She thinks Lisa needs more challenge. I tell Lisa she can keep the tape until we come back the following week, and she is happy about that. She continues watching it while we leave.

FOR MY THIRD and final interview with Lisa, it is early evening when we arrive at Lisa's home. She and her mom have just returned from vacation. Lisa slips out of the room, and her mom goes to get her. Lisa returns with a slice of bread and a glass of ice water. We sit down to begin our interview as she gobbles down her snack. I ask if she has eaten her dinner and she replies she has not. I suggest we can wait until she has eaten, but she decides to continue. She eats hurriedly and then we begin.

I have my folder of magazine pictures and we go through these tonight. I show Lisa the first picture and ask her to tell me stories about what she sees happening in them. The first picture includes a man, a woman, and a baby.

Lisa looks at the picture and laughs. "The father has to work. And the mother has to take care of the baby."

"Okay. Good. What else?"

"The baby wants its mother."

"Okay. When mother takes care of the baby, what do the mother and the baby do?"

"Bottle and change clothes, change the diaper, all that."

"Okay, what else do they do?"

Lisa looks at her glass and sees that it has made a ring on the dining room table. She leaves the room and returns with a napkin. I ask her to tell me more about the family in the picture. She teasingly takes a deep breath and says, "I don't know."

"Do the mother and the baby go places? Where do they go?"

"Store."

"What else?"

"The store."

"When they go to the store, what do they buy?"

"Baby stuff."

Lisa has not begun to identify whether or not the infant is deaf or hearing, so I ask her, "Okay. Is the baby deaf or hearing?"

"Hearing."

"Is the mother deaf or hearing?"

"Hearing."

"Why do you think they're both hearing?"

" 'Cause they're not deaf."

"How do you know?"

" 'Cause there's no hearing aids." In this study, only the students who are mainstreamed mention hearing aids as an indicator that someone is deaf.

"Oh, if they have hearing aids, then that means they're deaf. Do all deaf people wear hearing aids?"

Lisa pauses for a while and then responds, "I think so."

"What about Dad?"

"He's hearing."

"Dad's hearing? Okay, how do you know Dad's hearing?"

" 'Cause he's not deaf."

"Because what?"

"They're all not deaf."

"Okay. Okay. Good. Thank you. That was good. Number two." She takes a minute to look at this new picture and seems unsure of it. I ask her, "Is that complicated?"

"I don't know."

"What's that man doing?"

"Drawing."

"What's he drawing?"

"I don't know."

"Is he drawing for fun or for work?"

"Work."

"Is he deaf or hearing?"

"He's hearing."

"How do you know?"

"I see there's no hearing aid." Hearing aids seem to be Lisa's primary indication of a person's hearing status.

"No hearing aids, okay . . . If you look at the picture of a deaf man and a different picture of a hearing man, is it hard to know who's deaf and who's hearing?"

She nods, "I don't see a hearing aid."

"What kind of job do you think he does?"

"Drawing."

"Drawing, okay."

Looking at the next picture, she tells me that the children in this picture are "playing."

"What kind of game are they playing?"

"Sorry."

"Are they deaf or hearing?"

She begins to sign "de . . ." and then changes to "Hearing. Hearing."

"They're hearing? Both hearing? How do you know?"

Once again Lisa identifies the people in the picture as hearing, " 'Cause there's no hearing aids."

"There's no hearing aids. Okay."

She looks again at the children in this same photograph with one child on the phone and another child sitting next to him with his head in his hands. "Waiting and waiting and waiting on the telephone, talking on the telephone."

"Uh huh. Okay. Sometimes do you see hearing people talking on the phone?" Lisa nods. "Do you understand what they're saying? Do you have to wait and wait and wait sometimes? Do you have to wait and wait and wait for hearing people to finish talking on the phone?"

"I don't talk on the phone."

I point to the picture of the boy who is waiting, "Suppose this were you. Pretend that's you, and this is a hearing person talking on the phone. How would you feel?"

"Bored." In her mainstream program, Lisa relies on her oral skills, and she has the same emotional response that most of the children in this study have about these circumstances: that waiting for hearing people to finish talking in an inaccessible situation is boring.

"Bored . . . What do you do?"

"I don't know."

We go on to the next picture. "Okay. Number four. What's happening?"

"Reading a book." Lisa holds the picture close to her face, then shrugs and puts it down.

"You don't know? Can you make up a story?"

"I thought she might be doing art, but she's not. I don't know." Lisa looks closely at the woman and two young children in this picture again and then she shrugs.

"Are they deaf or hearing?"

"Hearing."

"Hearing? All of them? What's that little girl doing?"

Lisa's interpretation of the sign in the picture is, "She's making I LOVE YOU."

"Trying to make I LOVE YOU? Is that the teacher or who is that?"

"The teacher or art teacher."

"What's the teacher doing?"

"Showing the I LOVE YOU to her."

"What's this person doing?"

The child in the picture we are discussing is looking in the opposite direction from the teacher and the child who is signing. Lisa says he is looking at something else: "Saw something."

"Okay. What do you think he saw?" Lisa shrugs. "Okay. If, um, that's the teacher and she's signing, and the girl's trying to sign I LOVE YOU, why would they sign I LOVE YOU?"

"For the family." Lisa's family communicates orally with her at home. I think here that she means learning to sign I LOVE YOU allows her and her family to communicate this message to each other.

She has indicated that the children in this picture are hearing. Can they possibly represent her sisters?

"For the family?" I ask. Lisa shrugs. "Why do hearing children learn sign?"

Lisa shrugs, "I don't know."

"Do you know any hearing children who sign?"

"I don't know."

"Hearing children in your school? Do they sign?" She nods. "Why do they sign, if they're hearing?"

"They know how to sign language. 'Cause they want to know how to do sign language."

"But why do they need to know?"

"Easy to sign for hearing and deaf . . . People know sign language . . . When I was in third grade, the people would ask how to sign something—'How do you sign that?' I would say, 'I'm not telling you.' " Lisa seems serious here. I don't have the impression that she says this to them in a teasing manner, but rather that she really does not want the hearing children to learn sign.

"You don't tell them?"

"They always want to know how to sign language."

"You don't want the other children to learn that?"

Lisa seems uneasy here. At home, Lisa's parents prefer that she use her speech, and they would like for her to improve her speech skills. Perhaps her discomfort here reflects her experience at home where spoken English is preferable to sign language. She picks up the next picture, but then continues, "Some people know."

"Some people know? And some people . . . Do you want some children to know how or not?" Lisa shakes her head. "You don't want hearing children to know how. Can you tell me more about that? Does it bother you? Does it bother you when hearing children sign?"

Lisa moves on to the next picture on her own, not answering my questions. She looks at this next picture, puts her finger on one of the children in a group and says, "Deaf."

"Is he deaf?" She moves her finger on the page, pointing to the entire group. "All of them?" She nods. "What are they doing?"

"Playing."

"Playing what?"

"I don't know."

Pointing at the adult in the picture, I ask, "Who is this?"

"Teacher."

I point to a group of children and Lisa says, "Kids."

"Deaf kids? Okay. Where are they?" Lisa shrugs. "Okay. Do you think that those children, if they're all deaf, do they have hearing friends, too? Or just deaf friends? Or what?"

"Both."

"Both? The hearing friends . . . How do they communicate with their hearing friends?"

"I don't know."

Again, Lisa does not seem eager to discuss her communication with hearing children. She indicated earlier that she doesn't want them to learn to sign. I am curious about how they do communicate and what issues exist for her, but further information is not forthcoming. I sense that Lisa is starting to become tired and appears anxious to get through the pictures. "Okay. We don't have to do them all. We can just do ten, and that's number six."

"I think he's deaf."

"You think they're deaf? What are they doing?"

"Talking."

"About what?"

"I don't know . . . vacation."

"Talking about vacation. What happened on their vacation?"

"I don't know . . . Florida."

"Florida. What did they do in Florida?"

"Party."

"Party? Have parties? Who was at the party?"

"Wedding."

"A wedding party. Who got married?"

"My Uncle Kevin."

"Your Uncle Kevin? Did you go to your Uncle Kevin's wedding?"

"? live in Boston."

"He's living in Boston?" She nods. "Did you go to the wedding in Boston?"

"Florida. In Florida was the wedding. And now he lives in Florida."

"That's far away. Have you been there?"

"I haven't gone to Florida . . . And I want to go to California."

"To California?"

"I've never," she says, indicating that she has never been to California.

"Maybe some day you will."

"Maybe not."

"Maybe not? What's in California?" Lisa voices without signs, and I don't understand her. I ask her to repeat for me, "What?"

She gestures and signs, "Whales and dolphins and seals."

For clarification, I ask, "Whale?" and I fingerspell the word. Lisa used a "w" on the top of her head as a sign for whale, a sign I had never seen before and I interpret it as a "local" sign that is probably used in her classroom.

Lisa fingerspells, "WHALES . . ." and then signs "and dolphins and seals."

"I see."

"And ride and ride."

"That sounds like fun."

"I want to go. And I want to go to Sea World. ?? Fun."

"You've been there before and it's fun?"

"In a different state."

"And what do you do there?"

"They have whales and dolphins. You watch the dolphin or whale show and they splash and they go up and you try and run away and get splashed."

"Sounds like fun . . . Okay, number seven." We move on to picture number seven. Lisa sets aside number six and holds the seventh picture up in front of her face.

"Deaf." She indicates that the two women in this picture are both deaf.

"They're both deaf. What are they doing?"

"They're using sign language." Initially, when examining the photographs, the first clue that Lisa notices about the characters that indicates whether or not they are deaf or hearing is the presence or absence of a hearing aid. Lisa looks for hearing aids first, above other possible indicators such as mouth movement or the visible act of signing. It isn't until the fourth picture that any of the characters are using sign language. It is at this point that she begins to see the use of sign language as an additional overt indicator of the person's deafness. The primacy of hearing aids to Lisa is an indication of her own perceptions of self. Having or not having a hearing aid appears to be more significant to her than whether or not a person uses sign language.

"What are they talking about?"

"School."

"What happens in school?"

"Some people don't know what to do." Unconsciously, perhaps, Lisa is referring to her own uncertainty at the beginning of a new school year in an unfamiliar situation.

"They don't know what to do in school? What do you mean?"

"Some people won't be at school, and they don't know. They need to know."

"Some people won't be there? And they don't know that? Who won't be there?"

"Some other people."

"Students? Children?"

"Other people. Some other people go to a different school. They go to a different school and they don't know what to do. They need ??"

I try to understand what Lisa is saying, wondering if she is talking about moving to a different school. "Are you going to a different school this year?"

Lisa shakes her head no.

"The same school?" She nods. "Do you know what to do?"

"Norwood ??" She tells me the name of her school and follows that with something else that I do not understand.

"Do you know what to do there?"

"I went there for third grade." Lisa was in the third grade last year at Norwood.

"Okay. It's the same school. But some other people won't know what to do. If they don't know what to do, who do they talk to? How do they find out?"

"Other people will help."

"Who will help?"

"I don't know. Some children, teachers."

"Are those children and teachers hearing or deaf?"

"I think both."

"Both? So they both help. Okay."

We move on to the next picture.

"Deaf." She shows me the hearing aid on one of the two young boys in the picture. The other child, who doesn't appear to have a hearing aid, is signing something. Lisa's perception in this picture is that while the child with the hearing aid is deaf, the child who is signing is hearing because she does not see a hearing aid.

"He has a hearing aid. So it's easy to know because he has a hearing aid," I say. Lisa nods. I point to the other person in the picture. "Is this person deaf or hearing?"

"That person's hearing."

"What makes you think he's hearing?"

"Sign language, so he knows what she said."

"Oh. Okay, and what are they talking about?"

"About fishing."

"Fishing?"

"About this big." Lisa holds her arms wide apart, signing "big," copying what she interprets the "hearing" child in the picture to be saying. No indications in the picture suggest that the topic of the children's conversation is fishing. I take her response to be based on her own experience.

"Do you fish?"

"Before."

"Did you catch a fish?"

"About this small." She holds her fingers close together and giggles.

"That small. That's funny. Do you like to fish?" She indicates she does with a nod of her head. "Who goes fishing with you?

"My friends."

"Deaf friends, hearing friends?"

"Hearing friends."

"Hearing friends. That sounds like fun. Who taught you how to fish?"

"My grandma."

"Your grandmother taught you? Did your grandma go fishing?"

"I don't know."

"But she taught you how?"

Lisa nods, but she seems to be tiring and running out of ideas, so we move on to the next picture.

She examines a picture of a young woman typing on a TTY and determines she is deaf. "Deaf."

"She's deaf? What makes you think she's deaf?"

"? Maybe her family, her grandmother or someone tell her what they said in typing."

"What's that called?"

"Typing."

"Do you know what this is?"

"I don't know."

"It's called the TTY. A TTY."

"TTY."

"Have you seen one of those before?"

She fingerspells, "At Rome school." This is not Lisa's school, but a school that her family had apparently visited.

"They have them there?" She nods affirmatively. "Did you use one?" She shakes her head.

Lisa tells me she doesn't use a TTY. She goes on to explain that her teachers help her use the phone at school. They set up two telephones, one with a headset for the teacher to listen with and the other for Lisa to speak into. The teachers then voice for Lisa what the other party is saying so that she can speechread. "I don't use one, talking, talking." She imitates holding the phone and talking.

"Can you talk on the phone? Do you? Can you hear other people on the phone?"

"Other hearing teachers tell me what they say." I am not clear how the teachers do this. I am trying to get a picture in my mind of the teachers on the phone telling her what people are saying. I tell her I don't understand and she expresses her frustration, "Rrrrgh."

"What? Are you upset with me?" Lisa makes loud breathing sounds. "Are you upset really?"

Lisa yells, "No," and grins as if to indicate she is teasing. Despite her grin, I think that her frustration with our communication is real, and I am actually relieved that she has expressed that frustration. "On the phone, other teachers, what my family says."

"So the teacher helps you understand what your family says?" She nods. "So you call your family from school on the telephone?"

She nods again. "Can you hear them a little bit or does the teacher interpret?"

"No."

"How does the teacher know what the family says?"

"She heard."

"So she listens on your phone? You two share?"

"Two telephones, side by side."

"Oh, and you talk to your family, and the teacher helps you understand. How does she help you understand?"

"She says what my mom says. What my family and my mom."

"So she just repeats what your mom says. Does she sign or just talk?"

"Just talk."

"And you like calling home and talking to your family?" Lisa pauses and looks at the file. "Okay. Number ten . . . The last one, okay. What's happening here?"

She looks at the group of schoolchildren sitting on the floor with an adult and says, "School. Hearing."

"Are they all hearing? Is the teacher hearing or deaf?"

"Hearing."

"How do you know they're all hearing?"

"No hearing aids."

"No hearing aids. Let me see. Yes, you're right. I don't see any either. Okay. Do you want to tell me a story about that one?"

She shakes her head no.

"No? Are you tired of telling me stories?"

Lisa nods. Seeing that she is tiring, I conclude our final interview.

"Okay, that's fine. We can stop. Thank you. You did a good job. A *real* good job."

IT WAS A struggle initially for Lisa to warm up and begin to open herself to me. As our sessions progressed, she became increasingly responsive. Communicating was a challenge. A great deal of effort went into that process; consequently, there was a lack of depth in the content. I wonder now, had I allowed one additional interview with Lisa, if I might have learned about her images of the future and other aspects of her life, topics that arose in interviews with other children. It would have been interesting to see if she had similar predictions for her future. I knew though, that Lisa was tired and growing frustrated, and I didn't want to impose further. Nonetheless, there is much to learn about Lisa's lifeworld from the data and the process that did occur. A wealth of information arose about Lisa's lifeworld out of the nonverbal dynamics and the communication processes observed in our sessions.

Lisa's parents recognize that she has communication challenges. Her mother told me that Lisa needs more help with her speech and that Lisa is initially afraid that people may not understand her. Lisa didn't present labels for hearing dogs, interpreters, or TTYs. I wondered if this was because of an actual lack of vocabulary and language skills or if it might have been due to more breakdown in our communication than I was aware of. I felt that by signing English and voicing clearly, I was matching her communication and linguistic needs. Her discomfort may also reflect her experience at home, where spoken English is preferable to the signing that took place in our session. She appeared to have good receptive sign language skills and was comfortable with oral communication, but was not fully using her expressive sign skills because of her family's oral communication preferences. Beyond vocabulary, insight, and expressive language skills, I wondered if perhaps she was also naturally reserved regardless of her choice of signed or spoken communication. Her mother confirmed Lisa's anxieties over communication in our first session, when she said that Lisa was afraid that she would not be understood. My perception is that all of the above factored in, some weighing more heavily than others, with communication being one of her biggest and, I would imagine, most painful challenges at this particular point in her development.

Lisa is certainly a very talented and active child. She is encouraged at home and provided with many opportunities to develop these talents. She told me about her school program and the many and varied activities she participates in with her friends and family. She shared that she has both deaf and hearing friends but did not comment on the quality of her relationships as much as the other children did. Perhaps this was an indication that Lisa was satisfied with the quality of her relationships as they are.

Initially, Lisa identified characters in the photographs as deaf if she was able to see a hearing aid and identified characters without hearing aids as hearing. To Lisa, the presence of a hearing aid was the primary overt indicator of someone's deaf or hearing identity.

Lisa, like most of the other children, appeared to take her deafness for granted. She knows that she is deaf, and she knows where other deaf children are. She has many things in common with other children in this study, including the varied recreational activities she participates in, the fact that she plays with both deaf and hearing children, the sense of boredom she experiences in communicatively inaccessible situations, and her perception that her mother helps out with communication at times. Moreover, like the other children, she feels loved by her parents, she experiences a bond and is comfortable in her relations with her deaf friends, and she uses overt indicators to assign deaf or hearing identities to those whom she observes. She is a happy, energetic, resilient, well-behaved, and likeable child who is surrounded by people who she knows love her.

9

Mary

MARY, WHO is eight years old, attends a nonresidential program for deaf students that utilizes a total communication approach. She is mainstreamed with hearing children for some of her classes and studies in a self-contained class with other deaf students at other times. Mary's parents, grandparents, aunts and uncles, and siblings are deaf; only a few distant relatives are hearing. Mary's parents are going through a divorce, and Mary lives with her mother during the week. With six children at home, her mom is very busy with their schedules.

Mary was born profoundly deaf, and her deafness is hereditary. Both of Mary's parents and all of her siblings are proficient in ASL, which is their native language. She has no additional disabilities. Mary is different from the other children in this study in that she is the only one with deaf parents. In addition to being immersed in Deaf culture, she is partially mainstreamed and appears comfortable among both deaf and hearing children. Being bicultural and bilingual, she is adept at ASL and Signed English, and she frequently uses simultaneous communication, signing in English and speaking at the same time.

It is interesting to note the uniqueness of Mary's bicultural and bilingual self in the stories she shares about her relationships with deaf and hearing peers, her family relationships, and the identities she issues to characters in the pictures she examines.

Mary's mother had suggested we meet somewhere other than home since she was concerned there would be too much distraction there. So I had agreed to pick Mary up at her home and transport her to a local community service center for deaf and hard of hearing people.

When I arrived at Mary's home, her mother answered the door. The six children were all seated in the living room and dining room. Mary and the other children were busy watching a captioned version of an after-school special on television. The youngest child, a two year old, interacted with me, babbling in signs, taking an interest in the papers I brought with me. He spelled "fx" for "fax" and then playfully inserted the paper between shelves as if faxing them.

Mary was finishing up her dinner. The oldest child sat quietly watching TV, ready to leave for her softball game. The second oldest, a boy, also watched TV while keeping an eye on his two-year-old brother. He got up at one point and pointed to my papers, which the toddler had started playing with, and signed, "That's hers."

As Mary and I left for our interview, her mother waved good-bye from the front porch and signed "I love you." Mary looked over her shoulder, signing "I love you" back to her mother until we turned the corner and disappeared from her mother's view.

℘

MARY HAS short brown hair, and today she is wearing a headband to keep her bangs off of her tanned forehead. She is a strikingly polite and very talkative eight-year-old child. Sitting in the front seat next to me, she carries on a conversation the whole way to our meeting place. She points out to me that there are holes hammered in the telephone poles because people were trying to sell things, and she tells me that her mommy and daddy are getting a divorce. She says she'll be going back to school soon and can't wait to see her friends. She shares with me that she has never been on videotape or TV before and that she is excited about our doing this.

One of Mary's first questions for me is if our interview site will be air-conditioned. She smiles exuberantly when I respond that it is, and she has been equally positive regarding the air-conditioning in my car. She tells me her air conditioner is broken and that her daddy is going to get it fixed. It starts to rain as we approach our destination, and we laugh about having to run to the building in the rain. We share an oversized umbrella as we run up to the entrance.

When we arrive at the building where we are scheduled to tape our interview, Mary walks quietly down the hall with me. As we approach the room I had reserved, a quiet, comfortable conference room with good lighting, cushioned carpet, and a nice oak table, she eagerly asks, "Camera in there?" We sit down with the camera rolling, and I make sure she understands the purpose of our meeting. Then all of a sudden the smoothness and naturalness of our earlier conversation in the car and the hall is gone, and our interview becomes awkward and formal. Mary struggles to draw herself, and when I see how it is becoming a task I ask if she'd rather not draw and just tell me a story. She smiles and agrees. She brushes her paper and pens aside but then gets stuck with the storytelling part.

Sensing her awkwardness, I decide to drop the formalities and just let the dialogue go where it will and then take opportunities to weave in some of my prepared questions as chance offers. I seem to have learned much more about Mary and her lifeworld when I was not conducting a formal interview.

"Tell me a story about yourself," I ask her.

"I can't remember, when I was little. I can't remember."

"Okay."

"My mom and dad talk about it, when I was little."

"Do Mom and Dad tell you stories about when you were little?"

"That's what Mom tells me, that when I was little I was really stubborn and wouldn't listen to my mom."

"Really?"

"And I would take off and run away. I would be bad mouth to my mother."

"Oh, okay, but you don't remember that?"

"But my mother told me, and now I remember."

"Oh. So tell me about your family."

"Well, a long time ago my sister, you know Barbara? My sister was little, and she wasn't born, then she was born in a hospital, and she stayed in the hospital, my mother stayed in the hospital when she was born, and then she almost died. But then my daddy tried to help, but the hospital said no, no, they couldn't help. Because she just had to die. Because my daddy tried and tried and tried, and we were very lucky that she lived . . . my mother was ready, the doctor was ready to give my mother a shot in her back, but then, you know, because she almost died, she had to suffer."

"But she was born then. Wow, you were very lucky."

"And we're happy that she was all right. If she had died, I would have cried and cried."

"Uh huh."

"The family cried."

"Mmhmm. And how old is Barbara now?"

"She's four."

As our interview progresses, Mary seems to become more relaxed. One of the things that strikes me about her is the amount of information that she reveals about her family in our interviews. It is clear to me that she has access to more family information than many of the other children do. This can be attributed to the fact that Mary's parents and most of her family members are Deaf and share a common language, ASL, which makes her family communication accessible. Since ASL was the first language learned by members of this family, Mary and all of her siblings have had access to information earlier in life than most deaf children. With 90 percent of deaf children having hearing parents, the language and communication patterns of hearing family members must be adjusted. This adjustment is often a long and drawn-out process. Since language and communication are not readily accessible in these families, the deaf child often experiences an early gap in information input. This gap results in many deaf children from hearing families not having the wealth of information about themselves and their families that Mary demonstrates.

Although Mary describes her father and brother as hard of hearing, they are deeply involved in Deaf culture, use ASL, and are part of a family with a long history of hereditary deafness. In reviewing my sessions with Mary, I am reminded of Meadow, Greenberg, Erting, and Carmichael's research (1981) comparing various mother-child dyads in families with deaf members, deaf children with deaf mothers, hearing mothers and deaf children using oral only communication, hearing mothers with deaf children using simultaneous communication (oral communication and simultaneous signing), and hearing mothers with hearing children. These researchers found that deaf children of deaf mothers and hearing children with hearing mothers were alike in that they were able to "carry on conversations about themselves, their mothers, and nonpresent objects and events" (p. 454).

"And you have an older sister, named Susan?"

"Yeah. She's almost eleven. She was born on May 5, 1984." She signs "1984" again, then adds, "Three, no, um four years before, um, above me she was born."

"And so your baby brother is two and one-half?"

"He's three." She goes on to tell me the names, ages, and birthdays of all her siblings.

"So is all of your family deaf?"

"Well, except my father, and my brother, they're hard of hearing. My mom and dad . . . My mom and me and my other brothers and sisters are deaf . . . I have cousins and nieces and everybody. And my two little cousins, or my nieces, they're hard of hearing, I mean hearing. Most of my family is deaf. Most of my family is . . . I have a puppy, named Boy, I don't know how many months. He was lost, and my mother saw this one puppy walking and lost. And he was crying and came right up. And they picked up the puppy and loved and was real close to my mom."

"So you take care of the puppy now at home?"

"Mmhmm. I feed the puppy and I do a lot with the puppy."

"That's nice. When your family goes out places, what do they do?"

"Well, sometimes we go out, and sometimes . . . We went to the state fair."

"Was it fun?"

"Oh, yeah, it was a lot of fun. But I was really tired. We didn't leave until ten, eleven o'clock. I was tired. I went to bed. I went to sleep in the car."

"At eleven at night. Wow, you stayed a long time at the fair. I bet you had fun."

"Well, we left at twelve in the afternoon and we stayed until eleven at night . . . And we ate and played a whole lot and had fun. And it was hot."

"Yes, oh, yesterday was very hot. Did it rain on you?"

"Oh, just a little bit. There was a downpour and then it stopped and then there was another shower and then it stopped . . . When we got there it was raining. And we stood outside in the cool. Then when it stopped and we could leave there and play. We had tickets and they put a wrist band around your arm. And if you got lost, they said if the kids got lost, they have security people with walkie-talkies around there. They have this, um, um, I forget . . . Most of the time I can't remember because I play so much. So I just forget."

"So, school, when does school start? August . . ."

"On the thirtieth."

"Tell me about school. What do you do at school?"

"Well, I work. And I'm in third grade. And my sister Barbara will be in preschool, and my little brother will be three. She's going to the [name of school], for, she got first prize."

"First prize? What do you mean?"

"It was her first time at the school."

"Oh. And is she excited about going there?"

"Yeah, yeah. She really wanted to ride the bus. And we play on the bus, it was, 'Do we play on the bus?' And it was, 'Yes! We get to go on the yellow bus!' . . . She was, like, 'Yeah! Yeah!' We were laughing."

"Uh huh. That's pretty funny. And what about your brother Christopher?"

"He goes to the fifth grade. It's his last day, um, last year of school there. But I have two years of school. Two more years."

Mary has been explaining to me that she and all of her siblings attend or have attended the same school. This school is a self-contained day school for deaf children, and for some classes the children are mainstreamed in a neighboring hearing school. I ask her to tell me more about the hearing school.

"That's a different school. It's far over."

"And it's both deaf and hearing? But the other school is all deaf?"

"It's mixed. It's mixed some. There's a little bit of hearing and hard of hearing, some, and some deaf . . . kindergarten or below kindergarten, they have a school for first, second, third, fourth, fifth grade, kindergarten, and on up."

"And do the deaf people tend to play together and the hearing people play or . . ."

"No. No, it's all mixed."

"It's mixed all the time. Oh, that's interesting. And do you prefer deaf or hearing?"

Rather than answering in terms of preferences, Mary says, "I have some friends who are hearing. And I teach them some signs."

Teaching hearing children to sign is apparently a strategy that Mary uses for building comfort and a sense of attachment in her social relationships with hearing children, and for enhancing communication with them. She appears to be proud of the number of friends she has made.

"And you like to help people communicate?"

"Yeah. We communicate. I have a lot of friends."

"And who are your friends?"

"Can I tell you my friends' names? . . . I've got a lot of friends . . . Should I tell you?"

"Well, it's up to you. Up to you."

"Some people live in another town . . . And some I don't know where they live and some I do. They live all over." She pauses and seems to have decided not to tell me their names. "There's lots."

"Hmm, what else do you want to tell me?"

"I don't know."

"Okay, suppose . . . Okay, we've got this camera going. Imagine that we are on a real TV show, tonight . . . and there was an audience of boys and girls, hearing people, hearing boys and girls. And you are on TV and they are all watching you. What would you want to tell them about?"

"I don't know. It wouldn't matter."

My attempt to set up a scenario where Mary could tell me what she would say to hearing children did not succeed. I could have redirected the question to clarify that it would be her chance to tell hearing children about herself, about being deaf, or about her family, but I give up too easily here and change the subject, moving on to explore another area of her lifeworld.

"What do you watch on TV?"

"At five, from five to five thirty, I watch the 'Power Rangers.' Do you know who the Power Rangers are?" I tell her that I do. Mary enjoys television superheroes just as some of the other children in the study do. She continues, "And from five thirty until seven, sometimes six thirty or seven, it's 'By the Bell.' "

"You like that?"

"Mmhmm."

I ask her if the show is closed captioned, and she responds, "Yeah. Sometimes they have captions and sometimes they don't. 'Cause the

TV man sometimes switches them off or on. Boy, I don't like that. I want them to just leave them on." Mary is eight years old and her response indicates that her reading skills are such that she benefits from closed captioning so much that it frustrates her when something is not captioned.

"Who's that? Who's the TV man?"

"You know. The man who works for the TV, closed captioning. It's off and on and off and on. And I get really tired of that. I tell them just leave it on. Just leave it on. I want everything captioned. But sometimes I can't have that."

I imagine that Mary envisions a lone male worker sitting at a desk somewhere who is responsible for determining which programs are captioned and which are not and switching the captions on and off as he sees fit. "I understand . . . Okay, let me see what else I want to ask about. Your school now has a mixture, but if you were the only deaf person . . ."

"No, I'm not. No, I'm not."

". . . what would you do? But suppose, just imagine *if* you were the only deaf person. If you could imagine that, just pretend. What would you do?"

"I'd make friends with the hearing people. I'd make friends."

"How would you do that?"

"Well, if I was bored, some hearing people might come over and ask me, 'Do you want to be my friend?' . . . No. I wouldn't have any problems. 'Cause I make friends real easily; it's real easy for me to do . . . Sometimes I'll have one special friend. Jenny, sometimes, and [Mary uses a name sign for someone I do not know] second. And sometimes we do different things . . . Sometimes people bother me. Like, I want to eat my lunch and they'll try to steal my lunch. What can I do?"

"Yeah, that's not nice."

"It's awful. She's a really bad girl that's in trouble sometimes . . . She's deaf. And then the first time at the mainstreamed class, you go into the class, A's class [A is apparently a name sign], class eight. So we go in second grade, and it's a hearing classroom, or . . . no, no, no, wait. Well, first grade, sometimes it's the mainstreamed school, sometimes you switch between different classes. There's mainstream classes and there's deaf classes and sometimes you switch . . . Yeah, now, last year, two years ago I did that. And now, last year, in second grade, I just went into mainstream classes. And now I don't know who the teacher is, I don't know what room or anything. I'm in a mainstream class, that's all I know . . . My sister knows. She knows who the teacher is, it's S [she uses a name sign for the teacher's first name] Ireland, rooms 11 and 12. Both of those rooms."

"And what do you think is the difference between a deaf class and a hearing class?"

"Well, you can go back and forth from one to the other for different hours. For different periods you can switch."

"And if you go into a deaf class and then you go into a hearing class . . ."

"Yeah, you just switch."

". . . do you feel different?"

"No. You just go into one or the other. They're both comfortable. 'Cause I have friends in both. I have a lot of friends."

"Sounds like your hearing friends really accept deaf students."

"Mmhmm. They want to learn sign. And so I say okay and I teach them . . . Yeah, sometimes I teach my friends. Or deaf friends. Then the deaf friends teach the hearing friends."

"Okay. Tell me about your teachers at school."

"Well, sometimes we play games. Sometimes we work and do math and stuff."

"And do the teachers sign?"

"Um, second grade was a hearing teacher. She knew a little bit of signs I taught her. First grade, yes, that teacher was for deaf kids and could sign. Deaf and hard of hearing."

"So second grade was a hearing teacher who didn't know any signs?"

"Just, I taught her some." Mary seems to take it upon herself to teach not only her hearing classmates, but also hearing teachers how to sign. At this point in Mary's development, she appears to take pride in her ability to teach her peers and teachers to sign.

"How did you understand her?"

"We had an interpreter."

"Oh, an interpreter. Was the interpreter good?"

"Mmhmm."

It appears that either Mary's first grade class was self-contained or the teacher who taught both hearing and deaf students that year could sign, but in the second grade the teacher she had for her integrated classes did not have sign language skills and a sign language interpreter was used.

"Okay. Can you tell me, were there any deaf students before in that class?" Mary shakes her head. "Oh, you were the first one? What was that like?"

"Well, sometimes we play games, and sometimes we don't . . . And we have a lot of work. A lot of work." Mary fingerspelled most of this sentence.

"Homework that you have to take home and do?"

"Yes. Every Monday."

"Every Monday you do homework? But not Tuesday, Wednesday, Thursday, and Friday?"

"Nope. Just on Monday. We have one homework on Monday. Sometimes we have two or three . . . And in second grade, my friend and I, we were the only two deaf people in a hearing class."

"So there were two of you."

"Uh huh."

"Well, that's interesting. And did you like having another deaf person in class with you?"

"I liked it." Mary appears to be comfortable with both deaf and hearing classmates.

"You don't have that anymore?"

"Well, I don't know. I don't know. Maybe I'll be the only one, but that's fine." This is summer vacation. School has not started yet, and Mary doesn't know if any of her classmates will be deaf.

I am intrigued by the simplicity and the enthusiasm that Mary expresses about her relationships with hearing peers. Mary stands out among the children in this study in regard to the positive feelings she communicates about her relationships with hearing children at school. Even though she subtly acknowledges communication barriers, which she attempts to overcome by teaching hearing peers to sign, at least she has discovered that doing so helps her deal with those barriers. Perhaps, though not consciously, she appreciates her sense of competence and mastery of her own language and culture, something that contributes to her uniqueness, a positive aspect of herself that she has to offer other children. Such a positive sense of oneself and one's abilities is an important achievement in childhood. I am reminded that some of the other children in this study also mentioned teaching hearing children and some teachers to sign. For some of them I worry that this is too big of a responsibility. I wonder if at some later time in these children's lives this coping strategy will translate into an unwanted burden. This is a responsibility that hearing children don't shoulder, except perhaps bilingual hearing children. Do bilingual hearing children also teach their language to their peers in play situations and to teachers? Do they engage in as much cultural and communication negotiation as these deaf children seem to be doing? This is a good subject to explore in further research.

I wonder if she can imagine that the brightness of her situation might not always be true for others. "When I was a little girl growing up, I went to a hearing school. And I didn't have any deaf friends there. And I was the only deaf person. And they didn't know any signing at all, and I didn't know how to sign either when I was growing up. I didn't know how. I didn't learn sign until I was nineteen."

"You didn't?"

"Can you imagine that?"

"Well, I don't know."

"Can you imagine? So it was real different for me when I was growing up. I think you're real lucky because you have a deaf family. What's the difference between a deaf family and a hearing family?"

"Oh, I don't know. My cousins and nieces and nephews and people like that, they have some friends and some families and friends. Really, my cousin is my good friend and we play together . . . One little girl who is three, I think, two or three, I don't know. She just loves me. That little girl just loves me. Every time I go over to her home she comes running up and gives me a big hug."

"That's really nice. So hearing people like you as well. It doesn't matter whether they're deaf or hearing."

"No, it doesn't matter."

"Now, suppose there's a hearing family and there's a deaf family. Are there going to be any differences?"

I believe Mary is responding here in terms of ability to develop friendships with hearing people. "No, you can still be friends. It doesn't make any difference, you can be friends."

"Now suppose there are hearing parents and the baby is born deaf. How would they feel?"

"Well, the baby was born deaf, and that would mean he would need to go to a deaf class and would sign. And then when the child grew up they'd teach him sign. So they would learn. They would know. It'd be real easy . . . Or sometimes if there's deaf parents and the kids are born hearing. Then what do they do? They have to learn speech. That's hard." Mary's response indicates that she envisions it would be easy for hearing parents to learn to sign and that things would be easy for the deaf child in a "deaf class." On the other hand, deaf parents might have hearing children and they would have to deal with speech, something she interprets as more difficult than learning sign.

"That's right. My little boy is one year old and he's hearing. Mmhmm. Imagine, I have a hearing baby. Can you imagine that?"

"What do you do?"

"Well, I teach him signs. Just like you teach your friends signs, I teach him signs. So that he'll sign for his mom."

"Or his dad . . . My mom and dad are divorced."

"Oh, I'm sorry to hear that."

"But every week, I take turns to go to my dad's or mom's."

"So you can visit both your mom and dad."

"Yeah. My dad moved." Mary tells me where her father moved and how far away it is.

"Is that hard for you, and the children in your family? Is it tough?"

She tells me, "Well, it is. But we can have vacations and we can go and visit."

"Do you know other boys and girls whose parents are divorced?"

"Oh yes. My friend Donna has a stepmother and stepfather. Her mother and her father were divorced and so she's got stepparents. Her father has a wife, and her mother has a, a husband. And so they're both remarried and so she has stepparents."

"So your friends know how you feel, right? Because they've been through something similar."

"And I wish my parents were still married, that they'd never divorced." She goes on to tell me her perception of why her parents got divorced. She seems to have a good understanding of what her parents disagreed about and what led up to their divorce. It is clear that her parents have spoken with her about what took place. I am impressed by the maturity of her perception. After talking about this for a bit we move on in our interview.

"Okay. If you were writing a book about deaf children, what would you write?"

"Um, I don't know. About friends."

"Could you tell me a story?"

"Fine." There's a long pause and then she asks, "Do you want me to write it down?"

"If you want."

Mary asks for a different kind of paper, which I don't have. She folds the paper she has, picks up a pen, and thinks for a moment before she begins to draw. She talks to herself as she is drawing, "Hope you get love."

I ask what she means and she responds, "Some kids are loved by their moms and dads. And most of us did . . . clean up our things. Clean the house, clean our rooms. Things like that."

"I'm sure you help your mom and dad a lot."

"Hmmm. Hmm."

Mary seems to run out of things to say, and we were running out of time. I ask her if there is anything else she wants to say before we finish for the night, and she says there isn't.

"So that's it. Okay. I think we're done. We're going to go out and get some ice cream and then I'll take you home."

Mary is eager to view her videotape, so we stop to watch it on the way out. She quietly watches the tape, and after about ten minutes says, "Let's go get ice cream."

On the way home, Mary shows me where her father lives. As promised, we stop for ice cream. She orders a double scoop of chocolate-chip cookie-dough flavored ice cream and politely tells me it is delicious. She finishes three quarters of her treat and is ready to go on home.

Mary invites me into her house to see her room when we get back, but I tell her that I need to pick up my little boy, and that if it is okay with her mother, then next time I would love to see her room. I tell her I will see her again in two weeks, and she said with a surprised smile, "Again in two weeks? With TV?" and I say yes. She says, "And then we can get ice cream again," so I agree. When we arrive at her house, I wait in the car as she goes to the door and her mother lets her in. We wave good-bye.

Once again, I pick Mary up at her home for our interview. Mary is in quite a different mood this evening. She seems more subdued than at our last meeting. She has just completed her first week back in school and may be tired. I think about asking about her mood, but I am afraid to make her concerned with any perceived expectations about her behavior and decide instead to ask her about school. She doesn't have much to say except that it is "fine" and "yes" she is happy to be back with all of her friends again.

This evening we have a different meeting room. It is not quite as comfortable as the room we had last week, but it is colorful. I tell Mary that this evening we will be doing something a little different, that I will show her pictures that I would like for her to tell me stories about.

"And I want you to look them over, take your time, and see what you think that picture is about. Who the people are, what they're doing, why they're doing whatever they're doing. Just create something for me, okay? This is picture number one." I ask her, "Who are those people?"

Although I am unaware of this during our session, the interpreter tells me afterward that Mary at times was apparently intentionally using an unnecessarily loud voice. She begins talking loudly here, "A mother and father and baby."

"Can you tell me what they're doing?"

"They're holding the baby. They're holding the baby."

"Holding the baby. And?"

"Hugging it."

"Hugging the baby. And then what?"

"Maybe they'll go to bed."

"Okay, the baby will go to bed. And? What else can you tell me about that picture?"

"There's the mother and father there." She shows them to me on the picture. "They love their son very much." As in our earlier interview, Mary speaks again of the love she imagines parents have for their children. This translates into the unconditional love she feels her parents have for her. This theme is repeated in the message that follows.

"What about that family? Do you think they're a deaf family?"

"No, they're hearing . . . They look like hearing people . . . They talk . . . Deaf people can't use speech." Mouth movement and the appearance of speech indicate to Mary that a person is hearing. Interestingly, Mary is using her voice as she tells me this. She frequently code switches when she discusses factors related to the overt and covert identities of the people she observes in the photographs. There are times when she signs without voicing, times when she signs and speaks simultaneously, and at other times, when she only vocalizes.

"Okay. I'm curious. You say deaf people have difficulty with speech, and it looks like they [the hearing people] are speaking. Right? Now suppose that the parents are hearing and the baby's deaf. How would the parents feel?"

"I don't know. Happy."

"Happy? And what about the baby? How would the baby feel?"

"Happy too." Like Alex, Mary's response to the question about the feelings hearing parents have toward their deaf children is very positive, contradicting much of the literature on this topic. Mary examines the next picture. She believes the mother in the picture is deaf and tells me in ASL, "The mother is telling the baby I LOVE YOU. And the baby boy, or something . . . I LOVE YOU to mother, like GOOD-BYE, I LOVE YOU. Saying I LOVE YOU to the mother. I LOVE YOU to the father, and to the whole family." Mary folds her arms as if she is holding a baby and voices something. I do not understand her and ask her to repeat. "Sometimes uncles or aunts or whoever."

I am curious about her perception of the toddlers. "One other question. Are both of those children deaf?"

"It looks like . . . Well, I don't know. This one [she points to the mother] looks like deaf. Looks like deaf, right there. I know who this one looks like. Looks like my neighbor, my friend, the girl. She's signing. She knows how to say I LOVE YOU . . . Yeah, so it looks like she's deaf."

I ask Mary how deaf and hearing families are different and she responds, "They'd be different because the deaf family can sign and the hearing people don't. So that makes a difference."

Mary looks at the next picture, a photograph of a deaf man with whom I am acquainted. He is working in his office. When I ask her what is happening in the picture, she says it is a picture of a hearing boy drawing something, "Because he looks like he's talking. No more difference."

"So he looks like he can talk. Suppose . . . he's deaf . . . tell me a story about that man . . . what do you imagine he might do? Does he have family?"

"Yep."

"So tell me about his family."

Here Mary voices without signing, "I don't know . . . I don't know if he's divorced . . . Might be divorced like my mother and father. I don't know . . . I think he probably has children but I think his children are hearing . . . Some hearing people have deaf children. And some deaf people have hearing children. But it's different."

"What kinds of things do deaf men do in their lives?"

"Some deaf people are in TV and they do sign language. They sign. And some sign for blind people . . . They do things for blind people and different things . . . Because they don't know what people are saying, when somebody's making a speech. And the blind person, the deaf-blind person holds their hand and so they can feel the signing." Mary is discussing hand-on-hand signing, or tactile sign language, which is used by deaf-blind individuals. She knows that deaf adults can work as interpreters for deaf-blind people.

"Now, when you grow up, what kind of work do you think you'll do?"

"I don't know . . . Maybe a, a helper."

"A helper?"

"Or a school bus driver or a schoolteacher or help people make their lives in the hospital where babies are born. I might work there."

"That's wonderful. Those are wonderful things to become. So deaf people can do those kinds of jobs? . . . Do you know deaf people who work helping people?"

"I don't know."

"Okay. Um, does your school have any deaf teachers?"

"Some of the hearing teachers know sign language . . . Yeah. Two. Two deaf teachers."

"Where?" Mary signed a couple of name signs that I was not familiar with. "Could you spell those names for me?" Mary repeats the name signs several times while voicing, but since I am unfamiliar with her school personnel I was not able to determine the names from the name signs alone and, of course, cannot hear what she is vocalizing. She says she doesn't know how to spell their names, but she tries, "Amann. Do you know who that is?"

"At your school?"

"No . . ." She spells out the name of the hearing school where the deaf kids are mainstreamed.

Thinking she is telling me that this hearing school has deaf teachers I am surprised.

"They're deaf? I didn't know that school had . . ."

She corrects me. "They're hearing in my school . . . I know some deaf teachers. I know them for speech." Then it becomes clear to me that when Mary uses the term "deaf teachers," she means teachers of deaf children who are not themselves deaf.

"Okay, you mean hearing but they teach deaf children." There are no teachers or professionals working at Mary's school who are deaf. Mary is fortunate to have adult roles models who are deaf in her own family and her parents' informal network of friends. This network contributes to Mary's sense of self, her self-concept, her identity, and her visions of her future.

She looks at the next picture and sees the board game called "Sorry" and says, "Oh, my cousin has the same thing here. The 'Sorry' game . . . And I know how to do that . . . Well, first, you start right here. Where it says 'start.' And you have four pieces that you put right there. And you take turns moving them out, depending on how many numbers. You need to have a one or a two. And then you can move them out. And if you don't have a one or a two, then you have to wait. And other people have their turns. And whoever gets a two, then they get to move out two spaces from the start. Then you'd be on the corner, and then other people can go. And then when your turn comes back around, if you get another number two you can go along like this. And then you get another number and you keep going on the board. All around until you get to this area right here. And that's home."

"So you really know how to play the game well." I point to the children in the picture and ask, "Who are those two children?"

"One boy and one girl." I ask her what the girl is doing and she says, "Talking on the phone to a friend. And the boy is bored." Mary imitates the boy's stance. "Because he's waiting for the girl to play . . . She's hearing . . . because she's using speech on the phone. You can see that." From this we know that Mary, like the other children in this study, would be bored in a situation such as this where she is left out of a conversation.

We move on to the next picture, and after examining it she tells me, "There's a woman and some children. And they're going around in a circle. Holding hands going round and round. And there's one boy standing in the middle of them all. And he's looking around at the circle, and kids are turning around and round and round." She holds up the picture to look more closely. "They're playing a game . . . mmm. I don't know. They're not signing . . ." Mary makes faces and shrugs. "I don't see . . ."

She seems indecisive about whether or not the children in the picture are deaf or hearing and I ask, "If they were deaf, what would they be doing?"

"Something different. Different things than hearing."

I point to the manual alphabet on the wall of the classroom in the picture and she says, "It's deaf spelling . . . Or maybe they're doing speech. Maybe they're just learning the ABC's." Here she vocally recites the alphabet. Learning and practicing speech is a part of Mary's routine.

"They're learning that in speech?"

"Or A, B . . ." She again recites the alphabet, stopping at J.

"So now do you think they're deaf or hearing?"

Mary shrugs, "I have some doubts. I'm not sure."

Moving on to the next picture, she says, "Number six. They're deaf. They look like they're deaf . . . This boy looks like he's blind. This one, they're deaf, and they're signing."

Mary holds up the picture and points, but I don't understand what she is indicating. She moves the picture in front of her face, hiding behind the picture. I am unaware that she is voicing but see that she is getting playful. Confusion begins to develop in our interview as I don't realize that she is vocalizing when hiding her face behind the pictures. She seems to be testing me. I'm not sure what her day was like today or what might be on her mind. Is she tired? Is she growing restless? Or is she enjoying knowing that she has me confused? Is she trying to figure out if I am really deaf? Can she hear her voice echoing in the room?

Unsure about her response, I ask, "What? This? Is there a sign? Their face? What is the face doing?"

She continues to hold the picture in front of her face and signs, "Talking . . . with signing."

"Talking and signing, both?"

She moves the picture away from her face, "They're using speech. Like 'How are you?' with their speech. Like people hear when they're discussing." Mary indicates that this child is deaf. "Deaf . . . because her grandmother is deaf maybe. I don't know. Looks older." This is a picture of a young person sitting opposite an adult who is signing. Mary's unique response here illustrates her sense of herself within a multigenerational Deaf family system. Being the only child in this study from a multigenerational Deaf family, she is the only one who shares an identification with an unknown child in a photograph based on the imaginary deaf grandmother she assigns to the child. At the same time, her bilingual identity is manifested through her indication that the deaf people in this photograph sign and talk.

When we go to the next picture, Mary indicates that the characters are deaf. "There's a man and a woman and . . ." She holds out the picture in front of her face and signs "Playing with their son . . ." and then vocalizes, "because they're signing."

"Ah, because they're signing. Okay. And they're both signing?"

She leans forward and looks at the picture again and signs, "This one's talking, and this one's not . . . You have to wait until one finishes talking, then that one can have a turn. You have to take turns when you're talking."

Mary's playfulness has made it hard for us to communicate. The difference in Mary's mood this evening is becoming more and more evident. Sometimes she hides her signs completely behind the pictures, making it difficult and at times impossible for me to understand her. I am not aware of how many times she voiced (without signing) behind the pictures.[14] This experience shows the

---

14. These passages may be confusing to the reader because they include the interpreter's voicing of what was not evident to me when Mary was not signing and had her face hidden behind the photographs.

importance of having an interpreter present even in sessions between a deaf researcher and deaf informants who share the same
language.

Mary holds the paper up and makes noises, and then she voices
and fingerspells "Boo."

"You're teasing?"

"I'm playing." Again, she vocalizes "Boo" behind the picture.

"Are you ready for number eight?"

Mary sets the previous picture aside and looks at the new one.
Leaving the picture on the table in front of us, she signs, "Sign Language American. Know why I know these are deaf? Because right
here." She points to a hearing aid.

"There's a hearing aid. Uh huh. That's how you know?"

"Yes. Yes. They're using sign language. They're using sign language . . . Both are deaf . . ."

Mary indicates that the woman in the next picture is deaf and is
using a TTY. "Maybe talking to her family." Once again Mary repeats "Boo" behind the picture, but I am unaware of this. She imitates talking on the phone like a hearing person. She continues
her imitation with the picture held up in front of face. She giggles.
Putting the picture down, she tells me she has a TTY at home.
"It's hard. It's a lot of work . . . It's about this big. My grandmother
has one of those big old funny ones she types on." Approximately
the size of a three-drawer file cabinet, some of the original West-
ern Union teletypewriters still used in a few homes today are
large, noisy machines that are difficult to type on. Newer ten-by-
thirteen-inch portable TTYs fit in the corner of a desk next to a
phone and are much more user-friendly than the older "clunky"
models.

Mary imitates typing, then hurts her nail.

"Do you call your grandma?"

"Sometimes."

Looking at the next picture, she offers, "It looks like . . . hearing."
She hides behind the picture again.

"What's the difference between them and you? They're hearing?
What's the difference?"

"Um, I don't know. They just look like they're hearing." She
holds the picture in front of her face and signs in front of it, "They
talk, talk, talk. Smile. Pretty class. Ha, ha, ha, ha, ha. Boo."

"You said they look like they're hearing because they're talking and they're smiling and they're pretty?"

"Yes." Mary continues to sign in front of the picture, "And big, big, big smile. There's the nose and eyes." She lowers the picture. "And . . ." she draws a smile on the table with her finger, "a big smile."

Mary holds another paper up in front of her again. This time I realize she is saying something behind the paper and I ask her to repeat.

"What? The interpreter and I can't see you if you sign behind that paper."

Mary puts the picture down but continues her teasing for a bit. We are not making much progress until she identifies a child she says is hard of hearing. This is something none of the children have talked about yet. She mostly voices, "A mother and a baby. The boy smiles. Hard of hearing."

"Hard of hearing. How do you know he's hard of hearing?"

Voicing, Mary says, "The mother's using speech."

Without her signing, I don't understand her the first time, "The little boy?" She doesn't answer. "The mother?" She shakes her head no. "No, so you think the little boy's hard of hearing?"

"Yes."

"Why do you think he's hard of hearing?"

Mary doesn't answer. She's making singsong noises behind the picture.

"Hard of hearing children and deaf, do they look different?"

"A little bit . . . They look, it makes a difference." She still has her face and part of her hands behind the picture.

"But I'm really, really curious now. Because we started talking about hard of hearing people. And I'm really curious about if you see a deaf person and a hard of hearing person and a hearing person. And the hearing person and the deaf person look different. Maybe the hearing person doesn't sign. Maybe the deaf person can sign. Maybe the hearing person talks, and the deaf person might not talk. But what about a hard of hearing person? How do you know that person's hard of hearing? How do you know?"

"Because they look like this . . . Because they talk. That means they're in an all hearing family . . . Maybe they're talking, or not clear signing . . . They wouldn't sign."

Before leaving, Mary asks to see her videotape. She points at the television. "Can we see my video?" We stay for a few minutes and watch part of her tape. Following this we pack up and start our drive back to her house. We stop for ice cream again on the way home, but this time at a different market. When we arrive at her house, her mother and siblings are not home yet from her sister's softball game, so we wait in the car in front of their house. To make the time pass, we take turns telling stories like *The Three Bears*, *The Three Little Pigs*, and *The Little Engine That Could*. After this, we play an alphabet game. We have reached the letter G when her family returns home. I walk Mary to the door and speak with her mother. I thank Mary and her mom for their participation and tell Mary I hope to see her again and that I am sure we will meet again at Deaf community events.

෫ඨ

     I PERCEIVE Mary to be the most bilingual, bicultural child in this study. Unlike the other children, she provides indications that represent dual perspectives of the identities of characters in the pictures. While they sign, they also talk and/or wear hearing aids. She also easily negotiates her communication and her "fit" in relationships among both deaf and hearing people.

Mary is an intelligent child who demonstrates mature language skills. She is bilingual and bicultural. She is a member of a Deaf family with a long history of ASL and Deaf cultural heritage. At the same time, Mary demonstrates a mastery of spoken and written English, and she reflects positively on her experiences with hearing peers in a hearing school and upon her relationships with hearing "others."

The quality and details in the information that Mary shares about her family show that she has benefited from the rich early language experience she enjoys at home, and she relates that she experiences a strong sense of positive regard from her parents and her family. Even though her parents are going through a divorce, Mary demonstrates warmth and happiness at home. She appears to have a good understanding of why the divorce occurred and doesn't show evidence of the self-blame or fears of abandonment that many children of divorced parents experience. She acknowledges her sadness about the divorce and her wish that things could be different, but at the same time, she talks about continuing positive involvement with both of her parents. I attribute her perspective to the family's ability to communicate and the strong language foundation that has been established at home.

Mary demonstrates a strong positive sense of herself both at home and in her relationships with deaf and hearing peers at school. She reports that she makes friends very easily with both deaf and hearing children. Once again, as is true for the majority of these children, Mary's responses to my interview questions seem to be saying, "Being deaf is really no big deal." From Mary's perspective, everything seems fine—with her, with her family, her school, and her home life. Given a hypothetical situation where Mary has to imagine that she is the only deaf child in her school, she says, "I'd just make friends with hearing students and teach them how to sign." It is clear that she experiences a high level of comfort with her lifeworld.

Although she considers herself to be Deaf, she sees hearing and hard of hearing people as different from her because they "talk" and either do not sign or do not sign clearly. It is interesting to note that while Mary points out this difference, she is frequently vocalizing; at times she vocalized without signs in our interview. Her point, perhaps, is not that she *can* talk, but that she is also adept at ASL, her first language, and that her family is Deaf. On the other hand, Mary also refers to a hearing teacher who signs and teaches deaf students as a "deaf teacher." Perhaps this indicates that Mary has two meanings for the term *deaf*; deaf in the sense of being culturally Deaf and, secondly, deaf in the sense of working with people who are deaf, such as teaching deaf students. This definition would place the teacher in the context of a community of people who are either deaf or who are involved in the community in some way. Alex's description of hearing family members who sign as deaf is similar to Mary's description of this "deaf" teacher. These individuals are *domesticated others*, people whom the deaf child is comfortable with and experiences a sense of attachment to because they share something similar, or because they are similar in some sense, regardless of their hearing status.

Self-direction and self-determination are evident with the children in this study when they are confronted with communication challenges. Mary takes it upon herself to teach hearing children and teachers how to sign. She has a sense of optimism about her future, and she is aware of resources available to her. She knows where other deaf children and adults live and even recognizes differences among deaf, hearing, and hard of hearing people.

10

Pat

TEN-YEAR-OLD Pat attends a residential school. He was born profoundly deaf and the cause of his deafness is unknown. His brothers and parents are hearing. Although it doesn't appear evident in Pat's interview, his parents report he has attention deficit hyperactivity disorder. Pat uses ASL, and his hearing family members are learning to sign. His parents report they make an effort to sign with him at home.

୧ୡ

IN MY first session with Pat, I share with him that I am in college and almost all done, but that my teachers have given me homework and that my homework is to write a book. I tell him that I am writing about deaf children and would like his help with it. I tell him I think it is really important because a lot of people have written books about deaf children, but most of the time the children didn't get to help by sharing their ideas and that his input is what will make this book special.

Pat is eager to get started. Before I can finish explaining the purpose of our meetings, he looks eagerly at the stack of paper on the table and says, "What's this paper for?"

"There's a lot of paper, yes. That's for you to draw something for me, okay? But I want to make sure you want to help me."

"Yup."

"Is it okay if we use the videotape?" Pat nods. "Is that all right with you? . . . Then later, I can watch the TV and we'll be on there. And I can remember what we talked about. That'll help me write my book."

"Okay, fine."

"Okay. There's one more thing . . . If later on you decide to change your mind, you don't want to help me, that's fine. Just let me know, okay?" Pat nods. "Okay. All right, now I have some questions for you. First, I'd like you to draw me a picture of a deaf child or a deaf boy, okay? Can you draw that for me?"

Pat turns to the interpreter, whom he knows from school, and says, "Oh, and tell her I'm a good drawer, all right?" He then points at something on the back of the pencil box. "Wow. Should I draw the same as this?"

"Well, I'd like you to draw a deaf boy."

"Like me?"

"Yes. Yeah, a boy like you."

Pat looks in the box while I take out the pencils and lay them out on the table for him to choose from. "Where's black? Where's black?" He finds his crayon of choice and begins to draw.

"Good?"

"Good."

He chooses another color and continues. Seeing that he is taking a lot of pride in his work and looks to me occasionally with a proud grin on the freckled face below his long red bangs, I continue to give him positive feedback as he draws. "That's good . . . you're a good artist . . ."

"I did the ears wrong."

"Oh, that's fine. What's wrong with them?"

"They're too big. It'd be better if they were smaller."

"Oh, you wish they were smaller?"

"Can I do a different one? Hmmm." He continues drawing and then decides to change colors. "Nope." When he finishes he has a very nice clear drawing of a boy's face that demonstrates his artistic talents.

"That's very good. Can you tell me a story about that boy?"

"Well, he's deaf. He's deaf."

"Okay. And . . ."

"Wait a minute. Deaf." As if he suddenly remembers something, he begins to draw more, indicating in the picture the sign for "deaf" on the boy's face. "Deaf. Deaf."

"That's great. Wow. That's great. You're right, you are a good artist. Can you tell me more, some kind of story about that boy?"

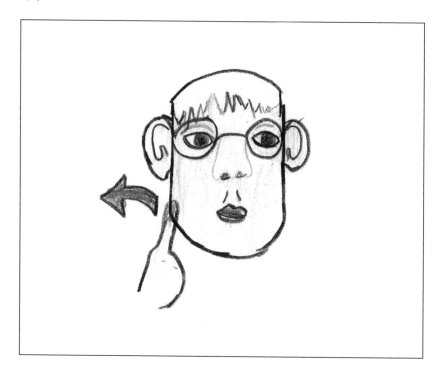

"Well, hearing are different from deaf . . ." He asks if I want him to draw the clothes and begins drawing more. "I'm going to put learn, deaf, and you know, signing and fingerspelling, you know? Signing and fingerspelling? . . . He's deaf, so he . . . Well, it's kind of hard, kind of hard." Pat pauses and I am unsure what he is struggling with and then wonder if he wants to draw the sign for "learn" in his picture but has decided it is too hard. He seems to associate being deaf with signing since he wants to include signs in this picture of a deaf boy. As stated earlier, with children we can assume their drawings of deaf children reflect their own self-reflections. Thus, this may be a self-portrait of Pat.

"Well, can you tell me a story about his family?"

"Family." Pat picks up a pencil. "Ummm, family. Here in [name of state], deaf, deaf." He draws more.

"That's great. Okay. How old is that boy?"

"Umm, is he my age? . . . Eleven. I guess eleven."

"And that's how old you are?"

"I'm ten. I'm ten."

"Okay, you're ten and he's eleven?"

"Oh, oh. I forgot glasses, I forgot glasses." He begins to draw glasses on the boy's face.

"Okay, great. So does that boy have a family? Does he have a family?"

"My family. My family."

"Who's in his family?"

"Well, there's the class and the teacher . . ." He names a deaf teacher at his school, "part of my family. And Steven, and me and umm, umm, I dunno."

Pat seems to be referring to his class at school as a family. I am confused here and try to clarify just what he means. "Your class or your family?"

"My, my, in my family, in my family . . ."

"Who's that?"

"And my family. They're different. My family for my class. There's two different ones. There's my class family, but not [he names a teacher from a different class], 'cause she's in a different class." Pat's reference to his class as a family implies the level of comfort and closeness that he feels with them. Accepting that, I want to learn more about how he perceives his own family. We have trouble moving away from his analogy of his class as a family but eventually succeed in doing so. It is possible that Pat's reference to his class as a family indicates a lack of understanding regarding the concept of family, but I am inclined to believe that this is more of an example of the sense of attachment he feels in relationships with domesticated others.

"Okay, can you tell me a story about your family?"

"Family?"

"Yes, family. Who's in your family?"

"My class?"

"Your family."

"Family, oh, there's . . ." He names a dorm at his school. "The house and the bed and lots of friends and fun in that dorm."

I ask, "How many people are in your family?"

"I dunno."

"Mom and Dad and . . . Do you have a mother and father and sister and brother?"

"My mom and dad, my brothers, my family."

"Okay, Mom and Dad and one brother? No sisters?"

"No, no. Just boys. Well, there's a boy, and me, and a boy, and then Mom and Dad. And my dog."

"Okay. So how old is the youngest boy?"

"Umm, five."

"Five. And you're ten?"

"Uh huh."

"And Mom and Dad, they're hearing?"

Pat nods. "And they . . ."

"And then you're deaf."

"Well, no, well, my brothers are hearing. My brothers are hearing." I have been using my fingers to indicate family members. Pat reaches across the table to point at individual fingers. "That's my brother. That, that person represents my brother. That's my mom and dad; they're hearing. And then a brother who's hearing. And I'm deaf. All, and they're all hearing. And they talk." Pat imitates a person talking. "And my dog, too." Pat didn't hesitate to tell me that his hearing family members talk. As with the other children, talking appears to be a significant characteristic of hearing people, part of the way the deaf children in this study determine who is hearing and who is deaf.

"Can you tell me a story about your dog?"

"My dog, he listens and he hears things. And he knows, when he hears a sound he goes running over and looks. And we know that he's heard something. And barks." Here Pat imitates a dog barking. "And then we go and see what's going on." Pat has a hearing dog at home just as I do and I tell him so.

"I have a dog at home, too. And my dog listens for me. Do you enjoy playing with your dog?"

Pat has been drawing. He picks up his picture and moves it toward me. "Done . . . Um, we have one week of school. One more week."

"Next week, yeah. You're almost done. During the summer what will you do?"

Pat picks up his drawings in front of him. "Um, um, um," he points at a drawing. "There's a horse. Um, you know, what do horses say? They make a noise. Horses, horses, what noise do they make? They, they do something with their lips."

"Oh, yeah, okay. Well, I don't know. I've never heard what kind of sound a horse makes."

"They put their lips together like this." Pat imitates a horse neighing.

"Can you hear them?"

"Um, I, uh, with a hearing aid. I have a hearing aid I might hear something."

I don't see that Pat is wearing a hearing aid, so I ask, "But you don't use it here?"

"No, no. Ummm . . ." He returns to his animal stories, ". . . and rooster, they make a noise, roosters make a noise." He imitates a rooster crowing. "They crow, and they make a noise that people can hear."

Because of Pat's interest in animals, I wonder if he lives on a farm. "Do you live on a farm? Do you have a farm at your house?"

"Nope. No, but my friend."

"Oh, I see. A friend's house. Where's your home?"

"My, um, I live at home in a house."

"What town?"

"It's, um, um, it's, um . . ." Pat spells out the name of his town letter by letter.

"Is that far?"

He tells me his address and his phone number. "It's 2276. And my phone number is 555- um, 679-7777. That's it."

"Oh, you've got it memorized. That's good. That's important. Okay." Pointing to Pat's drawing of himself I ask, "How did this boy become deaf?"

In response to my question, Pat tells me more about being deaf, but not how he became deaf. "Um, it's different from hearing. He has to practice speech, he has to practice talking, so he can communicate. He has to practice, and he has to practice talking." This response is similar to a comment that Angie made about needing to practice speech. Lisa and Mary also mentioned having speech lessons. Pat's response seems to indicate that a major difference between deaf and hearing people is that when you are deaf, you have to practice your speech.

"Uh huh . . . ?"

"He's in [name of state]. He's here in [name of state]. People all over the state. There are lots of adults and some of them are hearing and some are hard of hearing."

"Uh huh. There are."

"And I might be hard of hearing."

"Are you hard of hearing?"

Pat looks at Marilyn, who is voice interpreting into the camera microphone. "Am I hard of hearing, Marilyn?" But Marilyn, staying in her role, doesn't reply.

I step in. "She doesn't know. Okay. Were you born deaf or later become deaf?"

"A long time ago. A long time ago."

"When you were a baby?" Pat nods. "Uh huh? You were deaf?"

"Uh huh. And then I grew up." Earlier, the drawing of a deaf boy that Pat completed indicated a strong sense of identification as a deaf person. He has told us already that deaf and hearing people are different from each other. Now, however, it appears that he is not quite sure if he is deaf or hard of hearing. Most people who are profoundly deaf have some residual hearing. I don't have information on how much Pat actually hears or if he benefits from hearing aids, which as he indicated, might help him hear a horse's neigh. I wonder if he thinks that because he hears some sounds, that he might be hard of hearing. His question, "Am I hard of hearing?" indicates that while he knows the differences between hearing and deaf people (hearing people talk; deaf people sign and have to practice talking), he is not quite sure what it means to be hard of hearing.

For reasons unknown to Pat and his family, Pat was born profoundly deaf. Like Angie, another child whose history is unknown, Pat can only speculate as to why he is deaf and the rest of his family is not. I ask him, "And do you know why you're deaf?"

"I don't know. Maybe I forgot how to talk or something. Maybe, I dunno. Or, um, I don't like milk. I don't like milk at all. I can't drink milk. And orange juice is my favorite. And pop. I like pop. I like to drink pop. Both of those . . . I'll drink orange pop. Orange, that's my favorite. But, it's different, it's different." It seems that since Pat was born deaf he is associating my question with things about his babyhood. I was curious how he learned these things about his early childhood.

"Uh huh. And how do you know that?"

"A long time ago I saw it. I saw it. I looked up. My mom, my mom, I had my eyes barely open. And I was sleeping. When I was a baby. And my mom was there."

"Okay. Do you know how you happened to be born deaf?"

"I don't know. I don't know. But now I know."

I show him his drawing of himself and ask, "And when this boy grows up, when he gets to be a man, an adult . . ."

Suddenly Pat interrupts enthusiastically and begins writing. "Wait a minute, wait a minute." He is now writing with his right hand and signing with his left. "Ten, and you wait and you wait and you wait, and now I'm eleven, and you wait and you wait and you wait and wait, and then you wait and wait and wait some more until you're thirteen, and you wait and you wait some more, and you wait and you wait some more, and you wait and you wait some more, sixteen, and you wait and wait and wait, then you wait and wait and wait and wait. And you wait and wait. My . . ." He is writing. "You're very big, and . . ." He writes "twenty," then says "When you're twenty years old."

"What will that deaf man do when he's twenty?"

"You have to wait a long time and get very big. But you have to wait and you have to be patient. Eleven, and you wait and you wait and wait and you're eleven for a long time. And then you're twenty, twenty-two, twenty-one, twenty-nine, no wait, um twenty-nine." Pat holds up his picture in front of the camera. "Okay, that's enough."

"Okay, good. Now, this deaf boy, when he's twenty, what kind of job will he have? Will he work?"

"Um, he'll work at a house. And he'll work and work and work and work, and some of it'll be hard, and he'll know lots and lots of stuff . . . Lots of different things. Lots of things. You know, like all over."

"Like what?"

"Oh, different things. There are many different things, all over. And many places to live. Here's, like, like, here, okay?" He begins to draw again. "Where's green? This is Disneyland." Pat is drawing a map. "Okay, this is our state. And that's where Mickey Mouse is." He continues to draw. "Now, this is, it's different. It's got to be different 'cause it's the water. It's the water and there's a lot." I had asked Pat to tell me what the deaf boy in the picture would be doing when he was an adult. His storyline began with his chronological movement through the passing years, arriving at adult vocations and ending with a trip to Disneyland. Is he telling me that deaf people can travel all over and work any kind of job? Or is he just stopping for a break at Disneyland on the way to adulthood, which would actually prove to be true to his own experience since he did go to Disneyland with his family?

"That's good. Do you want to show that one to the camera?"

But Pat is still busy drawing, "Wait, wait, wait. Gotta wait. Now wait." He is still drawing.

"Have you been to Disneyland?"

"Yeah. I have." He is busy completing his drawing.

"When? When did you go?"

"It was fun. It was so much fun."

"Was it recent?"

"It was, we had to go for about an hour."

"Did you drive?"

"Uh, let's see, right, left, east, north, south, um." Pat continues to write and sign. "Uh, east, west, east, east, and north. And, wait . . . that's it. In bed, you know, the pirates . . . Pow. Wait." He points to pictures on the papers he has drawn. "And that and that . . ."

"What is that?"

"That's, you know, it's the pirates and they've got the money hidden . . . And all the pirates, well, they were a long time ago . . . And they died and they were buried. It's sad." Pat continues to draw and makes comments while he is drawing. "And they . . . wait . . . that . . . that . . . okay . . . I'm just making this up. I'm just making this up, right? Okay, you go south, like that." He taps his pencil on the paper as he indicates the places he is talking about. "I'm just making it up, okay? It's not real. And you fly there, and then you go over here. You fly. This is the same. And then you take a boat. And you go like this, real far, real far. And finally . . . and then you find it and you go back and do that part, then you do that part, and then you're back home. It's fun to play. That's it."

"That's good. That's really good." Pat gives me the paper. "Okay, thank you. Do you want to show the camera?" He agrees, so I hold his drawings up in front of the video camera. "Thank you. Now, this deaf boy, when he becomes an adult, when he becomes a man, will he work?"

"His favorite thing is to be a policeman."

"A policeman?"

"That's my favorite thing. Or a fireman, a policeman, uh, ride in a helicopter, umm. Fox, that's another one of my favorites. And Mickey Mouse. Those are my favorites." Pat knows there are many vocational possibilities for deaf adults, but he has some favorite images of himself in the future.

"Wonderful. This man, will he get married? This boy, will he get married?"

"He got married, yeah."

"He's married?"

"No, not really, no . . ."

"Okay, if this boy got married, will he have children?"

"Um, he's got to wait 'til he gets big . . . Um, when he gets big, real big, real big. And days and days and days and days and days and days and days. Many, many days. And, one, two, three, four, um, lots and lots. And then he's gonna be a policeman. 'Cause that's my favorite."

"Okay. I was wondering if someday he has children, will they be deaf or hearing? Will they be deaf or hearing? What do you think?"

"Um, deaf. Or hearing. Lots of people. There are lots of people and they're all different."

"Yes, they're all different. Okay. I had something else I wanted to ask you. That deaf boy is ten now, right? And does he have friends?"

"Mmmhmm."

"Deaf friends or hearing friends?"

"Deaf friends . . . and hard of hearing, and some, I don't know."

"Can you tell me a story about his friends?"

"Nope. Nope, no stories."

"Or how they play?"

"No, I'm done. He just has friends, that's it."

"Does this deaf boy play with hearing children sometimes?"

"Uh huh. Yeah, he might go to a different place, a different class. 'Cause he gets tired of working; there's too much work. And . . . he gets tired of working. And then he goes to bed. Monday, Tuesday,

Wednesday, Thursday . . . Monday, Tuesday, Wednesday, Thursday, Friday, and he sleeps. And then he goes home on Friday and Saturday and Sunday and has fun. That's what he likes." Metaphorically, Pat may be telling me that he is tired and wants to stop.

"He likes to go home?"

"Yeah. That's my favorite thing."

"Your favorite place is home rather than here?"

"Yeah. Yeah, now it's Friday. And there's only one week, it's the last week, only one more week of school. And then I go home. And I can, I can swim, go in the water and stuff . . . it's fun. I play and play and play around and it's fun."

"Uh huh. I see."

"Um, on Monday . . . Now, next week, got Monday, and then next week. And I just have to wait that long and then school's finished." Pat stands up, ready to leave. "I want to go to computer now. I want to go to computer. I want to leave."

"Yeah. Three months off, too. Okay, all right, we're done. And I'll see you again on Monday, okay? And then I'll have some different things for you to do, okay? And . . ."

Pat is anxious to get back to his class activities. He looks at the camera and waves "Bye." He starts to leave then he turns around and says, "Wait a minute, wait a minute." Pat looks through the camera lens and sees me. He puts his hand in front of the lens and signs, "Pat is leaving. Bye-bye. Okay?"

"Bye, see you Monday."

THE FOLLOWING week, I return to Pat's school to meet with him for the second time. It is a warm, inviting spring day, the kind of day that makes school children prefer to be expending their energy in the great outdoors. He enters the room full of bounce and vivacity. I greet him with a smile, "Hello, how are you?"

"Fine!" He sits at the table in the same spot where he sat last week.

"Can you tell me what you've been doing since last week?"

"Umm, I'm here again. Umm, I want it to be short so I can go to art."

"Oh, your art class is now, hmm?"

"So I want to go there."

"Yeah, you really enjoy art."

"Yep. I like art."

"You like that class. What do you do in art?"

He tells me the name of his art teacher. Wanting to get started with his drawings here in his meeting with me, he reaches for my folder, not knowing that I have a different plan for him this week.

"This is different than last week. You won't be drawing, but I have some pictures, and I want you to look at the picture and tell me a story."

"That's boring. That's boring." Nonetheless, Pat looks to see what is in the picture, and he starts to share his perception of the picture with me, "The baby's crying, and the dad's giving him something . . . The baby's crying 'cause he wants his mom."

"Baby's crying because he wants Mom? Why does he prefer Mom?"

"He's crying and the dad will give him to Mom and then the baby will feel better."

"Is the baby hungry?" He nods. "Okay. Who are those people? Who are the mother and father and baby?"

"There's, they're hearing maybe."

"Are they all hearing?"

"Oh, I don't know. Deaf or hearing. Either way. It doesn't matter. They might be deaf or hearing or hard of hearing."

"Okay. If the baby's deaf, if the baby's deaf and the parents are hearing . . ."

In keeping with his intention to keep this session short, Pat moves quickly through the pictures. He pulls out a picture of a man at work and he says, "Oh, they're drawing. The man is drawing. He's drawing, he's really good at it. And there's a lot of work, drawing funny things and Mickey Mouse or a bunch of different things . . . And he's a very good artist. And the next picture." With the deaf man in this picture sitting at a drawing table, I can imagine that the children would be reminded of Walt Disney, and this is where I think he is getting the image of Mickey Mouse. Pat seems willing to cooperate but eager to get though our interview today and get back to class.

"Okay, number three."

"I have, a boy who's talking on the phone and a girl who's bored who's sitting there. She's bored. She's kind of complaining about it. And the other person's talking on the phone and the gal's just sitting there like, oh, nothing to do. And they're friends and they want to have fun." Pat is the last of the interviewees and, again, his interpretation of the deaf child's mood in this picture is boredom.

"Are they hearing or deaf?"

"Deaf and hearing . . . This one's hearing; this one's deaf. Or I don't know, that one could be deaf or hearing. I don't know." Pat quickly moves on to the next picture. "And for this one, this sign, it's I LOVE YOU. It's the sign I LOVE YOU. . . . They're telling a story from a book. And they're telling a story and it's got the sign I LOVE YOU. And that's the sign I LOVE YOU . . . Maybe the mother wanted to say 'I love you' or . . ."

"Is that the mother?"

"Oh, it's just different people. That's a schoolteacher. But there are other people."

"Okay. Okay, fine. And number five. What's that?"

"Umm, hearing or deaf, explain about their home and where they live, if it's a farm or whatever. Lots of different possibilities. I dunno, they might have cows or horses or different things . . . They're deaf."

"Both deaf?"

"Yeah."

"How do you know?"

"They're learning. They're learning. They, they memorize things. And they're just looking at each other and one's teaching and, um . . . And they're really pained because they're thinking and thinking and thinking and thinking. And they're doing a lot of hard work. And they're, like, wow, my head hurts from all this."

"So they get a headache from thinking a lot 'cause it's a lot of work?"

"Yep."

Pat picks up the next picture, looks at the back of it, and indicates something. He then turns it over and indicates a typing movement, "Ah. It's typing on the phone. Putting the phone on the TTY. And that's for deaf people to have phones. So they can type and have the letters go across. And they type and type. And that's it."

I ask him whom they might be calling and he tells me, "Uh, calling a car. They're calling for a car." Pat moves on to the next picture. "And this is a girl. And that's the father, the teacher. And they're playing. And learning. And smiling. And they look at each other, and it's real comfortable and real fun."

"So where is that? Is that teacher in a school? Are they in school, in class?" He nods. "And are they deaf or hearing?"

"Oh, hearing or deaf. I dunno."

"You don't know which. Okay. And, if they're hearing, the people in that class . . ." Pat picks up all the pictures and holds them in front of him. "Pat . . . Okay. If they're hearing children in that class and there's a class of deaf children, what's the difference between those two classes?"

"Ummmm, I just want this to be short, okay? I want to go to art. I want to go to art."

"Okay. You really want to go to art class, right?"

"Can I go?"

Seeing that Pat has not really been invested in our interview and how important his art class is to him, I end the interview and give him a thank you card for his help. As he gets up to leave, he once again looks at the camera and says, "Bye."

彩

ALTHOUGH THE time spent with Pat was short because of his enthusiasm to return to his classes, I was able to collect enough data to gain some insight into Pat's perceptions of himself and others as well as his lifeworld.

It was clear that Pat saw himself as different from hearing people. He said that he plays with both deaf and hearing children and anticipates boredom during interactions with hearing children that are not accessible to him. He expressed comfort in his environment at his residential school, and I believe he considered his classmates to be like a family. He was eager to return to and participate in his classes, even though he viewed learning as hard work. He clearly preferred to be in class than in his interview with me. Pat told us that life with his friends at school is fun.

Since it is not known how he became deaf, Pat was only able to speculate about why he is deaf. He did know that he was deaf as an infant, and he seemed to associate his fantasies about the reason for his being deaf with his infancy. Pat identified himself as deaf, and he even labeled the picture he drew for me with the sign DEAF. However, he also questioned if he might be hard of hearing.

Pat had very good artistic skills and took much pride in his ability to draw pictures for me. He was assertive in his communication and autonomous in his desire to return to his art class. He imagined a future for himself as a policeman or a fireman.

Pat, like other children in this study, specified differences between deaf and hearing children as being equated with speech and sign, which are visible and readily observable clues to a person's hearing status. He reiterated this connection when he was unable to explain how he became deaf and speculated that perhaps he had forgotten how to talk. It is interesting to note the perceptions of the children on the reasons why or how they became deaf and what actual information they have or do not have about this aspect of their beings.

11

So What You Are Saying Is . . .

One day the Town Mouse visited his cousin Country Mouse. Country Mouse gave him a nice dinner. Town Mouse said, "This is very dull." He invited Country Mouse for his dinner. They walked a long way. He saw a huge house and fancy food. They started to eat. Then something terrible . . ."It is a cat!". . . Country Mouse doesn't want to live there. He likes his own food. The end.

Pakuna Spady, age 7

PAKUNA SPADY, a student at Kendall Demonstration Elementary School in Washington, D.C., shared her version of Aesop's *The Town Mouse and the Country Mouse* for a class assignment. This story symbolically tells us that while the characters may both be mice and therefore members of the same group, they have different likes and dislikes, different cultures, and different preferences—as do the children who participated in this study. The contexts of their lives are different, and they make different choices in life.

The purpose of the research presented in this book was to explore deaf children's views of their lifeworlds. Like the fable above, the stories of Alex, Angie, Danny, Joe, Lisa, Mary, and Pat tell us that while the children are members of a group of deaf and hard of hearing schoolchildren between the ages of seven and ten, each of them is unique. Each child has a different family and particular cultural, educational, social, biological, psychological, and communication realities that became a part of this study. These differences tell us much about who these children are as individuals. Yet, in spite of their differences, similarities or themes in the lifeworlds of these children were discovered. In their interviews, these children revealed images of themselves and others and images of their communicative interactions.

During the course of the interviews, the children told about the paths they and their families take to deal with and prevent unpleasant experiences. They also described how they create positive experiences. I call the themes in this category of positive stories *pathways:* the strategies the children and their families devise to steer through a system of communication and attitudinal, interpersonal, and ecological influences.

A CHALLENGE TO TRADITIONAL VIEWS

Overall, the results of this study challenge negative beliefs and expectations often noted in the literature and that society has accepted about the self-perceptions and lifeworlds of deaf and hard of hearing children. The children who were interviewed had many positive experiences, relationships, self-perceptions, and expectations for themselves, as well as healthy coping styles. Their themes of attachment, domesticated others, infinity, and pathways contradict many of society's expectations that without speech and hearing, deaf and hard of hearing children will not be happy, intelligent, fully functioning, and contributing members of society. Despite the traditional categories (i.e., cultural, medical, or audiological categories) in which researchers have placed deaf and hard of hearing children, the children in this study have described in their own voices how they determine their identities, the identities of others, and who they see as similar to or different from them.

The literature regularly discusses the shock, sadness, anger, and disbelief that hearing parents experience on learning that their children are deaf. Some authors state that this grief process may cause negative responses, such as behavior problems and poor self-esteem, in deaf children. However, Mary, who has Deaf parents, and Alex, who has hearing parents, imagined that hearing parents would be happy or excited when their deaf baby was born. Angie has hearing adoptive parents, and she reported that the parents would worry but would work at learning to sign. Joe, a child of hearing parents, also reported that parents would worry. All of the children had responses that indicated loving relationships with their parents. This viewpoint on parental attitudes differs from the picture presented in much of the literature in which deaf children see their parents as not making communication accommodations, as denying or rejecting the child's deafness, or as having negative views of their children. The children in the study seemed secure in their relationships with their parents and sure of their love and acceptance even though some of them acknowledged their parents had needed to learn new methods of communication and sometimes worried about them.

Another assumption that seems to underlie much of our literature about deaf children is that the children are expected to have either good or bad experiences in specific educational settings or when adopting one language or communication method over another. The children in the study appeared to have both positive and negative experiences regardless of the type of educational program they attended or of the way in which they communicated, and they all had learned positive ways of coping regardless of the school's setting or communication philosophy.

Spatial negotiation was discussed in chapter 3 as an activity in which children act to create a comfortable line of sight necessary for effective communication and visibility. The children I observed in their classrooms moved around in their physical space to create a visually accessible environment in which they could all see in order to communicate. They moved their chairs, asked others to move, and checked with each other to make sure they could see the teacher and each other.

IMAGES

From the interviews with the children in the preceding chapters, several important overall characteristics were observed. Most of the children appeared to be happy, fulfilled youngsters who are involved in play, relationships, and school and who have positive images of their futures. The residential students, Danny, Pat, and Alex, and three mainstreamed children, Lisa and Angie, whose parents are hearing, and Mary, who has Deaf parents, gave the impression through their stories that being deaf is *no big deal*. The residential students' attachment to their milieu and their eagerness to return to their classroom activities was expressed through such statements as, "I want to go back to art class," and "I want to go to computer class." Mary also expressed a positive perspective of her relationships at school through her discussions of the many friends she has and how she eases in and out of her mainstreamed and self-contained classes. Lisa also did not report any overt conflicts in her educational placement or in her relationships with classmates, although behaviorally she appeared to struggle somewhat with communication and experience some apprehensiveness about deafness. To Lisa, school was just "okay"; she had both deaf and hearing friends but considered a deaf child to be her "best friend." The children also had pleasant experiences to share about family outings, such as trips to the state fair and vacations.

Most of the children conveyed strong positive perceptions of self. Joe's direct verbal expressions of hurtful experiences in relationships with hearing classmates, his concerns, uncertainties about himself, and his worries for his future seemed to be unique among the children in this study. He and Angie, who was adopted, both apparently became deaf in early childhood from illness. Their age-appropriate confusion about the implications of past and possible future illness in their lives and the lives of others was an underlying theme for them. Despite this anxiety, Joe and Angie, like the other children, still offered many positive images of themselves, relayed many strengths, described a variety of enjoyable activities and relationships, and projected positive images of their futures.

The seven children in the study conveyed a sense that deaf and hearing children are different from each other, and the majority of them did not view being deaf as a problem. The children told stories about difficulties they face, but they frequently seemed to view these difficulties as experiences and challenges shared by hearing people as well. Thus, while the children demonstrated a variety of problem-solving strategies, such as the self-directed behaviors of writing and teaching others how to sign, finding other deaf children to play with, or playing on their own, they did not see resolving whatever communication or relationship barriers they faced as being their sole responsibility. In addition, they reported that teachers, other children, their mothers, sisters, coaches, or interpreters helped when communication was inaccessible.

A continuum of comfortable and uncomfortable images and experiences with extremes on both ends was perceived. For example, Mary, who is mainstreamed and has Deaf parents, appeared to be very comfortable with both deaf and hearing children at her school while Joe, who is also mainstreamed and has hearing parents, reported many uncomfortable experiences with hearing children.

Differences occurred in the perceptions that the residential children, the child of deaf parents, and the mainstreamed children of hearing parents had about themselves and their lifeworlds. Mary, a child of Deaf parents, presented the most information about herself and others in her lifeworld. Alex and Danny, two residential children who have no additional reported physical disabilities and whose primary caretakers sign proficiently, also shared much information. The children with attention deficit disorders, Angie and Pat, and one who is mainstreamed and communicates primarily through speech, Lisa, shared less information about themselves and their lifeworlds. Joe, also mainstreamed and with hearing parents, considers himself hard of hearing and has the most hearing of any of the children. Joe offered more information about himself than the other two profoundly deaf mainstreamed children of hearing parents. The amount of information the children shared seemed to be influenced by the presence or lack of attention deficit disorder and by clear and effective language and communication at home and school.

These children take being deaf for granted. They are not preoccupied with the fact that they are deaf. They are immersed in the world of childhood and all of its enchantments. They experience the warmth and love of family and friends, they laugh at life's absurdities, and mourn its inequities. With youthful resilience they address their developmental challenges and adversities. They confidently anticipate their futures and were able to name a variety of career choices, some of which involved advanced education. Joe specifically stated the wish of attending Gallaudet University, and Angie mentioned attending a hearing college.

Just like other children, they are consistently involved in play, and many of their stories indicated that they are able to participate in, problem solve, and negotiate their interaction and relationships through play. Their play activities involve both interactive and solitary activities. At times some of the children reported retreating to solitary play when interactive play was not accessible.

Images that the children presented include *attachment* and *domesticated others, alienation* and *disparate others, infinity, overt* and *covert identity*, and *images of communication*. These images revealed common themes that tell us about the individuals, their lives, their relationships, how they determine who is deaf and who is hearing or hard of hearing, what they think about their futures, and what their communication experiences are like.

Attachment and Domesticated Others

In this study, the children shared their feelings about themselves and their feelings in the company of others. Their reports included situations where they felt a sense of attachment or belonging. These attachment experiences occurred primarily in relationships with what I call *domesticated others*. Domesticated others include people whom the deaf or hard of hearing child sees as accepting and with whom the child feels comfortable. Domesticated others may be someone the child sees as similar to himself or herself regardless of whether or not the person is deaf. A deaf child may accept hearing persons as deaf or as similar to himself or herself because of their ability to sign fluently (Alex's acceptance of hearing family members who sign as deaf: "Well, hearing and deaf both, because they sign and speak both"). A child may perceive other deaf or hard of hearing children as being like him or her. Joe's companions ("Sometimes me and my friend, this other boy named Carl. He's deaf like me and he talks too . . .") are two examples of domesticated others. The child may or may not be consciously aware of the other person's hearing status. Rather, this designation is based on what the child sees and interprets about the person, as well as the child's comfort with and acceptance of the person.

Several other examples of this perception arose in the interviews: Pat's report that his class of deaf students at school was like a family; Angie's communication that deaf children are not shy in the company of other deaf children; Alex's and Mary's explanations that hearing parents feel happy or excited when their deaf baby is born;

Mary's report that the hearing status of others doesn't make a difference in their feelings about her, that she has both deaf and hearing friends and feels comfortable with both at the school where she is mainstreamed; Mary's strong positive feelings about her family and her perception of her parents as loving and caring for her; Danny's reported comfort in the company of his deaf friends as well as in situations where he discovers that hearing children can sign; and Joe's identification with his deaf friend.

Alienation and Disparate Others

Besides reporting feelings of attachment with domesticated others, some of the children also reported situations where they experienced a sense of alienation in relationships with disparate others. *Disparate others* are people whom the child sees as different from him or her, regardless of hearing status, or from whom the child feels alienated. An example of disparate others was provided by Mary, whose family is deaf; she reported that people who are hard of hearing were different from her. Joe, a hard of hearing child whose family is hearing, also reported viewing a deaf classmate whose family is deaf as different from him. Further, the children gave several examples of their views of hearing children as different from themselves, for example, Pat's "Well, hearing are different from deaf . . . it's different from hearing." Another example of relationships with disparate others includes Alex's view of his hearing grandparents as different based on their lack of signing skills.

The children also gave examples of situations where they felt uncomfortable or alienated when others did not appear accepting or respond positively to them. For example, Danny had this to say: "Well, he might be kind of nervous and . . . yeah, a little unsure. Because they're hearing and they might not know . . . he might not know how to use his voice, . . . maybe not comfortable . . . kind of shy, kind of embarrassed, and kind of hesitant. A little bit afraid if no one signs."

The children may or may not be consciously aware of the hearing status of disparate others when these uncomfortable or inaccessible interactions take place. If the child is aware of or has a belief about the hearing status of this other person, the child's attitude could but does not necessarily imply a prejudiced or ethnocentric view. For most of the children, the difference between themselves and disparate others seemed to be just an ordinary fact of life.

Thus, it is important to note that feelings of alienation and the experience of relationships with disparate others should be seen only as one element of the children's lifeworlds. It should also be noted that children from a variety of backgrounds and educational programs reported both positive and negative experiences and relationships.

Infinity

At times the children shared their visions of their futures through stories about the pictures they drew or observed and in answer to direct questioning. *Future stories* is a term I use to indicate the manner in which the children depicted what appears to be a sense of infinity. The children's future stories centered primarily around vocational and parenting issues. Educational aspirations were also revealed by Joe, Angie, and Danny, who anticipate going to college. The stories imply that the children primarily see their hearing status as unchanging as they grow older. Joe indicated that a deaf child's hearing may improve or that he could develop an additional disability as he got older.

The children spoke about their futures in a quite self-assured manner. They appeared to take it for granted that they would grow up to become contributing members of society, living independently, continuing their education, working, and having families. Vocationally, all but Lisa conveyed the anticipation of a career. The fact that she did not mention work, however, does not mean that she does not foresee a career for herself. The children's ideas about their careers included being a policeman, a fireman, a school bus driver, a teacher or helper, taking care of animals, playing football, working in a grocery store, being a doctor, an actor, or an artist. Danny explained that deaf women could have a variety of careers. Only one child suggested that being deaf may limit career choices.

These children anticipate living separately from their parents. Marriage was mentioned by some of them as a possibility. The parents of most of the children in this study were divorced. Mary, who has Deaf parents, was able to explain the reason for her parent's divorce and saw divorce as a possibility for deaf adults. My perception is that her insight is due to a keen awareness of the world and because of the common language she shares with her family in which divorce has occurred.

The children mentioned the prospect of having either deaf or hearing children, and one child, Angie, stated a preference for deaf children. Mary knew that "some hearing parents have deaf children and some Deaf parents have hearing children." Although she did not state a preference for either, she acknowledged the possibility that her children could be hearing, an experience quite different from that of her Deaf parents since all of their children are deaf. Joe, a mainstreamed child of hearing parents, said, "I never thought about it," when asked if he imagined he'd have deaf or hearing children, and he also did not mention a preference. Angie said she would use a baby-cry signaler to alert her to her baby's cries when she has children. Other children mentioned teaching their hearing children to sign. The information obtained in this study about the children's preferences regarding whether or not their children are deaf or hearing is consistent with the research by Miller, Moores, and Sicoli (forthcoming), which concluded that the majority of the college students they surveyed had no preference for the hearing status of the children they might have in the future.

Covert and Overt Identity

The children in the study were asked to tell stories about what they thought was happening in pictures of individuals and groups cut out from magazines. Often, the children would indicate what they thought to be the hearing status of people in the pictures. When they did not volunteer that information, I asked for their impressions. These children had their own categories and methods of determining who is or is not deaf. They named various visible objects or actions as clues to whether or not a character in a picture was deaf or hearing. These visual indicators represented the *overt identity* that the children assigned to those they saw. A person's *covert identity* is the actual identity that a person adopts for himself or herself, that which is not visible.

Some of the children noted visual indicators—such as visual alerts, electronic devices, and the visible activity of signing or mouth movement—as indications of the deaf, hard of hearing, or hearing identities of the people in the pictures. Hearing aids were specified as visual indicators only by the mainstreamed students, not by the residential students. Use of speech and/or sign language as a visual indicator of identity were recognized by children from both mainstream and residential settings. The visible act of speaking usually symbolized to the children that the person could hear, and when signing was used the children usually suggested the person was deaf. Telecommunication devices for the deaf (TTYs) were also recognized by both residential and mainstream students as indicators of hearing status.

In looking at the pictures, the children chiefly noted differences between people who can hear and those who are deaf. Mary and Joe made distinctions between Deaf and hard of hearing children. For example, Mary, a Deaf child of Deaf parents, viewed hard of hearing people as appearing different from her because they talk, do not sign, or do not sign clearly. Joe, a hard of hearing child of hearing parents, viewed Deaf children in Deaf families as not having hearing aids. And Pat, who particularly enjoyed drawing, illustrated a Deaf boy actually signing DEAF.

The overt identity that the children interpreted from the pictures they saw did not always agree with the covert identity of the observed person. For example, Alex saw hearing family members as Deaf because they sign, but his own mother had indicated that she was hearing and signs. Other children decided that a Deaf man in a picture was hearing because there were no visible clues that he was Deaf: "I think he's hearing . . . 'cause he doesn't have a hearing aid on." Another application of overt versus covert identity can be seen where a deaf child may at first determine from observation that the person being observed is hearing because of mouth movement, or the person is seen talking, but the observed may actually be a hard of hearing child of Deaf parents and consider him- or herself culturally Deaf.

These types of gaps between overt and covert identity may cause an incongruence of images between the observed and the observer. These incongruent images have the potential to either delay or facilitate the achievement of harmony in relationships. A deaf child may approach a person she thinks is deaf because she observes the person signing. When it becomes clear the signing person is hearing, the child may have already made a new friend as a result of their mutual language. I have repeatedly observed these types of identity misreadings among people who are deaf, hearing, and hard of hearing.

A person's overt and covert identities are often revealed over a period of time. When hearing aids are visible before signing takes place, a person may at first be perceived by other deaf individuals as hard of hearing (because of their hearing aids) and later be accepted as Deaf (their covert identity) when they are seen skillfully using ASL in association with other Deaf people. People who consider themselves hard of hearing or deaf (covertly) and who learn to sign later in life but do not appear to be native signers are often mistaken as hearing. Once the observer and the observed become acquainted, the covert identity becomes clearer. With all the discussion of identity that occurs in the literature today, this particular theme appears to be of importance. Attempts by professionals to determine a deaf person's identity through scales and indexes or to develop criteria in the literature to decide who fits or doesn't fit a particular identity category impedes a person's basic psychological freedom. Processing and developing one's own identity is a fundamental human need essential to healthy growth and development. Regardless of what criteria professionals or others describe as essential for identity categories, people have the right to and will continue to establish their own individual covert identity and their own means of determining who fits in which category.

Images of Communication

Several findings arose from this study related to communication. The children in this study were quite articulate. Most of them expressed themselves with little difficulty. Although this sample of children was selected because they were considered particularly able to communicate in this type of interview, and some of them required more encouragement than others, each presented communication strengths.

An interesting gender issue arose from this study as well: it was evident from the children's stories that it is the mothers and sisters who often serve as interpreters for them in social situations. Lisa reported that her mother helps her understand spoken communication at a hearing church service, Danny noted several times that his younger sister interprets for him at times when he is with hearing children, and Angie said her mother could help out when she is with hearing friends who do not sign. A few of the children perceived their hearing parents as making a strong effort to communicate with them. Each of the children reporting on this level of parental effort had parents with good to excellent signing skills.

The amount and quality of information that the children shared about their lifeworlds varied on a continuum, with a Deaf child of Deaf parents having the richest amount of information to share. Mary, who has Deaf parents, and Alex and Danny, who both attend a residential school, had more information than the oral main-streamed children of hearing parents. The amount of information that the children had about themselves appeared in this study to be based on (1) the solidity of their communication foundation at home and school and (2) the presence or absence of the disability of attention deficit disorder. Joe, who was mainstreamed and hard of hearing, was the oldest of the children in the study and shared a great deal of information with me. At the same time, he sometimes seemed confused because of information gaps that made it difficult for him to put certain facts into perspective. For example, he told stories about another deaf child who developed what he believed to be cancer and was concerned that the cancer was related to the child's deafness. Not having more information about the child's sit-uation, Joe concluded that he could also be vulnerable to cancer.

While being deaf appeared to be taken for granted by these chil-dren, *play* was a consistent activity for these children, and their play involved both deaf and hearing children. Communication occurs in the process of play, and according to the children in this study, both deaf and hearing children find ways to communicate in their play activity. Play appeared to be at the forefront of their stories.

"It's not whether you are deaf or hearing, it's how you communicate" was the message that these children conveyed. For example, Alex's statement that people in a deaf boy's family are deaf and hearing both because they sign indicates the importance of signing in regard to a person's designated identity. Danny's story about a deaf and hearing child also illustrates this point: " 'Yeah, I can sign, I can sign. I'm hearing but I can sign' and then the deaf boy would, well, they would become friends and they could be on a football team . . . 'cause they can sign together" and "Oh, the boy would feel really

good and be surprised too" (when he saw that the hearing children sign). Mary commented that hard of hearing people communicate differently than deaf people: "Because they talk, that means they're in an all hearing family . . . Maybe they're talking, or not clear signing. . . . They wouldn't sign." Joe told of a Deaf friend from a Deaf family who is different from himself and his family because "They sign all the time. They just sign. . . ." Angie talked about the effort that her parents made to learn to sign. Pat told us that his family members are hearing "and they talk." In addition, he drew himself signing DEAF. The presence of sign language in these children's lives was obviously significant to them.

PATHWAYS

The children in this study developed positive *pathways* for negotiating their relationships with disparate others, for interacting with friends and family, and for meeting their daily informational needs. Pathways include use of visual alerts and electronic devices; relationships with peers, family members, cultures, or professionals; recreational activities; autonomy; adoption of heroes; and the use of sign language or other means of communication.

Visual Alerts and Electronic Devices

Many realities of modern society are based on the assumption that everyone benefits from sound. Telephones and doorbells ring, fire and smoke alarms blare, and language is spoken all around us in conversation and on television. Hearing people take these sound-based designs for granted. Those who are deaf and hard of hearing have found ways to change these discriminatory designs. Professionals in audiology, medicine, and rehabilitation have often used the terms *adaptive devices*, or *auxiliary aids*, to refer to electronic devices used by deaf people. However, these terms imply a deficiency, as if the mechanisms are used to compensate for the inability to hear. *Visual alerts*, on the other hand, seems to be a more appropriate and positive term as it reflects the taken-for-granted attitude that the children in this study have about being deaf.

As may be expected, vision is especially vital to those who are deaf or hard of hearing. During my visit to Kendall Demonstration

Elementary School in Washington, D.C., the students were studying the importance of light and visual means of receiving information from our environment. "Eye contact is important to deaf people" and "Why light is important to deaf people" were two of the
captions decorating the walls. In this study, nine-year-old Danny,
who is still learning to read, thoroughly and dramatically described
the actions he observed on television's "Teenage Mutant Ninja Turtles" despite his developmentally appropriate inability to fully benefit from his closed captioned television. His attention to visual details generated the same attachment to the television superheroes
that hearing children have.

A number of other visual devices are commonly used by deaf and
hard of hearing people to enhance communication, including hearing ear dogs, flashing signalers, sign language interpreters, and
TTYs. The children in this study mentioned all of these in their
stories. They know what is available to them in terms of visual alerts
and electronic devices for communication and signaling.

Relationships

The children also discussed a variety of relationships available to
them. They mentioned friendships with other deaf children, as well
as friendships with hearing children, particularly those who sign.
The children experience acceptance in relationships with deaf peers
or they value the comfort that they anticipate in those relationships.
Danny, Alex, Mary, and Angie all appear to appreciate their relationships with deaf peers. Joe mentioned his deaf friends in a positive light and, while he seemed to be dealing with a lot of teasing
from hearing children at school, he reported that he would like to
go to the college where deaf kids go. I interpreted Pat's account of
his class as a family to mean that he values the positive experiences
he has with his classmates as a peer group. Lisa reported that her
best friend is deaf.

Some of the children, including Danny, Lisa, Angie, and Alex,
explained that their mothers or sisters would help them communicate with hearing people when there was a communication gap.
Lisa, Angie, Danny, and Alex also said they would retreat to the
comfort of play and companionship with family members if they

ran into obstacles elsewhere. Some of them also reported using sign language interpreters.

Recreational Activities

The children enjoyed a variety of recreational and leisure time activities. They mentioned soccer, football, baseball, basketball, vacationing, fishing, gymnastics, playing tag, Nintendo, playing with toy guns and race cars, watching closed captioned television, reading, shopping, bike riding, swimming, traveling in the car with parents, attending the theater, playing with a boomerang, catching bugs and bats, playing with pets and relatives, going to the fair, playing on the computer, and attending church services. Obviously the children don't see being deaf as an obstacle to their successful participation in these events. Their enthusiasm for play and participation in these leisure activities was similar to that of any child.

Autonomy

The children frequently displayed a strong sense of self-direction or self-determination, as it is sometimes called. They often took responsibility for themselves in situations where barriers existed. The children asserted their autonomy in a variety of ways, such as motivating themselves regarding their school work, isolating themselves from situations where barriers existed, and at other times choosing to participate in more accessible or comfortable relationships. If the children found barriers in their play activities with other children, they sometimes directed hearing group members to more action-oriented play activities, taught sign language to hearing peers and teachers, asked hearing peers to write, and initiated play themselves instead of waiting for hearing children to invite or include them. Speechreading, telling others when they did not understand, and making a choice to attend a church that offers interpreters or signing pastors were additional examples of assertiveness. For example, in dealing with possible communication and attitude barriers in situations with hearing children, Danny described a possible scenario where hearing children would tell him to "go away." Danny at first isolated himself, then he made a decision to ask his mother to interpret; he also determined he could create an activity that was action oriented and did not require much communication. In a later discussion, he decided he could play with his sister. Danny knows he has options and is ready and able to make decisions about those options.

Angie reported she would ask other children to play with her even if it means they might sometimes need to write to communicate. Alex, Angie, and Danny explained that they would use writing as a tool for communication if necessary. Alex, Mary, and Joe all said they teach hearing children to sign. Joe explained that he takes the initiative to tell others to slow down when he doesn't understand them. In my interviews with Lisa, she made decisions to get up and look for information that would help her answer my questions. Pat made a decision to end our interview when he wanted to return to his art class. All of these actions were based on autonomous decisions that the children made for themselves. All of these decisions were positive ones and reflect the strength and abilities of these children.

Heroes

Danny, Alex, Mary, and Joe all told stories about superheroes or heroes. Danny recounted a very detailed story about Ninja Turtles. Even though he is still too young to understand everything that is captioned on television, this type of show is very action oriented and Danny had no trouble describing what takes place. Alex and Mary talked about Power Rangers, and Joe told me about football players.

Use of Sign Language

For the majority of the children, learning and using sign language was seen as valuable in their relationships. The children described situations where they taught other children to sign as well as situations where they valued peers and family members who were able to sign with them. Writing came in handy for Alex, Angie, and Danny when others did not sign.

Use of sign language was valued by this particular group of children because the parents of these children chose educational programs that utilize signing; thus, signing became a part of their lifeworlds. Only one child's parents in this group appeared to be ambivalent about this choice and expressed concern that their child

needed more speech training. This child struggled with her use of sign language. It would have been instructive to see this particular child's responses within the context of her experiences and communication realities. Had there been more children in this sample who relied entirely on oral communication, we would have been able to obtain more information about the experiences of "oral deaf" children. It would be valuable to repeat this study with a group of predominantly oral children to see what their descriptions of their lifeworlds are.

Summary

The children in this study demonstrated similarities or themes. Most compellingly, they showed themselves to be happy, self-confident, and fulfilled children in the process of successfully developing pathways for negotiating relationships with hearing others. From listening to the voices of these uniquely individual children, we learn that they do not always see themselves, their lifeworlds, and their experiences as researchers have traditionally described them. These children have strengths, they have positive experiences, and they enjoy positive relationships. The children in this study are mostly happy and involved in their environments, they experience autonomy, and they have healthy means of dealing with and changing potentially unpleasant experiences. They believe they are loved by their parents, and they have confidence in their futures. They know that they are deaf and understand that there are differences between and among themselves and hearing others.

The children in this study also have uncomfortable and unpleasant experiences and relationships, and they have established healthy ways of dealing with these experiences. The negative expectations and perceptions that society has traditionally held for children who are deaf do not appear to match the beliefs that these children have of themselves, their relationships, their futures, and their general lifeworlds.

12

*I*nto the *F*uture:

New Directions for Research and Practice

"What would you like to draw?"
"Is it my decision?"
"If you want."
"My decision?!"

—Interview with Danny, age nine

PERHAPS ONE of the most meaningful elements of this research was that the children told us in their own spirited voices what was important to them. Here, they had the chance to share their stories and images of their lifeworlds. The children were the artists, the builders, the creators, and the teachers of the lessons in this book.

This study represents a new direction in research, one that values the participation of deaf and hard of hearing children. Research that respects the participation of the people it seeks to understand needs to continue if we truly want to comprehend the multiple meanings of being deaf or hard of hearing. This direction is critical if we want to gain insight into the meanings and experiences that children derive from the policies, programs, philosophies, attitudes, relationships, and other environmental elements that society presents to them.

Professionals in a variety of fields could be led to new practices by seeking the children's perspectives. I hope this book will help professionals understand that the children have their own views of their lifeworlds and that their participation, their strengths, and their perspectives should be valued and their uniqueness respected.

STRENGTHS

In contrast to the problem focus of much of our literature in deafness, these children's stories showed us that they have many strengths. One of the messages herein is that we need to attend to and respect the strengths of these children, which includes their ability to "tell it like it is" and to be our teachers.

It is time for us to move away from the negative images and expectations that society at large and many professionals who work with these children hold of them. These negative images have included the notion that deaf children have low self-esteem, mostly troubled images of themselves and others, primarily distorted relationships with the world, and a life full of negative experiences. While the research presented in this book showed that some uncomfortable experiences and relationships do exist, it is important to recognize these children were mostly happy and had many affirming experiences, comfortable relationships, confident images of their future, and positive pathways for transcending whatever unpleasant experiences arise.

As discussed in chapter 2, existential theory suggests that people have the freedom and responsibility to transcend whatever uncomfortable or alienating experiences occur in life (Frankl, 1969). The pathways of the children in this study show that they use that freedom and to creatively or defiantly transcend whatever uncomfortable or alienating experiences they have and to create positive experiences and meanings. For centuries we have spent so much time arguing over the right way to raise deaf children and the right language and educational approaches to use that we have forgotten that each child is unique. While these children were able to tell us about their similarities, they were also able to tell us about their many differences, and our programs, policies, philosophies, and models need to take these into consideration. Culture, language, biology, cognition, legislation, socioeconomics, education, communication, technology, family, social environments, and time all play an important part in these children's lives and their perspectives on their lifeworlds. These ecological elements were preserved in the children's profiles in each of their chapters and explained in chapter 2.

We need to recognize that these children have many strengths that we must address and illuminate. This forces a change in traditional ethnocentric views and encourages the adoption of a strengths perspective.

RESEARCH AND FURTHER STUDY

This research demonstrated the potential of qualitative methods to overcome some of the limitations of traditional research and overcome the tendency for researchers to collect data from others in deaf children's lives rather than from the children themselves. It demonstrated these children's capabilities in communicating their realities through qualitative methods and phenomenological interviews.

This study attempted to acknowledge the personal and professional self of the researcher in the context of this investigative process. In any study, the biases and the context of the researcher's self must be acknowledged and controlled. Those who read research findings on deaf and hard of hearing people also need to be informed of these and other ecological contexts that exist in the research process.

The qualitative method and techniques used in this study can help researchers understand the experiences of diverse groups of deaf and hard of hearing children, their parents, and families. This study could be repeated with specific groups of deaf and hard of hearing children based on gender, race, educational placement, and communication and language orientations, as well as with children who are adopted, in foster care, or with cochlear implants. It would also be instructive to learn more about the nuances of childhood (e.g., play). Additional studies could also explore ways to enhance and increase opportunities for domesticated relationships and ways to reduce the number of disparate relationships and alienating experiences that children face. It might be enlightening also to look at the families of these children (including the child as a member and participant, of course), in order to explore and describe the diverse lifeworlds of the entire family.

Additionally, this study could be replicated with hearing children from diverse groups. For example, the lifeworlds of children with disabilities and children from various cultural backgrounds could be explored using the qualitative methods applied in this study. Also of potential interest to researchers is the fact that the next generation of deaf and hard of hearing children will have a new set of contexts within which to explore their lifeworlds, as environments continue to change.

REFLECTIONS ON INTERVIEW TECHNIQUES

The social, cognitive, and language realities of the children in this study were diverse. This diversity called for flexible interviewing techniques. I have successfully used metaphors in stories in many psychotherapeutic situations with children who are deaf and hard of hearing in order to solicit information. Unfortunately, this method was not successful with two of the children in this study when they were asked questions in complicated metaphorical ways (e.g., in assigning personality to inanimate objects). However, the children in this study were able to tell me stories about the deaf children in the artwork they created. They also told me stories about children they imagined to be deaf in pictures they reviewed. Direct questioning and probing for deeper information in the children's art and stories were also largely successful. Generally, the art and storytelling techniques used were effective in collecting information about these children and their lifeworlds.

REFLECTIONS ON THEORY

In chapters 1 and 2, ecological and symbolic interaction theories were briefly discussed as frameworks for understanding the contexts of this study. The pathways of the children in this study show that they take the responsibility to creatively or defiantly transcend whatever uncomfortable or alienating experiences they have and

to create positive experiences and meanings in their various situations. As the study progressed, it became apparent that ecological,
symbolic interaction, and existential theories are useful for understanding the meanings that these children have of themselves and
their lifeworlds.

Historically, we have looked for existing theories and models of
development and applied them to children who are deaf and hard of
hearing. Today, ethnic, bicultural, and biracial identity models are
applied to children who are deaf and are largely accepted. However,
we still need to develop our own models of development for deaf
children. Qualitative methods that include prolonged observation
and in-depth interviews that do not apply theory prior to data col-
lection can help us accomplish this.

It appears from the stories of the children in this study, as well
as my own childhood experiences and the data presented in recent
research on the reflective experiences of deaf adults (e.g., Bradford,
1991), that many information gaps exist for deaf and hard of hearing children in the process of developing a mature perception of
self and identity. If this is true, then it must be addressed at home,
in school, and in professional practice with children who are deaf
and hard of hearing. These information gaps can be filled with sen-
sitivity to the impact they can have on a child's growing sense of
self, with efforts to create communicatively accessible environments at home and school, through the provision of role models,
association with peers, parent and family education programs, and
through additions to our curriculum that address these issues for
the children.

AND FINALLY . . .

In chapter 1, I told of three little girls who approached me one afternoon many years ago and asked, "What is it like to be deaf?" By
now, these little girls are all grown up. I hope they have a chance
to read this book and that I finally have been able to shed some
light on their question. While deaf and hard of hearing children
are diverse, it is beneficial to recognize their similarities. These
similarities can pull us together, panethnically, as we move into
the future with respect for our diversity and work together to con-

tinue to transcend or transform whatever barriers lie before us. Exploring the experiences and perspectives of adolescents who are deaf using research methods similar to those used in this study will lead us to a deeper understanding of the developmental issues and tasks faced by deaf children and adolescents in their formative years.

REFERENCES

Akamatsu, C. T. (1993/1994, winter). The view from within and without: Conducting research on deaf Asian Americans. *Journal of the American Deafness and Rehabilitation Association* 27 (3), 12–16.

Allen, T. E. (1986). Patterns of academic achievement among hearing impaired students: 1974 and 1983. In A. Schildroth and M. Karchmer (Eds.), *Deaf children in America*. San Diego: College-Hill Press.

———. (1999). Personal communication.

Allen, T. E., and Schoem, S. R. (1997). *Educating deaf and hard of hearing youth: What works best?* Paper presented at the Combined Otolaryngological Spring Meetings of the American Academy of Otolaryngology, Scottsdale, Arizona, May 14, 1997.

Andrews, J., and Jordan, D. (1993). Minority and minority-deaf professionals. How many and where are they? *American Annals of the Deaf* 138, 388–396.

Baum, L. Frank. (1994). *The Wizard of Oz*. New York: Puffin Books.

Berger, P. (1963). *Invitation to sociology*. Garden City, NY: Doubleday.

Bradford, T. (1991). *"Say that again, please!"* Dallas: Bradford.

Bronfenbrenner, U. (1979). *The ecology of human development: Experiments by nature and design*. Cambridge: Harvard University Press.

Christiansen, J. B., and Barnartt, S. N. (1995). *Deaf president now! The 1988 revolution at Gallaudet University*. Washington, DC: Gallaudet University Press.

Christiansen J., and Leigh, I., (Forthcoming). *Cochlear implants in children: Ethics and choices*. Washington, DC: Gallaudet University Press.

Cohen, O. (1993). Educational needs of African American and Hispanic deaf children and youth. In K. Christensen and G. Delgado (Eds.), *Multicultural issues in deafness* (pp. 45–68). White Plains, NY: Longman.

———. (1997). Giving all children a chance: Advantages of an antiracist approach to education for deaf children. *American Annals of the Deaf* 142, 80–82.

Cohen, O., Fishgrund, J., and Redding, R. (1990). Deaf children from ethnic, linguistic, and racial minority backgrounds: An overview. *American Annals of the Deaf* 135, 67–73.

Coles, R. (1990). *The spiritual life of children*. Boston: Houghton Mifflin.

Cooley, C. (1970). *Human nature and the social order*. New York: Schocken Books.

Cose, E. (1999, June 7). The good news about black America. *Newsweek*, 40.

Crane, J. (1999). Other's attitudes. *World Around You* 20 (5), 13.

Dolnick, E. (1993). Deafness as culture. *Atlantic Monthly* 272, 37–53.

Emerton, R. G. (1996). Marginality, biculturalism, and social identity of Deaf people. In I. Parasnis (Ed.), *Cultural and language diversity and the deaf experience.* (pp. 136–145). Cambridge: Cambridge University Press.

Evans, J. F. (1998). Changing the lens: A position paper on the value of qualitative research methods as a mode of inquiry in the education of the deaf. *American Annals of the Deaf* 143 (3), 246–254.

Flexer, C. (1999). *Facilitating hearing and listening in young children* (2nd ed.). San Diego: Singular Publications.

Foster, S. (1989). Social alienation and peer identification: A study of the social construction of deafness. *Human Organization* 48 (3), 226–235.

———. (1993/1994, winter). Outsider in the deaf world: Reflections of an ethnographic researcher. *JADARA* 27 (3), 1–11.

———. (1996). Communication experiences of Deaf people: An ethnographic account. In I. Parasnis (Ed.), *Culture and language diversity and the deaf experience* (pp. 117–135). Cambridge: Cambridge University Press.

Frankl, V. E. (1969). *The will to meaning: Foundations and applications of logotherapy.* New York: New American Library.

———. (1984). *Man's search for meaning.* New York: Simon and Schuster.

Gallaudet Research Institute. (2000). *Regional and National Summary Report of Data from the 1998–1999 Annual Survey of Deaf and Hard of Hearing Children and Youth.* Washington, DC: Graduate Research Institute, Gallaudet University.

Gardner, R. A. (1993a). *Psychotherapy with children.* Northvale, NJ: Jason Aronson.

———. (1993b). *Storytelling in psychotherapy with children.* Northvale, NJ: Jason Aronson.

Germain, C. B., and Gitterman, A. (1996). *The life model of social work practice* (2nd ed.). New York: Columbia University Press.

Glickman, N. S. (1996). The development of culturally Deaf identities. In N. S. Glickman and M. A. Harvey (Eds.), *Culturally affirmative psychotherapy with Deaf persons* (pp. 115–154). Mahwah, NJ: Lawrence Erlbaum Associates.

Glickman, N. S., and Harvey, M. (Eds.). (1996). *Culturally affirmative psychotherapy with Deaf persons.* Mahwah, NJ: Lawrence Erlbaum Associates.

Glickman, N., and Zitter, S. (1989). On establishing a culturally affirmative psychiatric inpatient program for Deaf people. *JADARA* 23 (2), 46–59.

Grosjean, F. (1996). Living with two languages and two cultures. In I. Parasnis (Ed.), *Cultural and language diversity and the deaf experience* (pp. 20–37). Cambridge: Cambridge University Press.

Harvey, M. (1989). *Psychotherapy with deaf and hard of hearing persons: A systemic model.* Mahwah, NJ: Lawrence Erlbaum Associates.

———. (1996). Utilization of traumatic transference by a hearing therapist. In N. S. Glickman and M. A. Harvey (Eds.), *Culturally affirmative psychotherapy with Deaf persons* (pp. 155–167). Mahwah, NJ: Lawrence Erlbaum Associates.

Heward, W., and M. Orlansky. (1992). *Exceptional children: An introductory survey to special education* (4th ed.). New York: Merrill.

Holcomb, T. K. (1997). Development of Deaf bicultural identity. *American Annals of the Deaf* 142 (3), 89–93.

Hughes, M., and D. H. Demo. (1989). Self-perceptions of Black Americans: Self-esteem and personal efficacy. *American Journal of Sociology* 95 (1), 132–159.

Humphries, T. (1996). Of deaf-mutes, the strange and the modern self. In N. S. Glickman and M. A. Harvey (Eds.), *Culturally affirmative psychotherapy with Deaf persons* (pp. 99–114). Mahwah, NJ: Lawrence Erlbaum Associates.

Isenberg, G. (1996). Storytelling and the use of culturally appropriate metaphors in psychotherapy with Deaf people. In N. S. Glickman and M. A. Harvey (Eds.), *Culturally affirmative psychotherapy with Deaf persons* (pp. 169–183). Mahwah, NJ: Lawrence Erlbaum Associates.

Jacobs, L. (1974). *A Deaf adult speaks out.* Washington, DC: Gallaudet University Press.

Lane, H. (1984). *When the mind hears: A history of the deaf.* New York: Random House.

———. (1992). *The mask of benevolence: Disabling the Deaf community.* New York: Alfred A. Knopf.

Lane, H., Hoffmeister, R., and Bahan, B. (1996). *Journey into the Deaf world.* San Diego: DawnSignPress.

Lantz, J. E. (1986). Family logotherapy. *Contemporary Family Therapy* 8 (2), 124–135.

Leigh, I. (1999). Inclusive education and personal development. *Journal of Deaf Studies and Deaf Education* 4 (3), 236–245.

Levine, E. S. (1960). *The psychology of deafness.* New York: Columbia University Press.

categories [handwritten marginalia]

————. (1981). *The ecology of early deafness: Guides to fashioning environments and psychological assessments.* New York: Columbia University Press.

Lincoln, Y. S., and Guba, E. G. (1985). *Naturalistic inquiry.* Newbury Park, CA: Sage Publications.

Mead, G. H. (1934). *Mind, self, and society.* Chicago: University of Chicago Press.

Meadow, K. P. (1968). Parental response to the medical ambiguities of congenital deafness. *Journal of Health and Social Behavior* 9, 299–308.

Meadow, K. P., Greenberg, M. T., Erting, C., and Carmichael, H. (1981). Interactions of deaf mothers and deaf preschool children: Comparisons with three other groups of deaf and hearing dyads. *American Annals of the Deaf* 126, 454–468.

Meadow-Orlans, K. P. (1969). Self-image, family climate, and deafness. *Social Forces* 47, 428–438.

————. (1980). *Deafness and child development.* Berkeley: University of California Press.

————. (1983). *Meadow-Kendall social-emotional assessment inventory for deaf and hearing-impaired students manual.* Washington, DC: Gallaudet University.

————. (1990). Research on the developmental aspects of deafness. In D. Moores and K. P. Meadow-Orlans (Eds.), *Educational and developmental aspects of deafness* (pp. 283–298). Washington, DC: Gallaudet University Press.

Medoff, M. (1979). *Children of a lesser god.* New York: Dramatists Play Service.

Miller, M. S., Moores, D., and Sicoli, D. (Forthcoming). Preferences of deaf college students for hearing status of their children. *JADARA* 32 (3).

Moores, D. F. (1987). *Educating the deaf: Psychology, principles, and practices* (3rd ed.). Boston: Houghton Mifflin.

Padden, C. (1980). The deaf community and the culture of deaf people. In C. Baker and R. Battison (Eds.), *Sign language and the deaf community* (pp. 89–103). Silver Spring, MD: National Association of the Deaf.

————. (1996). From the cultural to the bicultural. In I. Parasnis (Ed.), *Cultural and language diversity and the deaf experience* (pp. 79–98). Cambridge: Cambridge University Press.

Padden, C., and Humphries, T. (1988). *Deaf in America: Voices from a culture.* Cambridge: Harvard University Press.

Parasnis, I. (Ed.). (1996). *Cultural and language diversity and the deaf experience.* Cambridge: Cambridge University Press.

————. (1997). Cultural identity and diversity in deaf education. *American Annals of the Deaf* 142, 72–79.

Paul, P. V., and Jackson, D. W. (1993). *Toward a psychology of deafness: Theoretical and empirical perspectives.* Boston: Allyn and Bacon.

Piaget, J. (1952). *The origins of intelligence in children.* New York: International University Press.

Pollard, R. Q. (1993/1994, winter). Cross cultural ethics in the conduct of deafness research. *JADARA* 27 (3), 29–41.

Pray, J. (1999). Personal communication.

Ramsey, C. L. (1997). *Deaf children in public schools: Placement, context, and consequences.* Washington, DC: Gallaudet University Press.

Redding, R. (1995). Factors influencing academic and behavioral expectations of teachers in classes for deaf and hard of hearing students with diverse racial, ethnic, and linguistic backgrounds. Doctoral dissertation, Gallaudet University, Washington, DC.

————. (1997). Changing times, changing society: Implications for professionals in deaf education. *American Annals of the Deaf* 142 (3), 83–85.

————. (1999). Personal communication.

Rosenberg, M. (1990). The self-concept: Social product and social force. In M. Rosenberg and R. Turner (Eds.), *Social psychology: Sociological perspectives.* New Brunswick, NJ: Transaction Publishers.

Sacks, O. (1990). *Seeing voices: A journey into the world of the deaf.* New York: HarperPerennial.

Saleebey, D. (1992). *The strengths perspective in social work practice.* New York: Longman.

Schein, J. D., and Delk, M. T. (1974). *The deaf population of the United States.* Silver Spring, MD: National Association of the Deaf.

Schildroth, A. N., and Hotto, S. A. (1995). Race and ethnic background in the annual survey of deaf and hard of hearing children and youth. *American Annals of the Deaf* 140, 96–99.

Schlesinger, H. S., and Meadow, K. P. (1972). *Sound and sign: Childhood deafness and mental health.* Berkeley: University of California Press.

Self Help for Hard of Hearing People, Inc. 1995. Position statement on residual hearing. *The SHHH Journal* 16 (5), 36.

Sheridan, M. A. (1995). Existential transcendence among deaf and hard of hearing people. In M. D. Garretson (Ed.), *Deafness: Life and culture II: A Deaf American monograph* 45. Silver Spring, MD: National Association of the Deaf.

————. (1996). Emerging themes in the study of deaf children. *Dissertation Abstracts International* 57/07 (January, 1997), 3254.

———. (1998). *Mental health assessment of deaf and hard of hearing persons: A transactional deafness paradigm.* Paper presented at the First World Conference on Mental Health and Deafness, October, Gallaudet University, Washington, DC.

———. (2000). Images of self and others: Stories from the children. In P. E. Spencer, C. J. Erting, and M. Marschark (Eds.), *The deaf child in the family and at school* (pp. 5–19). Mahwah, NJ: Lawrence Erlbaum Associates.

Spencer, P. E. (2000). Every opportunity: A case study of hearing parents and their deaf child. In P. E. Spencer, C. J. Erting, and M. Marschark (Eds.), *The deaf child in the family and at school* (pp. 111–132). Mahwah, NJ: Lawrence Erlbaum Associates.

Stokoe, W. C. (1960). *Sign language structure: An outline of the visual communication system of the American deaf.* Buffalo: Department of Anthropology and Linguistics, University of Buffalo.

Stokoe, W. C., Casterline, D., and Croneberg, C. (1965). *A dictionary of American Sign Language on linguistic principles.* Washington, DC: Gallaudet College Press.

Sussman, A. (1992). *Characteristics of a well adjusted deaf person or: The art of being a deaf person.* Paper presented at the Statewide Conference on Deafness and Hard of Hearing, April, North Carolina Department of Human Resources, Raleigh, NC.

Tatum, B. D. (1997). *Why are all the black kids sitting together in the cafeteria? And other conversations about race.* New York: Basic Books.

Tucker, B. P. (1998). *Federal disability law in a nutshell* (2nd ed.). St. Paul, MN: West Group.

Van Den Bergh, N., and Cooper, L. B. (Eds.). (1986). *Feminist visions for social work.* Silver Spring, MD: National Association of Social Workers.

Vernon, M. (1988). Psychological assessment. In P. V. Paul (Ed.), *Ohio symposium on deafness: Critical issues on health, mental health, education and vocational rehabilitation.*

Walsh, J. (Forthcoming). Social work practice and mental illness: Symbolic interactionism as a framework for intervention. *Journal of Applied Social Sciences.*

Winefield, R. (1987). *Never the twain shall meet: Bell, Gallaudet, and the communications debate.* Washington, DC: Gallaudet University Press.

Zieziula, F. R. (1982). *Assessment of hearing-impaired people.* Washington, DC: Gallaudet University Press.

Index